A Psychoanalytic Approach to the Feminine

A Psychoanalytic Approach to the Feminine sees Houari Maïdi dissect the concepts and characteristics of the feminine in both males and females, separating them from womanhood and femininity, and equipping readers with the tools to better understand pathologies such as masochism, narcissism, depression, and paranoia.

Starting from Freud's binary depiction of gender identity through the lens of bisexuality, Maïdi seeks to redress the way in which traditional psychoanalysis considers sexual characteristics. He separates the feminine from gender, showing how historically misogynistic theories in psychoanalysis have potentially damaged the progress of the field, as well as female and male analysands alike. Depictions of the feminine are considered through their relationship with traumatic seduction, mourning and melancholy to address questions related to different clinical and psychopathological representations.

Using clinical vignettes throughout, this book is essential reading for psychoanalysts and those interested in the intersection between gender and analysis.

Houari Maïdi is a psychoanalyst and professor of psychopathology, psychoanalysis, and clinical psychology at the University of Burgundy Franche-Comté, France.

A Psychoanalytic Approach to the Feminine

Houari Maïdi

LONDON AND NEW YORK

Designed cover image: © Getty Images

First published 2025
by Routledge
4 Park Square, Milton Park, Abingdon, Oxon OX14 4RN

and by Routledge
605 Third Avenue, New York, NY 10158

Routledge is an imprint of the Taylor & Francis Group, an informa business

© 2025 Houari Maïdi

The right of Houari Maïdi to be identified as author of this work
has been asserted in accordance with sections 77 and 78 of the
Copyright, Designs and Patents Act 1988.

All rights reserved. No part of this book may be reprinted
or reproduced or utilised in any form or by any electronic,
mechanical, or other means, now known or hereafter invented,
including photocopying and recording, or in any information
storage or retrieval system, without permission in writing
from the publishers.

Trademark notice: Product or corporate names may be trademarks
or registered trademarks, and are used only for identification and
explanation without intent to infringe.

British Library Cataloguing-in-Publication Data
A catalogue record for this book is available from the British Library

ISBN HB: 978-1-032-53907-2
ISBN PB: 978-1-032-53737-5
ISBN EB: 978-1-003-41424-7

DOI: 10.4324/9781003414247

Typeset in Times New Roman
by codeMantra

Contents

	Introduction	**1**
1	**The riddle of the feminine**	**5**

The feminine and femininity   5
Hatred of the feminine or horror feminae   6
Freud and the woman   7
What does a woman want?   9
The feminine in Freud, Winnicott, and Lacan   10

2	**The feminine and castration**	**25**

Psychic bisexuality   25
Masculine–feminine, activity–passivity   27
Narcissistic feminine   29
Feminine narcissism and traumatic homosexuality   29
Sidonie: 'The young homosexual'   30
Freud's analysis   31
Lacan's position   32
Aesthetic encounter   32
The feminine as legacy   33
Natacha   35
Pauline   36

3	**From the guilt of being feminine to the feminine being of guilt**	**42**

Julie: 'As though it's my fault for being born!'   44
Nadia: 'You can't do anything for me'   49
Olga: 'I fail at everything I do'   52

4	**The feminine victim**	**59**

Trauma and seduction   61
Feminam hostia   63

vi Contents

The victim and the law 65
The sacrificial feminine and the sacred 66
Oedipus the scapegoat victim? 67
Victimology and organisation of the personality 68
Feminine masochism in Baudelaire 69
Freud and the notion of victim 72
The victim and their innocence 74
The victim is a martyr of the unconscious 75

5   The melancholic feminine   **79**
Pathological grief and the pain of a bitter mother 81
Melancholia and primary narcissistic trauma 83
Pathological grief and melancholic organisation 85
Melancholy of fate 86
Loss and guilt 87
Suicide, autosadism, and melancholia 88
Maternal passion 89
Grief, melancholic sacrifice, and the feminine 90
The 'diabolical' feminine: hysteria and melancholia 90
The melancholic tear: neither living nor dying 91
Double figures and narcissistic relationships 91

6   Can you be innocent if you love someone guilty?   **94**
Hainamoration in the love relationship 95
The love-hate connection in persecution 96
Mrs E: 'Loving hurts, because since the time of sin, it means being
   crucified for someone else.' 98
Narcissism, feminine masochism, and paranoia 100
Love in persecution, love of persecution 101
Hatred of paternal castration 103
Hatred of the diabolic masculine as a substitute for the father 104
Cruelty and delight or masochistic enjoyment of the feminine 107

7   Feminine destiny   **111**
Body of destiny and destiny of the body 113
'I missed a step': bad luck or doomed birth? 113
Negative narcissistic exception 114
Fate and the mother 115
The fate of transplantation: Solution and/or problem 116

Contents   vii

Ambiguity of gift, debt and guilt   118
Negative therapeutic reaction   119
Sublimation: A bastion against destiny?   120

8   Feminine hypochondria   123

Hypochondria and melancholy   123
Hypochondria, actual neurosis   125
Transnosography: hypochondria/psychosis   126
Feminine masochism, narcissism, and hypochondria   127
Primary homosexual relationship and hypochondria   128
Justine: 'I can't stand being me any more'   *128*
Sophie or hatred of the mother   129

9   Feminine paranoia   133

Passivation and feminisation of Schreber   133
The narcissistic feminine and paranoia   134
Is the paranoiac a 'true' victim?   135
Seduction, femininity, and paranoia   137
Feminine masochism and paranoia   139
Projection and paranoid persecution   140
Lacan's foreclosure of the Name-of-the-Father   141
Primitive homosexual hatred and paranoia   142
Seduction, frustration, and harassment in feminine paranoia   143
Daniel   144
When the worst is yet to come in persecution   147
Transformation, division, and splitting of the self   148
Logical loss and the logic of loss   148
Stolen thoughts and lost identity   150
The body hears   151
The anxiety of being 'forsaken'   152
Feminine masochism and persecution   153
Paranoia somatica   *154*
Mephitic Mephistopheles in the paranoid body   156
Anxiety about the loss of knowing/having [savoir/avoir]   *157*
The 'disseminated' body   157
'You have to die in order to live'   *158*
Regression, castration, and anal eroticism   159
Sacrificial giving, masochism, and megalomania   161
Feminine or 'Sacrifixion'   *162*

viii   Contents

10   Feminine masochism   **168**

Rousseau's feminine masochism   169
Masochism and dreamlike punishment   170
The desire for displeasure   171
Sadomasochism of compulsion neurosis   172
Moral masochism, the need for punishment and unconscious
  guilt   173
Active masochism: Negativity in treatment and in life   174
Feminine masochism as the negative of sadism   176
Masochism and introjected or auto-objectal
  narcissistic sadism   177
The return of primary masochism   179
At the edge of displeasure: Jouissance   180
Repetition compulsion, the displeasure principle, and the death
  drive   181
Melancholy or death masochism   183
Death masochism and instinctual disintegration   184
Life masochism or the primacy of moral conscience and Eros   185

Conclusion   **189**

References   *195*
Index of names   *205*

Introduction

It is never an easy task to produce a book on the subject of the feminine and femininity. The reader may quite legitimately be surprised. Discussing this 'disagreeable' question may not always 'sound friendly', as Freud himself confessed in his 33rd lecture on 'Femininity'.[1] In this key discourse from 1933, he described the problem of the feminine as 'obscure' and femininity as a 'dark continent'.

What is 'woman'? What does it mean 'to be a woman'?

Could it be that 'woman', without being limited to reductive ideas or vague representations, is indefinable, much like the notion of 'beauty'?[2] Is there something unsayable, 'inexpressible', something indeterminable about woman?

'Woman' is not an emotion, an experience, something ineffable, but a 'reality'. The reality of woman is generally characterised in the first instance by specific features rooted in the anatomical body. A woman is distinguished first and foremost by a body that is 'hollowed out', with an 'active receptivity' quite distinct from the passivity described by Freud. Secondly, and most commonly, femininity is determined through reference to social criteria: the roles, functions and qualities reserved for women in different places and times (countries, cultures and eras). These criteria are transmitted from one generation to another by the conscious and unconscious investment in the girl by her parents, her environment, and by the girl's identification with the phantasies of which she is the object. We are most certainly what has been made of us.[3]

Beyond the reality (the facts) of a woman, there is also a cult of the 'feminine ideal' and a famous myth of the 'eternal feminine' which combines various imaginary representations of women (such as the myth of the mother, the virgin, the earth, mother nature, the motherland, etc.). The myth of the 'eternal feminine' seeks to entrap women in a difficult ideal by challenging the subjectivity of women and the specificity of their condition.[4]

Freud was particularly interested in the idea that psychological differences between men and women are the result of anatomical differences that determine their evolution in different ways.

Taking Napoleon Bonaparte's famous dictum[5], and giving it a twist of his own, Freud liked his expression 'Anatomy is destiny'. The destiny of an individual who 'bears' a particular anatomical sexual difference at birth.

DOI: 10.4324/9781003414247-1

2 Introduction

In my book *La plaie et le couteau*[6] [The wound and the knife], I stated more broadly that 'the body is destiny'.[7] It is, in fact, the body in its anatomical–physical totality, which, beyond heredity, will largely determine the trajectory of our lives, as an absolute, fundamental, and unique inheritance. In this way, destiny is, as it were, already established. It is, therefore, both pre- and post-corporeal, because not only does it 'make' the body, but the body, through its own specificity, acts on the 'destinal' life.

A body is both destiny and 'destinal' because, beyond the question of the distinction attributed by fate to the anatomical sexes and their psychological consequences, it also mercilessly seals the course of a whole life.[8]

This 'destiny' is not definitive, but relative. It is continuously being reshaped by the interactions we have with our environment, its injunctions and expectations, an environment that is not only emotional but also societal and sociological. Throughout our lives, we never stop questioning this destiny, sometimes rebelling against it. It could be said that we are both encountering and countering it.

Some authors, particularly Jean Laplanche,[9] have challenged Freud's biological 'misdirection' by giving priority to phantasy. Indeed, although he defends the fundamental idea of psychic bisexuality, Laplanche primarily focuses on anatomical difference.

It is true that beyond the question of anatomy, the 'feminine' opposed to the masculine is evoked as a 'principle', particularly in Taoism and Eastern thought. Jung's opposition between animus and anima is also based on these same fundamental ideas.

Our era, which is so concerned with gender equality following the claims of feminism in the 1960s, raises more questions about equal rights (social, professional, political, etc.) without denying the question of *difference*.[10]

The question of the specificity of the sexes has long occupied both traditional and scientific thought. Many have come up against (and sometimes still come up against) these archaic *themata* that look at the issues of like and unlike.[11]

Freud did not shy away from the subject of the difference between the sexes and gendered identity, yet his theoretical development, despite regular revision and reworking, provoked a great deal of controversy and debate from the outset and continues to divide psychoanalysts today.[12]

There have always been 'conflicts' and even envy caused by the difference between the sexes, leading men and women to fantasise about the supposed advantages of 'the other's body'. This is always accompanied by the feeling of being dispossessed and disadvantaged by these so-called advantages.[13]

In this sense, the antagonisms that can be conjured by each of the anatomical sexes inspire the idea that woman considers man's 'strength' to be her 'weakness', and man considers woman's 'weakness' to be his 'strength'.[14]

So, to take an example, in representational systems women are imbued with an image of uninterrupted jouissance. Women are thought to be endowed with a kind of 'surplus' jouissance, or 'sur-jouissance'. Women are thought to have unfavourable and evil powers of a hybristic nature. Women are likened to immoderation, extravagance, 'excess', to being 'too much'.[15]

Introduction 3

This idea is ancestral. It belongs to archaic thought, and we find it in the mythology of classical antiquity and in fairy tales.

An example is Tiresias, the blind soothsayer of the city of Thebes, who, according to legend, had the 'advantage' of experiencing both sexes, and testified that while pleasure from love consisted of ten parts, men enjoyed only one and women nine. This idea is echoed in certain accounts of imaginary history. One tale from *The Thousand and One Nights*, for example, recounts particularly bewitching and allegorical points of view between two dreamlike fables, such as this in extract: '[…] just as desire in women is much more intense than in men, so their intelligence is infinitely quicker to grasp the relationship of the charming organs'.[16]

Freudian thinking is along the same lines. Even the great discovery of psychic bisexuality is said to be 'much more pronounced in women than in men'.[17]

Furthermore, there's a link between the 'riddle of the feminine' and that other problem: 'mysterious masochistic tendencies'.

This work seeks to deal with certain 'images', figurations or expressions of the feminine in both men and women. The feminine, which is both a clinical and a metapsychological concept, should not be confused with that of woman. Yet, the feminine does reflect the most deeply rooted common representations of woman and constitutes its foundation. That is why I thought it would be useful to begin this book with the riddle of the feminine and the question of castration, with the 'feminine in woman'.

In the chapters that follow, the feminine and some of its images are examined in their intimate relationship with a number of essential themes, such as traumatic seduction, narcissism, depression, grief and melancholia, as well as the defensive organisation of a hypochondriac or paranoid nature.

This is what I propose to study, and to try to understand from a theoretical and clinical perspective, in the following chapters. Similarly, I shall present certain clinical observations throughout, in order to challenge the theory, and vice versa.

Notes

1 Freud (1933a).
2 See Maïdi (2012).
3 Even if, as Jean-Paul Sartre (1963) rightly said in his book *St Genet, Actor and Martyr*: 'What is important is not what people make of us but what we ourselves make of what is made of us.' We are what we make of what others wanted to make of us.
4 In Book 1 of *Le deuxième sexe* [The Second Sex], Simone de Beauvoir (1949) made a remarkable attempt to deconstruct this myth of the 'eternal feminine'.
5 Napoleon Bonaparte coined the aphorism 'Geography is destiny'.
6 Maïdi (2003b). See also, 'Body of destiny and destiny of the body' in Chapter 7, 'Feminine destiny'.
7 Maïdi (2000).
8 It is therefore possible to argue that an original trauma, in the sense of an ordeal from birth rather than because of birth, is at the heart of human destiny. Present in every subject, this traumatic experience of primordial 'being' will largely influence one's direction and vital path. Original, pre-established destiny affects and traumatises the subject from the very first encounter with their environment.

4   Introduction

9 Laplanche (1987a).
10 Is this the famous 'To be or not to be'? although it doesn't really evoke fundamental existential anguish, but, rather, the question: Why am I, rather than not being (existing) in the face of what I have to confront. It also brings to mind Alfred de Musset's Lorenzaccio when he exclaims: 'This crime is the only thing that binds me to existence'.
11 From an anthropological point of view and with regard to the systems of representation relating to difference between the sexes, the reader can refer to the work of Françoise Héritier (1996).
12 These issues are directly related to morals and societal references, such as so-called 'marriage for all' which has divided psychoanalysts. It is essentially the notion of 'marriage' between people whose choice of object is of the homosexual orientation that has split many psychoanalysts.
13 Cournut-Janin & Cournut (1993).
14 See Jean Cournut (2006).
15 Remember that Enlightenment thinking was also moving in the same direction. In the 18th century, Diderot described women as beings of passion and instinct and Rousseau was convinced of their insatiable sensuality.
16 Quoted by David (1973), p. 244.
17 Freud (1931b).

Chapter 1

The riddle of the feminine

The feminine and femininity

The feminine encompasses representations of childhood pertaining to weakness, hollowness, castration, containment, and 'active' receptivity. It is defined by its intrinsic, *in principio*, welcoming mode. It is linked to the function of relative and incomplete 'passivity' and the reception of the object. Traditionally, cultural and religious representation of the feminine is likened to a receptacle, a hollow object, a 'weaker vessel',[1] even though 'fragility' does not, in itself, automatically have a pejorative connotation. An object's value is in no way diminished if it is 'fragile'. On the contrary, it can be enhanced.

However, prior to the dominant phallocracy, we should not forget the much older cult, dating back to prehistoric times, of the mother goddess who was dethroned by the phallocratic gods. In these cults, the image of the woman was linked to motherhood, in turn associated with fertility (and therefore with harvest). Statuettes (such as the 'Venus of Lespugue') do not portray her as hollow but instead she is filled out, with protruding and rounded (full) forms. She thus represents the principle of life, of origin, before this is transposed into the phallic principle: does life originate from the seed or from the one who makes the seed bear fruit? ('Blessed [...] is the fruit of thy womb, Jesus!', is said in the Hail Mary.) In this respect, the myth of the Virgin Mary is interesting, because it portrays the image of the pure mother begetting, without sexual intercourse, a Christian transposition of the mother goddess.

It is worth noting that common phallocracy guided Freud (1905d) in his association of the castration complex with what he called *Penisneid* (penis envy).[2] This idea has become widely accepted. Since then, to my knowledge, no psychoanalyst has really evoked and seriously analysed a counterpoint, the *Uterusneid*.

Similarly, with few exceptions, theological, philosophical and even psychoanalytical thought has regularly displayed some degree of phallocentrism. The primacy of the phallus is an ancient notion that largely predates psychoanalytic thinking.

In the beginning was man. This clearly identified masculine form contains the feminine within it. According to the Bible, God brings forth woman from man (and not through man). 'Yahweh Elohim caused a torpor to fall upon / Adam, who fell asleep, / And He took / one of his ribs (or sides = Tasalotav) / and He closed up the

DOI: 10.4324/9781003414247-2

6 The riddle of the feminine

flesh in its place. And Yahweh Elohim built / the rib (Tzela) which He had taken from Adam / into a woman, /and He brought her to Adam. / And Adam said: "This time, / bone of my bone, flesh of my flesh, / she shall be called Ichah / (woman) for from Ich (man) it was taken' (Genesis, II, 21–23).

The book of Genesis makes man first, and woman second. Indeed, if we refer to Genesis, man (the first man) is not [*n'est pas*] from woman, but woman is born [*naît*] from man. The woman came out of the man. Consequently, man was not created for woman, but woman for man. From this point of view, woman is considered to be part of man's body. From the very beginning, the supremacy of man over woman, the preponderance of the masculine over the feminine, is expressed without ambiguity.

The specificity of the sexes is rapidly affirmed by the primacy of *having* over *being*. In other words, having, or, on the contrary, deprivation and lack, will become the differential sign that conveys existential meaning. While sexual gender does not reflect anatomical sex, its use is striking in terms of the differentiation of natural bodies.

As a result of monotheistic religious culture, the woman has from the outset been condemned to two punishments: the 'fault' and original sin: 'In pain you will bear children'[3] — 'Your desire shall be contrary to your husband, but he shall rule over you.'[4] Very early on, 'being a woman' and the notion of 'fault' are deeply associated.

Similarly, medieval condemnation of women was applied even more widely and with unparalleled cruelty. Her very appearance and 'make-up' were banished, rejected, and imbued with evil elements, all with extreme violence. Preachers of the Middle Ages (13th–15th centuries) were unequivocal in condemning beauty treatments. In contrast to moral qualities, the repression of 'make-up' practices in women who aspired to 'beauty' was irredeemable. This medieval intolerance demonised the embellishment of women, linking it with lust and depravity. For a very long time, physical beauty was considered to be the inspiration of the 'diabolical' and the 'malignant'.[5]

Hatred of the feminine or *horror feminae*

This hatred of the 'feminine' in women was fuelled by genuine persecution. In this respect, the notorious *Malleus Maleficarum*[6] (The Hammer of Witches, 1486) is an illuminating treatise on phallocentrism. This book, written by two Franciscans, Jakob Sprenger and Heinrich Kramer, was approved and recommended by Pope Innocent VIII in 1484, and served as a reference for several centuries. It was responsible for thousands of innocent women being burnt at the stake as 'witches'. In no instance were the theories of these publicly celebrated and widely quoted 'theologians' disavowed. They wrote:

> What else is woman but a foe to friendship, an inescapable punishment, a necessary evil, a natural temptation, a desirable calamity, a domestic danger, a delectable prejudice, an evil of nature, beautifully varnished. … And it should

The riddle of the feminine 7

be noted that there was a defect in the formation of the first woman, since she was formed from a bent rib, that is, a rib of the breast, which is bent as it were in a contrary direction to a man. And since through this defect she is an imperfect animal, she always deceives … [When Eve replied to the serpent], she showed that she doubted, and had little faith in the word of God. And all this is indicated by the etymology of the word; for *Femina* [woman] comes from *Fe* [to produce] and *Minus* [less] since she is ever weaker to hold and preserve the faith.[7]

In his work about witches, which could be described as proto-feminist, Michelet[8] tried to rehabilitate these creatures and de-demonise them.

To try and understand the issue and the concept of the 'feminine', a diversion into philosophical thinking is also indispensable.

In his remarkable text *In vino veritas*,[9] Søren Kierkegaard, who greatly inspired the work of Lacan, formalised with corrosive mockery the strangeness of femininity, the '*dit-femme*'.[10] He asks not what a woman is, but what it is *to be* a woman. In his view, the feminine being is confronted with the very difficulty of its definition, in the sense of the following question: 'How does one become a woman?' The feminine is not, but becomes it, after the fact. For Søren Kierkegaard, the woman is, above all, an object of fantasy. This is in line with Simone de Beauvoir's renowned expression: 'One is not born a woman, but becomes one.'[11]

Similarly, the ideas of both Arthur Schopenhauer[12] and Friedrich Nietzsche[13] greatly influenced Freud in his work to understand what he eventually called 'the riddle of the feminine'.[14]

For Schopenhauer, woman is 'will' but also the '*sexus sequior*', that is to say, the secondary sex in all respects.

Nietzsche, on the other hand, compares women to truth 'which is founded on not letting the foundation be seen'. For the male philosopher, truth is as unreasonable, natural, and unknowable as a woman, the object of his desire. The Nietzschean metaphor of 'woman as truth' meets another symbol with a clearly disadvantageous tone, that of the *Baubo*,[15] a vulgar Greek demon that represents female genitalia. According to Nietzsche, women embody mysterious and irrational forces.

Freud and the woman

In the development of his work, Freud was greatly inspired by German philosophers, in particular from the Romantic and 'melancholic' period.

In his *Three Essays on the Theory of Sexuality* (1905d), he writes with considerable value judgement:

The significance of the factor of sexual overvaluation can be best studied in men, for their erotic life alone has become accessible to research. That of women – partly owing to the stunting effect of civilized conditions and partly owing to their conventional secretiveness and insecurity – is still veiled in an impenetrable obscurity.[16]

8   The riddle of the feminine

In 'Some Psychical Consequences of the Anatomical Distinction between the Sexes' (1925j), Freud adds:

> I cannot evade the notion (though I hesitate to give it expression) that for women the level of what is ethically normal is different from what it is in men. [...] Character-traits which critics of every epoch have brought up against women – that they show less sense of justice than men, that they are less ready to submit to the great exigencies of life, that they are more often influenced in their judgements by feelings of affection or hostility – all these would be amply accounted for by the modification in the formation of their super-ego which we have inferred above.[17]

In his seminal text *Civilization and Its Discontents* (1930a), Freud argues that women are guided by their natural and irrational instincts. Thus, he argues that

> women soon come into opposition to civilization and display their retarding and restraining influence – those very women who, in the beginning, laid the foundations of civilization by the claims of their love. Women represent the interests of the family and of sexual life. The work of civilization has become increasingly the business of men, it confronts them with ever more difficult tasks and compels them to carry out instinctual sublimations of which women are little capable.[18]

In his lecture on 'Femininity' (1933a), Freud states that anatomy cannot account for femininity, nor will psychology 'solve the riddle of femininity'. 'The explanation,' he adds, 'must no doubt come from elsewhere, and cannot come till we have learnt how in general the differentiation of living organisms into two sexes came about'.[19]

> Throughout history people have knocked their heads against the riddle of the nature of femininity... Nor will *you* have escaped worrying over this problem – those of you who are men; to those of you who are women this will not apply – you are yourselves the problem.[20]

Men seem to be confronted with the irresolvable nature of this riddle, and so too are women, because, according to Freud, they themselves are this riddle: that is to say, they are, in a certain way, incapable of thinking about their own enigmatic nature. There is something of a phallocratic tautology here: as woman is designated a riddle, she cannot think of herself as such!

In 'Female Sexuality' (1931b), as well as in his lecture on 'Femininity' (in 1933a), two fundamental psychoanalytical concepts emerge in our comprehension of femininity: the castration complex and the idea of passivity.[21]

In 1933a, Freud states:

> In recent times we have begun to learn a little about this, [how a young girl becomes a woman] thanks to the circumstance that several of our excellent female

colleagues in analysis have begun to work at the question. The discussion of this has gained special attractiveness from the distinction between the sexes. For the ladies, whenever some comparison seemed to turn out unfavourable to their sex, were able to utter a suspicion that we, the male analysts, had been unable to overcome certain deeply-rooted prejudices against what was feminine ...[22]

In this same lecture, Freud adds: 'If you reject this idea as fantastic and regard my belief in the influence of lack of a penis on the configuration of femininity as an *idée fixe*, I am of course defenceless'.[23]

Two years earlier, Freud had admitted that the 'impression of castration' was 'confused and contradictory'. He wrote: 'In truth, it is hardly possible to give a description which has general validity. We find the most different reactions in different individuals, and in the same individual the contrary attitudes exist side by side'.[24]

According to the founder of psychoanalysis, the woman herself denigrates herself and 'begins to share the contempt felt by men for a sex which is the lesser in so important a respect, and, at least in holding that opinion, insists on being like a man'.[25]

Not only does Freud reflect the positions of Schopenhauer and Nietzsche, for whom woman is only instinct and nature, but he also appears at times to share the Nietzschean conception of woman as identified and associated with truth, the enigmatic, and the inscrutable.

In 'The Dissolution of the Oedipus Complex', he writes:

How does the corresponding development take place in little girls? At this point our material – for some incomprehensible reason – becomes far more obscure and full of gaps.[26] ... It must be admitted, however, that in general our insight into these developmental processes in girls is unsatisfactory, incomplete and vague.[27]

However, if all libido is by its very nature, like all instincts,[28] active, and hence inherently masculine,[29] in women as in men, Freud uses euphemistic signifiers such as 'shortcomings', 'veils', and 'mysteries' in relation to women.

What does a woman want?

According to Jones, Freud's exact words to Marie Bonaparte[30] were: 'The great question that has never been answered and which I have not yet been able to answer, despite my thirty years of research into the feminine soul, is "What does a woman want?"'[31] *Che vuoi?*

It is specifically on *wanting* that Freud's awkward question focuses, *not on desire* as if it were an impossible question to answer, as the 'wanting-woman' is impossible to satisfy. Freud seems to be at a loss when it comes to the 'wanting-woman', the *What does a woman want*? For wanting is above desire. Wanting is associated with the notion of will, which expresses an unconditional and indisputable imperative. Yet, there is no other destiny for the will than that of desire. The will is something impossible to fulfil. Men and women are in the same situation, that of irremediable symbolic castration.

10   The riddle of the feminine

Thus, the 'wanting-woman' would be a form of denial of lack, even denial of the self, the non-fulfilment of the self in an impossible quest to be 'Whole', to be fulfilled and grandiose, without lack, a nostalgia for the omnipotence of early childhood.

What is questionable about this Freudian approach is the phallocentric, or masculine centred, vision, according to which for centuries we have only heard men talk about women, femininity, and so on. It is as if they wanted to exorcise their own fear of the feminine mystery. But why have so few women spoken for themselves, in their own name, about their own nature and sexuality? Why was this phallocentric dictatorship imposed for so long? It took perhaps Marie Bonaparte (herself of aristocratic origin) for women to start talking about sexuality as a woman, and it took Simone de Beauvoir and then the feminist movement for women to grant or claim the right to speak for themselves. Why this more or less explicit ban on women thinking, as if they could only be identified by their impulsive and irrational nature? How did Freud's Jewish origin influence his phallocentrism? Why did men arrogate to themselves the primacy of scientific thought, artistic creation, and the search for truth? Might the great Nietzsche have feared that this 'truth' held by women would dethrone the male quest for truth? Is it the case that science and truth are masculine in nature?[32]

What a lot of ideological assumptions lie behind these meta-psychological questions!

Beyond our intellectual honesty, this focus on the feminine, and not on the woman, remains a masculine approach and question …

The feminine in Freud, Winnicott, and Lacan

Freud: The phallocentrism of sexuality

Freud has been regularly criticised for his conception of sexuality structured exclusively on the model of masculinity and phallicity. He has often been reproached for his constant reference to psychosexuality as being infinitely male in origin, and continuously 'active' even when the purpose of the instinct takes on a 'passive' aspect. The activity/passivity distinction has no direct relation with the sexual differentiations of an anatomical or physiological nature.

Freud consistently held a phallic view of sexuality and libido: he wrote

> There is only one libido, which serves both the masculine and the feminine sexual functions. To it itself we cannot assign any sex; if, following the conventional equation of activity and masculinity, we are included to describe it as masculine, we must not forget that it also covers trends with a passive aim.[33]

It should be noted that the admission of a desire of a 'passive' nature somewhat modifies the representation of 'activity' as naturally masculine. 'Passivity' would be considered as being on the 'feminine' side. For Freud (1924d), the feminine signified passive, masochistic, castrated, enduring coitus and childbirth. If the

The riddle of the feminine   11

masculine is the culmination of the series: active, sadistic, phallic, the feminine is the culmination of the series: passive, masochistic, castrated.[34]

According to Freud, the feminine arises consecutively to the pre-genital stages of libidinal, oral, anal, and phallic development:

> At the stage of the pre-genital sadistic–anal organization, there is as yet no question of male and female; the antithesis between *active* and *passive* is the dominant one. At the following stage of infantile genital organization, which we now know about, *maleness* exists, but not femaleness. The antithesis here is between having a *male genital* and being *castrated*. It is not until development has reached its completion at puberty that the sexual polarity coincides with *male* and *female*. Maleness combines the factors of subject, activity, and the possession of the penis; femaleness takes over object and passivity. The vagina is now valued as a place of shelter for the penis; it enters into the heritage of the womb.[35]

He based his sexual theory on three major premises:

1. The existence, in both sexes, of a phallic stage determined by the presence or absence of a penis: masculine–phallic as opposed to feminine–castrated. The clitoris, mistaken for a shortened, 'stunted'[36] and depreciated penis, is thought to embody the only usual sexual organ for girls.

   Nevertheless, the vagina, and fundamentally the womb, 'remain for a long time unknown' to the girl.[37] The vagina will only take on its reality as the 'dwelling place of the penis' during coitus; the uterus will be revealed by menstruation and childbirth.

   At the anal–sadistic stage,

   > ... the aggressive impulses of little girls leave nothing to be desired in the way of abundance and violence. With their entry into the phallic phase the differences between the sexes are completely eclipsed by their agreements... We are entitled to keep to our view that in the phallic phase of girls the clitoris is the leading erotogenic zone.[38]

   It is worth noting that, in accordance with Lou Andreas-Salomé, Freud associates vaginal sensations with 'cloacal' sensations.[39]

   Consequently, for Freud, only the male genitalia (represented by the phallus) play a role in psychosexual development (in the phallic phase).

2. For Freud, in both sexes, the first object is, therefore, the mother. Castration anxiety, and the fear of 'emasculation', compel the young boy to separate from the mother. The 'anatomical' feminine of the latter is despised and devalued. The penis-organ is overestimated. *A contrario*, the young girl feels she will never possess this desired and valued organ.

   > They feel seriously wronged, often declare that they want to "have something like that too" and fall a victim to "envy for the penis" [*Penisneid*],[40]

12   The riddle of the feminine

> which will leave ineradicable traces on their development and the formation
> of their character and which will not be surmounted in even the most favour-
> able cases without a severe expenditure of psychical energy.[41]

The girl will also withdraw from the mother and seek refuge in her father, from
whom she hopes for a child. The girl resents her mother for the lack and incompleteness. This could explain the complicated, ambivalent, and devastating relationship between the two mother and daughter protagonists.

Studies on the 'feminine' by female psychoanalyst students of Freud led him to
connect the positive forms of the mother–daughter relationship, particularly to the
determining value of the pre-oedipal formations of female sexuality. Thus, Freud
sets out in his 1933a lecture on 'Femininity':

> A woman's identification with her mother allows us to distinguish two strata:
> the pre-Oedipus one which rests on her affectionate attachment to her mother
> and takes her as a model, and the later one from the Oedipus complex which
> seeks to get rid of her mother and take her place with her father … But the phase
> of the affectionate pre-Oedipus attachment is the decisive one for a woman's
> future: during it preparations are made for the acquisition of the characteristics
> with which she will later fulfil her role in the sexual function and perform her
> invaluable social tasks.[42]

3. The phallocentric view of sexuality is also asserted in the context of *psychic
   bisexuality*, which is both 'bodily in origin' and the result of real or phantasised
   processes of identification with the two parents:

> [Science]... draws your attention to the fact that portions of the male sexual
> apparatus also appear in women's bodies, though in an atrophied state,[43] and
> vice versa in the alternative case. It regards their occurrence as indications
> of *bisexuality*... You will then be asked to make yourselves familiar with the
> idea that the proportion in which masculine and feminine are mixed in an
> individual is subject to quite considerable fluctuations. You cannot give the
> concepts of 'masculine' and 'feminine' *any* new connotation. The distinction
> is not a psychological one; when you say 'masculine', you usually mean 'ac-
> tive,' and when you say 'feminine', you usually mean 'passive'.[44]

Note here that Freud has established an entanglement of the feminine and the masculine in psychic bisexuality. There is no such thing as male or female purity.

The castration complex on becoming a woman

Since castration anxiety is at the root of the formation of the superego, its lack will
enhance the deficiency of the superego in women:

> I cannot evade the notion (though I hesitate to give it expression) that for women
> the level of what is ethically normal is different from what it is in men. Their

super-ego is never so inexorable, so impersonal, so independent of its emotional origins as we require it to be in men. Character-traits which critics of every epoch have brought up against women – that they show less sense of justice[45] than men, that they are less ready to submit to the great exigencies of life, that they are more often influenced in their judgements by feelings of affection or hostility – all these would be amply accounted for by the modification in the formation of their super-ego which we have inferred above. We must not allow ourselves to be deflected from such conclusions by the denials of the feminists, who are anxious to force us to regard the two sexes as completely equal in position and worth; but *we shall, of course, willingly agree that the majority of men are also far behind the masculine ideal and that all human individuals, as a result of their bisexual disposition and of cross-inheritance, combine in themselves both masculine and feminine characteristics, so that pure masculinity and femininity remain theoretical constructions of uncertain content.*[46]

The current debate and controversy over 'gender theory' shows that this issue is far from being resolved on an educational or societal level!

Are there specifically male and female psychic functions? Would sensitivity and tenderness, for example, be precisely feminine in nature, like so-called 'female intuition'?

The fundamental notion of psychic bisexuality still remains attached to the gendering of 'qualities', which are, moreover, abstract concepts. Neuroscientific discoveries do not provide evidence of significant gender differences in brain function. Behind the opposing notions of masculine/feminine, there is no clear opposition of related concepts, for instance: drive/reason, feeling/reason, nature/culture, etc.

It should be noted that the ideas of Melanie Klein,[47] centred around the primacy of the maternal breast, are in total opposition to those of Freud. For Klein, the girl will usually desire the penis because of instinctual feminine demands, under the dominance of orality. The oral deprivation produced by the bad breast creates in the little girl the desire to possess the penis that is controlled by the mother.

Thus, the coveting of the penis is both secondary to an oral frustration and linked to the desire for a visible organ, the completeness of which she can perceive during the castration anxieties that women are not spared. The oral desire for the paternal penis, created by the frustration of the breast, would be the paragon of genital, vaginal desire. The introjection of the paternal penis, and the identification with this oedipal object, will form the linchpin of the female superego. The girl will be more obedient towards her father than the boy, and her superego, inversely to Freud's assessment, will become more austere. Female masochism results from the reversal of sadism against bad inner objects. Klein opposes the 'good' to the 'bad', instead of the opposition 'phallic' and 'castrated' or 'having' and 'lacking'. The indisputable value of Klein's work is to have countered the phallic organisation of psychosexuality to set up a female maternal order. However, although closely related to the clinical setting, Kleinian theories remain at the stage of metapsychological speculation.

14 The riddle of the feminine

Winnicott: 'Pure' feminine and masculine

For Winnicott, the child 'exists' long before they are born. Very early on, the 'good enough' mother who must welcome them will provide them with life's essential needs. She will give them the indispensable conditions of existence and transmit to them a real capacity to 'be'.

At the threshold of life, the 'pure feminine',[48] with no imprint of the masculine, does not yet know otherness, diversity, or the foreign object. It is unaware of the masculine and the difference between the sexes. It experiences only the feminine because the mother is a woman. At this time, the absolute feminine is foremost. It is a total, omnipotent feminine, that the mother 'gives' to her child to see and experience.[49]

It is quite possible to compare the phase of the 'pure feminine' described by Winnicott and the primary (or pure) narcissism, set out by Freud in these terms:

> ... the ego, in which at first the whole available quota of libido is stored up. We call this state absolute, primary *narcissism*. It lasts till the ego begins to cathect the ideas of objects with libido, to transform narcissistic libido into object-libido.[50]

Following Winnicott, we could say that the pure feminine coincides with Freudian *pure*, primary narcissism. It occurs at a time when instincts are not yet directed towards a specific external object.

On the other hand, the feminine precedes the libido, which Freud claims is quintessentially male. In this sense, it is not a question of a pure feminine linked to an instinct since, according to Winnicott, the instinct does not exist before the formation of the self. At this stage of omnipotence, subject and object become one. They are coalescent, hence the notion of 'subjective object'.

The pure feminine is formed and merged with the mother's breast. By virtue of its condition and its primordial relationship with the mother, the child, whether boy or girl, represents the 'pure feminine'. In a sense, the child 'is' the breast, even before being able to take it.

It is only when the child, of either sex, understands that the object does not belong to them (as a separate, objectively perceived object), and ardently desires and vigorously takes the breast that they gain access to the masculine.

What is it that guides the child to the breast, the mouth to the nipple? This natural, innate search comes from within. It is rooted in the interiority of the body. For Freud, instincts are forces that 'exist behind the tensions caused by the needs of the id ... [and] represent the somatic demands upon the mind',[51] while, for Winnicott, instincts are secondary to this pressure.

Winnicott brought new views to bear on the advent of the feminine and the masculine. He has been criticised for neglecting the role of the life and death instincts and their anchorage in the body. Yet, in his posthumous work *Human Nature*,[52] he insists on the predominant role of the instincts.

The riddle of the feminine 15

In this work, Winnicott gives an important place to instinctual forces and movements. He writes: 'Freud... put forward... the importance of instinct and the significance of childhood sexuality. Any theory that denies or bypasses these matters is unhelpful'. He identifies instinct with the animal instinct: 'the stirrings of instinct... like any other animal'.[53] It is worth recalling that Freud explains the instinct as a borderline concept between the psychic and the somatic, linked to the notion of representing.

According to Winnicott, the masculine emerges with the discovery and coveting of the 'other' object. In the same way, the move towards the masculine in the infant boy is thought to result from a reverie of the mother who distinguishes the sex of her son while he himself is not yet aware of his difference. It is the mother, the maternal object, who consciously or unconsciously assigns the child to a psychic sex, a determined gender.

The 'pure masculine' is a conquest of 'having' and a constraint upon the act of 'making'. As with Freud, the masculine is, according to Winnicott, characterised by activity. It is a transition from 'the being that is made' (passivity) to 'making so as to be', (activity), an 'asserting' of one's difference. This shift away from passivity and passivation, and the search for activity is true for both girls and boys. The 'pure masculine' would, therefore, be secondary to the 'pure feminine'. There is always a 'pure feminine', regardless of the child's gender, in the child's very first relationship with the mother.

However, if through a failure of the maternal figure[54] (mother or her substitute), the pure and essential feminine is not successfully constructed, the child will not be able to acquire a sufficient narcissistic base that will allow them to face separation and to establish the masculine dimension of their psychic life.

The development of the girl and the boy

There are, therefore, two reasons for the inequality between the development of girls and boys:

1. Prior to differentiation, the assimilation–identification with the mother facilitates the formation of a pure feminine, a form of archaic and essential nirvana (primary narcissism) where being is sufficient, but which will create the foundations of a subsequent ability to better overcome disappointment, separation, lack, and attainment of the 'capacity to be alone'.

   While the primordial care object has been able to give the child the potential to delude itself, it will later be able to endure its disillusion in order to conquer the pure masculine, which is determined by the ardent desire to seize the breast-object, the partial object of lust.

   The transition to the secondary masculine on an unstable and vulnerable foundation of 'pure feminine' will only allow a simple appearance of psychic balance and gendered identity.

2. In contrast, girls can only be accommodated in relation to what they lack, with respect to what is 'hollow' or 'negative'. Consequently, it is necessary for them

16 The riddle of the feminine

to provide themselves at all costs with a penis-object equivalent, an investment in the whole body, a love object, or a child. Their fulfilment results from this. The condition and position of girls appear more precarious and their narcissism more uncertain. They will be less autonomous in relation to the invested objects, whereas boys, comforted by the presence of their penis, will feel more complete.[55] One can see that Winnicott's point of view is close to Freud's.

According to Winnicott, the phantasy of oral activity is not necessarily 'erotic' at the beginning.

Ambivalence would be achieved more through transformations of the ego than through the development of the id, when the child moves from 'ruthless love' to 'concern' for the other.

The anal and urethral stages, which result from the good or bad properties of the excreted substances, is followed by the phallic stage, which concerns the boy, and 'the boy' within the girl, the masculine aspect of the feminine.

The genital stage unfolds later on to the pre-genital stage from which it will retain the marks. The genital stage is previously linked to penile turgidity in the boy which provokes castration anxiety in relation to the maternal love object and paternal rivalry. It naturally tends towards desires for penetration and fertilisation with the representation of a 'real love object'.

It is worth remembering that, for the boy, castration anxiety is relatively tempered and peaceful compared to archaic, unimaginable, and 'dissecting' anxieties.

Given the lack of a visible castratable organ and the absence of the castration anxiety attached to it, girls may have a problematic path to take that 'presents opportunities for homosexual development'. Winnicott agrees here that, contrary to what he states in *Playing and Reality* (1971a), 'there is ample space for *unhappiness*[56] and *distress*[57] in the little girl'.

However, he does emphasise the positive and effective form of penis envy in the girl and the conquest of its representation and equivalence.

We can assume that the boy will be more uncomfortable in constructing a distinct gendered identity and that he will retain a mark that is either moderate and common, or the opposite, solid and rebellious, repelling the break with the primary object.

It proves more convenient for the girl, whose sexual identity is similar to the mother's, formed in the past, to continually preserve the imprint of the primordial relationship.

Nevertheless, the girl will be confronted with the demands of the desire for the paternal object during the Oedipal stage, whereas the young boy will be able to return to and rediscover an object of the same sex as his first love.

For Freud, since masculinity comes first, it is the girl who will have difficulty abandoning the relationship with the primary object and for whom psychic bisexuality will be easier. This debate – feminine or masculine in the most archaic period – is still ongoing. The question of whether the renunciation of the primary object is easier for girls or boys is not settled.

The riddle of the feminine   17

Certainly Winnicott, like Freud and other psychoanalysts, finds it difficult to distinguish between the reality of psychic bisexuality and identifications with parents of both sexes on the one hand, and the need to consolidate a gendered identity consistent with anatomical singularity on the other. It should be noted, however, that sexual roles in human beings are not always related to sex defined by organs.

Making or being masculine or feminine?

The debate remains open. Is the feminine more achievable for girls than the masculine for boys?

Clinical references do not generally indicate this. Women, like men,[58] sometimes have a predisposition for 'making' (as though) rather than 'being' (this or that). Women, like men, have had to rid themselves of their primary identification with the mother, but more laboriously, as is shown in the clinical setting. Is it subsequently more difficult to carve out a secondary female identity?

Winnicott, nevertheless, emphasised that the female experience requires only a 'simple' psychic disposition, in so far as it is supported by the original identification with the mother. Structuring female identity would be 'easier' and would require less psychological work than conquering the masculine, which first requires detachment and is later based more on having than on being, hence the common preoccupation of men to constantly prove that they have not been castrated (cf. the male injunction: 'Show that you've got some...').[59]

Despite this, in *Human Nature*, Winnicott is forced to point out that there are several obstacles that girls face in acquiring their identity as adult women.

The initial stage, signified by the 'pure feminine' makes no distinction between the sexes. This difference exists in and through the mother's gaze. Through her phantasies, she 'sees' her daughter as similar to her own reality ('diminished' and far from omnipotent)... and the boy as endowed with the sex that she covets and idealises but whose difference she has to admit.

In 'Symbiosis anxiety and the development of masculinity", the American psychoanalyst Robert Stoller[60] (1975), well known in the gender studies movement, criticises Freud's assertion that the boy commits his life to heterosexuality from the outset. In total agreement with Winnicott, Stoller insists on the original consubstantial relationship with the mother, 'a woman with a female sexual identity', which he will have to dominate and overcome.

He insists on the importance of maternal desire for her son's access to a masculine sexual identity:

He writes,

I do not believe, that the sense of oneness with mother encourages even a primordial sense of maleness in the first months of life, but rather that this oneness must be counteracted. Only if a mother supports the development of masculinity will the oneness be pretty much overthrown as ego development proceeds. She will do this first because she wishes for and enjoys a masculine son.[61]

18   The riddle of the feminine

Stoller, like Winnicott, attributes considerable power to the environment. It has a decisive impact very early on. A baby does not exist on its own. A baby has no sexual identity of its own. Alone, a baby will not develop, or even survive. Thus, the influence of the mother, of the supporting maternal object, the *Nebenmensch* (the 'next-person'), on the child's sexual orientation from the very beginning, is undeniable.

Male or female gender

While the masculine or feminine gender encounters some ordinary and inherent 'turbulence' or confusion during adolescence, it is only firmly established as a function of the type and 'quality' of the relationship of sexuation, identification and assignment of a gender by an adult to the child. In this respect, Stoller (1985)[62] made it clear that it is the mother who chooses the sex of her child. The mother gives life, and offers her child a differentiated sex, an orientation in terms of sexual identity. Beyond the obvious anatomical difference, she gives the child a name and a gender identity.

Assignment to a gendered 'type' is associated with the granting of a first name. Those who choose the first name[63] assign the child to a position and function depending on their own imaginary world. This act will weigh on the child's future like a *destiny*, including in terms of sexuation. The name, therefore, represents not only the person who bears it (sometimes as a burden), but also determines a life plan. It is linked to a parental plan that needs to be appropriated in order to match and be in 'alliance' with the community, in the sense of a feeling of belonging to the group. Naming the child is an 'act' of transmission from the parents for a specific project and assignment to a determined sex which the child is destined to respect. Naming is an act of giving a destiny. The name can be a burden for the person who bears it. It is never neutral in the existence of a subject, as is the case, for example, with unisex names such as 'Taylor', 'Jordan', sometimes 'Alexis', as well as the completely fanciful and fantastical names given by some donors.

In this primitive transmission of the 'sexual', which takes place through the original seduction of the adult towards the child, *gender*, to be differentiated in psychoanalysis from *sex*, is also imposed on the child from the environment. Gender is acquired, addressed, and 'assigned'. A primordial environment 'assigns' gender in a message to be translated by the child. It is then through the body that the sexual adult is implanted in the child, in a way similar to that which sees the gender assigned to the child by the adult.

Jean Laplanche (2003) writes:

> Assignment is a complex set of actions which extends through language and the significant behaviours of those around us. One could speak of a continuous assignment or of a true *prescription*. Prescription in the sense of 'prescriptive' messages; hence in the sense of a message, or even a bombardment of messages.[64]

Gender, determined by assignment, therefore underlines the primacy of the other – the child before becoming a male or female subject is identified *as* – in the process of sexuation and gendered subjectivation. The adult stipulates that the child *be as*. They assign gender to the child and transmit to them '*le sexual*', which is not the sexuated. Here it is essentially a question of the *perverse infantile form of the sexual*. As the adult is constantly seducing the child who, initially passive, will enter into human sexuality in its fantastical value. This situation of seduction is referred to by Laplanche as the 'fundamental anthropological situation'.

Thus, *le sexual* would be defined, in effect, as that which is repressed and 'suppressed' by the adult and which is conferred on the child without the child's knowledge. *Le sexual*, as Laplanche names it, is related to the 'original seduction', i.e., the relationship between the adult ('endowed with an unconscious') and the child of infant sexuality ('*le sexual*'). The *sexual* is, therefore, a sexuality marked by unboundedness, overflow, and excitement.

'It is thus the *sexuated* [*sexué*] and also, above all, the *le sexual* of the parents that cause a disturbance in an assignment', writes Laplanche.[65]

Lacan: The primacy of the phallus

In his *Encore* Seminar in 1972, devoted in part to female jouissance, Lacan[66] considered two aspects, a masculine and a feminine, that any subject could possibly correspond with independently of their biological sex.

Lacan goes along with the monist thesis supported by Freud, and by some women psychoanalysts. In *Three Essays on the Theory of Sexuality* (1905d), Freud put forward the thesis of sexual monism and a 'male' essence of the human libido. Freud's 'phallicism' is based on the idea that the girl originally wants to be a boy. It should be remembered that this thesis about sexual monism was criticised and discussed by other psychoanalysts from 1920, particularly by Melanie Klein, supported in particular by Ernest Jones,[67] who put forward a dualistic thesis and a specific relationship between girls and their mothers.

The privileged organ of power is the penis which is, beyond an image, beyond a symbolic representation, the phallus. The male sexual organ, because it is visible and erectile, is immediately invested in by both boys and girls. For Lacan, as for Freud, the 'primacy of the phallus' is essential. It is common to both boys and girls. Lacan analysed these two aspects in relation to the phallic function. He went even further than Freud. He constructed a structural theory beginning with the primacy of the phallus and leading to some surprising insights. The father of the structure defends the existence of the signifying system whose function is symbolic. The vagina is said to embody a fragment of the real, not impregnated by the signifier.

Thus, he argues in *Encore*:

> That is what analytic discourse demonstrates in that, to one of these beings qua sexed, to man insofar as he is endowed with the organ said to be phallic – I said 'said to be' – the corporal sex (*sexe corporel*) or sexual organ (*sexe*) of

20   The riddle of the feminine

woman – I said 'of woman' whereas in fact *woman* does not exist, woman is *not whole* (*pas toute*) – woman's sexual organ is of no interest (*ne lui dit rien*) except via the body's jouissance.[68]

Lacan also explained:

I should say that strictly speaking there is no symbolization of woman's sex as such. In any case, the symbolization isn't the same, it doesn't have the same source or the same mode of access as the symbolization of man's sex. And this is because the imaginary only furnishes an absence where elsewhere there is a highly prevalent symbol.[69]

Not-Whole and the jouissance of woman

Lacan tightened up Freud's theory of the *primacy of the phallus*. As we have emphasised, it is a question of phallus and not of penis, that is to say, a symbolic representation of phallic power. However, for Lacan, contrary to what Mac Dougall[70] states, the phallus is associated with the masculine, with the presence of the penis. Woman is incomplete, 'not whole', but endowed with a mystery, an enigma, which she protects.

In *Encore,* he exasperatedly urges women analysts:

... Our colleagues, the lady analysts, do *not* tell us... the *whole* story! (*pas tout!*)... They haven't contributed one iota to the question of feminine sexuality. There must be an internal reason for that, related to the structure of the apparatus of jouissance.

In this same *Seminar*, Lacan later adds:

... There is a jouissance that is hers (à elle), that belongs to that 'she' (*elle*) that doesn't exist and doesn't signify anything. There is a jouissance that is hers about which she herself perhaps knows nothing if not that she experiences it – and that much she knows. She knows it, of course, when it comes (*arrive*)... all the time people have been begging them, begging them on their hands and knees – I spoke last time of women psychoanalysts – to try to tell us, not a word! We've never been able to get anything out of them. So we call this jouissance by whatever name we can come up with, 'vaginal' ...[71]

It is easy to conjecture that the inclination of women, effected on the 'visible' penis, is more practical to perform than that of men, which is more obscure, more anxiety-provoking, based on something unrepresentable and dangerous that underlies the phantasies of bewitching women: '... the vaginal orgasm has kept the darkness of its nature inviolate', Lacan stated.[72] He connects feminine jouissance to a link with God: 'Doesn't this jouissance one experiences and yet knows nothing about put us on the path of ex-sistence? And why not interpret one face of the Other, the God face, as based on feminine jouissance?'[73]

The riddle of the feminine   21

Lacan made it possible to overturn and go beyond this form of *doxa* according to which woman would be characterised by what is below [*en-dessous*], missing [*en-moins*], in relation to the phallic function. Thus, he asserts that woman has an 'additional jouissance', presumably furthering the thinking of Tiresias. Lacan emphasises: 'I believe in the jouissance of woman insofar as it is extra (*en plus*)'. He observes this jouissance through the ecstatic state of female mystics.[74]

The ecstatic face of the exuberant Saint Teresa[75], in Bernini's statue in the Church of Saint Mary of Victory in Rome is a paradigmatic model of this jouissance. A jouissance that is enigmatic even for the saint who experiences it: 'it is clear that the fundamental testimony of mystics is precisely that they experience it, but know nothing about it'.

The jouissance of the mystics is a divine jouissance in its broad polysemy. It is the expression of a feminine, accomplished in perfect narcissistic wholeness, which accedes to omnipotence, becoming One with God.

Throughout centuries of male domination, women have been denied female jouissance. And yet what if the 'jouissive' expressions of the mystics, concealed by religious legitimacy, presented the additional, ineffable jouissance of the woman in a supreme and divine way, without which there would be no risk of experiencing the fate of Tiresias?

The undeniable and indescribable 'oceanic feeling'[76] of this ecstatic state recalls the archaic phase of primary narcissism. Is it nostalgia for the primordial figure of the father as 'saviour' from the risk of annihilation by the omnipotent maternal *imago*?

In his famous *Encore* seminar, Lacan pursues his theorisation and elaboration on the mathemes of sexuation, which is the logical expression in the form of formulae derived from the theory of quantifiers that define the masculine and feminine position in their relation to the phallic function.

Lacan describes man as a symbol.[77] In this respect, Man can be written with a capital M, because he is completely subjugated to the phallic symbol. As for woman, Lacan depicts her as 'not-whole*'*, subject to this phallic function.

Lacan develops the symbolic and universal function of the symbolic phallus in his schema of sexuation,[78] which operates in every divided subject (S) as a *parlêtre* (speaking-being) subject to castration. The symbolic phallus equates to a signifier of desire and a signifier of castration. Sexuation forms the completion of an identification, which leads every speaking subject, whoever they may be, to ensure a sexuated identity, male or female. Man is limited to phallic jouissance alone.[79] Unlike man, woman has no limits to her jouissance. Woman does not exist. She is *ex nihilo.* The '*La*' in *la femme* is therefore crossed out (La). Furthermore, the not-whole woman is subjected to castration. She is under both the influence of phallic jouissance constituted by signifiers, and an additional jouissance of the Other which Lacan explains as being that of the body, and which he highlighted using the writings of mystics, women and men.

In a final deduction, Lacan reveals that 'Woman does not exist' as a stable and unalterable totality, any more than man is a master who could govern her by deluding himself into an illusory sense of omnipotence.

Notes

1 Cf. the Bible: 'Husbands, in the same way be considerate as you live with your wives, and treat them with respect as the weaker partner and as heirs with you of the gracious gift of life, so that nothing will hinder your prayers.' Peter 3:7.
2 Freud (1905d).
3 Note that this judgement contains both a curse: 'in pain', and a blessing: '…shall you bear children'.
4 (Gen. 3.16 : '*Mulieri quoque dixit : multiplicabo aerumnas tuas et conceptus tuos ; in dolore paries fllios et subviri potestate eris et ipse dommabitur tui.* ')
5 'Women are married to the devil' describes the misogynistic discourse in the first texts on the Sabbath (beginning of the 15th century).
6 Kramer & Sprenger (1486).
7 *Malleus Maleficarum*, (1486). English translation online at www.historymuse.net/readings/Malleus.htm
8 Michelet (1862).
9 Kierkegaard (2011).
10 The '*diffame*', according to Lacan's pun in On Feminine Sexuality, The Limits of Love and Knowledge, in *The Seminar of Jacques Lacan, Book XX Encore* (1972–1973).
11 In *The Second Sex* (1972), Simone de Beauvoir argues that male–female inequality is culturally determined, not innate.
12 Schopenhauer (1851). On women, in *Parerga and Paralipomena*.
13 Nietzsche (1887).
14 On this subject, see the article by George J. Makari (1991).
15 Nietzsche shows his great misogyny by referring to women harshly and pejoratively as *Baubo* or *Frauenzimmer*.
16 Freud (1905e), p. 151.
17 Freud (1925j).
18 Freud (1930a).
19 Freud (1933a).
20 *Ibid.*, p. 113.
21 Freud attempts to substantiate and justify his claims by referring to the work of female psychoanalysts. This includes studies by Helen Deutsch, Ruth Brunswick, and Jeanne Lampl-de-Groot.
22 Freud, S. (1933a), p. 116.
23 *Ibid.*, p. 132.
24 Freud (1931b), p. 233.
25 Freud (1925j).
26 Freud (1924d), p. 177.
27 *Ibid.*, p. 179.
28 Hence, libido is essentially masculine and its instinct inherently active.
29 This was supported by Françoise Dolto!
30 Marie Bonaparte was in intense search of her 'orgasmic fulfilment', and had three operations in Switzerland to have her clitoris repositioned.
31 Jones, E. (1961). Volume II, p. 474.
32 There may be a phallic fantasy behind this: 'penetrating' reality, sowing truth, fertilising words, the 'power' of the thought that rises up, and so on.
33 Freud (1933a).
34 Cf. Cournut-Janin & Cournut (1993).
35 Freud (1923e).
36 Freud (1940a).
37 *Ibid.* 'The development of the sexual function'. The vagina will only take up its reality as the 'home of the penis' during coitus, while the uterus will be revealed through menstruation and childbirth.

The riddle of the feminine   23

38 Freud (1933a), p. 118. As early as 1924, however, Karl Abraham cast doubt on the Freudian hypothesis:

> I have recently begun to wonder whether there is not already, at the moment of early childhood, a first vaginal outburst of the feminine libido, which is destined to be repressed, and which is then followed by the predominance of the clitoris as the expression of the phallic phase.

Cf. Letter to Freud, 3/12/1924 in *Œuvres complètes*, Vol. II. Paris: Payot, 1966.

39 Indeed, as early as 1916, in his book *Anal und sexual*, Lou Andreas-Salomé drew a connection between the vagina and the cloaca, referring to the passivity in the face of the drive to which women, in the absence of a reasonably outwardly directed aggressiveness, would be more fiercely attracted than men.

40 With respect to the notion of penis envy, we can, broadly speaking, consider the penis as representing the difference between the sexes, this being the first of the major distinctions. As André Green pointed out, it is not this 'small bit of flesh' that triggers interest, curiosity, and lust. It is the meanings it carries (the phallus). It is a sign, because it is 'visible', meaning something to someone.

41 Freud (1933a), p. 125.

42 *Id.*, p. 134.

43 Once again, Freud relies on the biological.

44 Freud (1933a), p. 114.

45 These are very ideological views! Nowadays, women lawyers or company directors would smile at this!

46 Freud (1925j), p. 258.

47 Klein (1932).

48 Winnicott (1971a).

49 Genetics teaches us that the foetus is originally female and is only differentiated under the influence of the dominant sex hormones.

50 Freud (1940a).

51 *Ibid.*

52 The texts were written between 1954 and his death in 1971, and, unfortunately the articles were not dated.

53 Winnicott (1988).

54 Maïdi (2008).

55 There is, however, another side to the coin: the risk of castration, of 'losing everything', whereas the girl would 'have everything to gain', because she has nothing to lose!

56 Emphasis added.

57 Emphasis added.

58 It is true that men are more often asked to 'prove' their masculinity, their *potenz*, as it is called in German. Potency is the hallmark of power. The 'potent' father is the one who has phallic power.

59 It is also odd to hear adolescent girls use the expression in French *Tu me casses les couilles* [You're breaking my balls] when boys or other girls annoy them. How often do we hear that! The question of castration is not absent from girls' vocabulary!

60 Stoller (1975).

61 *Id.*, p. 165.

62 Stoller (1985) summarises the assumed aetiology behind gender identity within five factors: a biological force; sex assignment; parental attitudes (how the child is perceived and raised); 'biopsychic phenomena'; and the developing physical self. There are also cultural and societal models. One only has to walk into a toy shop and see that there are separate departments for 'boys' and 'girls', with clear assignments: there will be no weapons of war on the 'girls'' shelves.

63 The father seems to be very involved in the naming process!

24 The riddle of the feminine

64 Laplanche (2003). Quote is author's own translation. Full translation can be found in *Studies in Gender and Sexuality Volume 8*(2), 201–219.

65 *Ibid.*

66 Lacan (1972–1973).

67 According to Ernest Jones (1933), pp. 1–33, the young girl is 'by nature' feminine from the start, the clitoris is a female organ and not a shortened penis, the desire for a child is a female desire and not a consolation for being deprived of the male organ. Ultimately, a woman is not a 'failed' man but a distinct creature.

68 Lacan (1972–1973), p. 7.

69 Lacan (1955–1956). The hysteric's question II *What is a woman?* p. 176.

70 Joyce MacDougall holds personal ideas that link Freud and Klein. She observes that boys experience envy of the father's penis as much as girls. The idea that his penis is too small triggers the same anxieties in men as it does in girls 'when they unconsciously cling to the dreaded fantasy that they are a castrated boy ... A boy's envy and admiration for his mother's body and sexuality is similar to a girl's envy and admiration for her father's penis and his sexual prowess.' In opposition to Lacan, she differentiates the symbol (phallus) from the partial object (penis): '*The phallus is not the symbol of the male sexual organ*, but that of fertility, complementarity, and erotic desire.' This is because '... male or female monosexuality remains a major narcissistic wound. To achieve a symbolic representation of sexual complementarity requires ... relinquishing the childish pleasure of *being* and *having* both sexes'. MacDougall (1996).

71 Lacan (1972–1973), pp. 57–75.

72 Lacan (1960). Propos directifs pour un congrès sur la sexualité féminine, in *Écrits*, Paris, Seuil, 1966.

73 Lacan (1972–1973), p. 77.

74 The feminine seems to be at the heart and in the body ('the flesh') of the mystics' jouissance. Ecstasy seems to be a sublimated reversal of orgastic jouissance. Cf. St Teresa of Avila, who speaks of a precise moment of divine ecstasy when an angel pierced her heart with an arrow, filling her with both pain and unutterable happiness. Saint Teresa's ecstasy may remind us of the amorous ecstasy of the Song of Songs, for it leads us to recognise the distinctly erotic sense of the poem, as if sexual ecstasy and spiritual ecstasy were ultimately one and the same sensation.

75 With his 'Transverberation of Saint Teresa' (1645–1652), Bernini succeeded tremendously in his magical treatment of marble, in the Baroque art of combining the various degrees of reality and the incursion of the divine into reality. This wonderfully demonstrative work is a marvellous revelation of the mystic experience and its role in 17th century Catholic piety. The statue represents God's love as a burning arrow piercing her heart. Bernini materialised this ecstatic image of Saint Teresa by depicting an angel with a golden arrow in his hand, like Cupid, leaning over her and smiling. The Angelic figure plunges the arrow into her heart or pulls it out. The face of the Saint indicates an anticipation of ecstasy or its plenitude. Ecstasy is embodied here in an almost voluptuous and fleshy way. This reveals a fundamental form of Baroque 'spirituality' in Catholic lands: the intimate union of the carnal and the divine, of earth and heaven, to which Bernini and Rubens both bear witness. Saint Teresa of Avila revealed this mystical experience in several booklets, recounting her physical reaction to spiritual illumination in very concrete words, which can be perceived in other notes by mystics.

76 Cf. Freud (1930a).

77 Lacan (1972–1973).

78 *Ibid.*, A love letter, 13th March, 1973.

79 Also to be differentiated from the phallic function. The question of femininity is one of not-whole, in the sense that a woman is not all inscribed in the phallic function.

Chapter 2

The feminine and castration

While women give the impression of escaping the risk associated with castration anxiety due to the specificity of their anatomy, they are also – perhaps especially – confronted by the threat of lack, loss, separation, and abandonment. This singular threat is inextricably linked to the fear of belittlement, devaluation, rejection, and non-recognition. All these elements have an eminently narcissistic value. It is an expression of life narcissism that is entirely usual, necessary, and tempered.

Castration anxiety in women concerns a series of losses that can affect her physical integrity (violation, intrusion, penetration), and her bodily narcissism (psychic injury). This anxiety is not typical of women, but tends to be more exacerbated. For this more intense fear in women recalls the lack, the original defect, the fundamental wound, whereas in men, it is specifically the loss of having that is feared, or, more precisely, of 'already having'. The rejection of the lack, of the feminine, operates in both sexes, but paradoxically it can seem more intense in women than in men. To use Aristotle's aphorism, is it not true that 'nature abhors a vacuum'? Is this not the equivalent of a 'hole'? A 'hollow' or 'hole' that is as symbolic as it is real.

On a more personal and extensive level, women fear 'losing' their beauty (Maïdi, 2012), their hair, putting on weight, growing old. Damage to the breasts in particular, for example through cancer or breastfeeding, is experienced as a symbolic castration; as are the menopause and a hysterectomy, which can cause melancholy and apathy.

However, more globally, female 'castration' anxiety would seem to be above all 'anxiety about loss of love from the object', as Freud emphasises in *Civilization and its Discontents*.[1]

Psychic bisexuality

The idea of bisexuality is ancient. It was evoked long before Freud. There is the myth from the banquet in Plato's *Symposium*, for example, that presents the combination, the conjunction, of the two gendered and separate body characteristics. The fantasy of androgyny is a form of mythical compensation for sexual incompleteness. It is a fantasy of the permanent union of the two 'opposite' sexes.

DOI: 10.4324/9781003414247-3

26   The feminine and castration

Man has always sought a fantastical or mythological satisfaction of a sublime[2] and hermaphrodite ideal.[3] The fantasy desire of the hermaphrodite, or androgynous ideal, is, therefore, an ancient phenomenon. It is a mythological, yet clearly psychological, hermaphroditism and androgyny. It is the expression of a fantasy which testifies to an idealising defensive activity and a psychic predisposition.[4]

Through the notion of 'psychic bisexuality,' psychoanalysis has, in a way, exhumed this old fantasy of an ideal androgynous self. It is worth noting that this concept – and problem – of psychic bisexuality has consubstantial links with the whole of psychoanalytic theory and practice. It is an essential concept in the psychoanalytic corpus. However, like many important concepts in psychoanalysis, the notion of bisexuality has undergone different fluctuations and evolutions.

Psychic bisexuality is easily justified. For in the unconscious, where there are no real boundaries, the difference between the sexes is not so distinct. In the psyche, the distinctive sexual typologies, those 'beautiful differences provided by nature'[5] tend to largely subside, or even disappear completely.

Freud talks of bisexuality in his correspondence with his friend Wilhelm Fliess. At Fliess's suggestion, Freud (1887–1904) initially considers bisexuality from its biological aspect. He supports the hypothesis of a conflict between masculine and feminine tendencies in every subject.

He seeks to draw certain 'psychological consequences' from anatomy, from the embryology of his time. Freud's prior propensity for biologism, even anatomism, leads him to consider bisexuality as a biological concept, which he envisages making a premise of the psychoanalytic clinic.

Thus, he writes in 'The Claims of Psycho-Analysis to Scientific Interests (1913j): 'We speak too of "masculine" and "feminine" mental attributes and impulses, although, strictly speaking, the differences between the sexes can lay claim to no special psychical characterization.'[6] Indeed, all that can be said is that activity and passivity are involved. The 'active' and 'passive' instincts[7] coexist in the psychic life and form an individual's bisexuality. However, beside the fact that these connotations are insufficient, they do not concern the instincts themselves, but the nature of their aims, and their constant association in our mental life is testimony to the bisexuality of each individual.[8] Bisexuality follows on from the clinical assumptions of psychoanalysis.

In this sense, Freud sees bisexuality as a basic universal predisposition, which can become markedly pathological when very pronounced. In an article entitled 'Hysterical Phantasies and their Relation to Bisexuality' (1908a), Freud sees in the bisexual nature of many hysterical symptoms 'an interesting confirmation of the hypothesis of a bisexual predisposition particularly marked in neurotics'.

The feminine and masculine have their source in the biological domain, but cannot be limited to it and stop at mere anatomical difference. Freud himself admits quite early on (1905d) that masculinity and femininity cannot be reduced to the biological.

In *Three Essays*, having underlined – in the context of a reflection on sadism and masochism – the great theoretical importance of the notion of a pair of antagonistic elements, he concludes:

> It is moreover a suggestive fact that the existence of a pair of opposites formed by sadism and masochism cannot be attributed merely to the element of aggressiveness. *We should rather be inclined to connect the simultaneous presence of these opposites with the opposing masculinity and femininity which are combined in bisexuality*[9] – a contrast which often has to be replaced in psycho-analysis by that between activity and passivity.[10]

Masculine–feminine, activity–passivity

In 1907a, Freud once again defines the masculine by activity and the feminine by passivity. However, in the same sentence he attests that the unconscious in men could not be fundamentally divergent from that in women (1907a).[11]

There is, however, a kind of 'competition' and conflict, for example between male and female identifications in hysteria (Freud, 1908a, 1909b). This leads Freud to increasingly assert the prevalence of the 'phallus' – which is not the penis, but an extracted symbol, detached from biological reality – for both sexes.

Freud then goes on to argue that, in the light of bisexuality, what is called masculine and feminine – and which narrows down to activity and passivity – does not cover the difference in the sexes, as anatomical gender has no specific psychic characteristics.[12]

Later, Freud (1919e) hesitates about the nature of this bisexuality: he speaks of 'masculine and feminine instinctual impulses' that may be subject to repression. In 1920, he states that the differences between the qualities of men and women are 'more conventional than scientifically justified'.[13]

Furthermore, as his thinking develops, Freud comes to recognise that while the phallocentric vision of sexuality within the context of *psychic bisexuality* is 'of bodily origin', it is also the result of identification with both parents:

> [science]... draws your attention to the fact that portions of the male sexual apparatus also appear in women's bodies, though in an atrophied state, and vice versa in the alternative case. It regards their occurrence as indications of a *bisexuality*... You will then be asked to make yourselves familiar with the idea that the proportion in which masculine and feminine are mixed in an individual is subject to quite considerable fluctuations … You cannot give the concepts of 'masculine' and 'feminine' any new connotation. This distinction is not a psychological one; when you say 'masculine', you usually mean 'active', and when you say 'feminine', you usually mean 'passive'.[14]

In 'Analysis Terminable and Interminable' (1937c), Freud ends up observing – due to the apparent difference in penis envy in women, and the refusal of passivity

28 The feminine and castration

in men with regard to other men – themes obviously linked to the 'inequality' of the sexes, 'something common to both sexes': the refusal of femininity, a refusal which, in the final analysis, refers to the fear of castration.

At the end of his life, Freud found himself faced with an unresolved puzzle: 'the great enigma of the biological fact of the duality of the sexes'[15] and the essentially biological psychic bisexuality.

Ultimately, Freudian psychoanalysis teaches us that the pure feminine and the pure masculine are myths on account of bisexuality. Human sexuality is a psycho-sexuality in which the feminine and the masculine succeed one another, oppose one another, are interlinked, forming psychic bisexuality, which reaches its apogee with the Oedipal organisation.

This conception has been taken up and sometimes discussed by certain authors with a complexion of its own. Thus, for example, Georg Groddeck calls for an awareness that 'in the being called man there is a woman and in the woman a man'.[16]

Winnicott, suddenly inspired, tells a male patient who is not homosexual:[17] 'I am listening to a girl. I know perfectly well that you are a man but I am listening to a girl, and I am talking to a girl. I am telling this girl: "You are talking about penis envy"'.[18] Surprised and momentarily dumbfounded, the patient then retorts: 'If I were to tell anyone about this girl, I would be called mad.' 'No,' replied the analyst, 'it was not that *you* told this to anyone; it is *I* who see the girl and hear a girl talking, when actually there is a man on my couch. The mad person is *myself.*' Here, Winnicott uses his countertransference, which is not defensive, with the aim of helping the patient get rid of his transference obstacle; so that the patient's transference can take effect. Winnicott captures the patient's transference within himself, and allows him to perceive, through projective identification, what the patient cannot express and cannot become aware of. Winnicott indicates that this maternal type of countertransference is required by the perceptive dimension of reality, that of the seen or heard. He states that he puts himself in the position of a 'mad' mother who expresses her 'mad' desire by perceiving her child in an altered way, due to her own disappointment at not having had a child of the other sex. The intervention of the analyst, through countertransference, allows the patient to understand that he has built his own defences around the 'madness' of his mother. This fragment of analysis also shows that other hypotheses are possible and plausible. Winnicott could also have placed himself in a paternal countertransference, that of a jealous and distrustful father who would contest the masculine sex of his son, that is, femi-nising him in the sense of castration at the level of phallus-castration.

Or a paternal countertransference of a father perceiving the penis envy of a boy who has to identify with a girl in order to have his desire to obtain a child from him understood. That is to say, in a passive homosexual position, having overcome castration anxiety.

These different positions are certainly to be questioned in an analytical treat-ment, which calls for transfers of investment and of identification.

Narcissistic feminine

In the absence of a visible phallic organ to invest in, narcissism in a girl can refer to her whole body. In his lecture on 'Femininity', Freud (1933a) states:

> We attribute a larger amount of narcissism to femininity, which also affects women's choice of object, so that to be loved is a stronger need for them than to love. [...] [the woman's choice of object] is often made in accordance with the narcissistic ideal of the man whom the girl had wished to become.[19]

Narcissism seems to be specifically on the feminine side. The importance of the theme of the feminine should be noted in the story of Narcissus. He seems to be dominated by his own femininity. He repels the love of numerous young girls. He is tormented by a female spirit, Echo, his twin sister, the source... Narcissus's love for the image he sees in the water is, in effect, female in type.

In this regard, we can note the use of the myth of Narcissus in nineteenth century French literature, taking as an example Jean-Jacques Rousseau, who wrote a play entitled *Narcissus, Or the Lover of Himself*[20] as an adolescent at the age of eighteen.

In this play, Narcissus is called Valère. He spends a lot of time looking in the mirror, and is accused by is father of 'strutting about in front of the mirror'.

Valère's narcissistic excitement is only determined when he comes across a lure of a different kind: a feminised portrait of himself, his face adorned in finery. Dressed and made up like a young girl in this portrait, he becomes infatuated with himself, and enamoured with his femininity, without recognising himself. Valère, considering the unrecognised portrait of himself, exclaims: 'My heart cannot resist... Frontin, tell me the name of this beautiful woman'.[21]

Not being in full possession of his capacity to discern and distinguish reality from his feminine aspect (like Narcissus gone 'mad'), he needs someone to help him discover his true sexual identity. Angélique, his father's ward, is the young woman chosen for this role and also the one intended by his father for betrothal.

Angélique succeeds in serving as a living mirror, and thanks to her 'narcissising' love for him, successfully becomes his wife, his double.

Feminine narcissism and traumatic homosexuality

Clinical experience shows that homophilic and homosexual inclinations are closely related to the theme, even the problem, of narcissism. Homosexuality is not a structurally homogeneous category. I shall dwell for a moment on the consubstantial link that combines homosexuality with narcissism in its traumatic aspect. Indeed, a connection between homosexuality and trauma can be found in Freud's text 'The Psychogenesis of a Case of Homosexuality in a Woman'.[22]

This paper presents the famous case of the 'young homosexual'. During the analytic work with this adolescent girl, Freud himself is in a period where he is

30 The feminine and castration

questioning the homophilia of his daughter Anna, who is in analysis with him. It is an unusual situation regarding the treatment of the patient, the so-called 'young homosexual', as Freud only accepts her at the insistence of the girl's father.

Sidonie: 'The young homosexual'

Sidonie is a 'beautiful and intelligent' eighteen-year-old girl from an upper middle-class Viennese family at the beginning of the twentieth century. She falls passionately in love with a woman some ten years older than her, Baroness Leonie Von Puttkammer, a socialite of noble origin, who leads a rather dubious life in Vienna as a '*coquette*'. The adolescent, despite knowing the bad reputation of this 'Lady', worships her and falls passionately in love with her. The girl makes no secret of this romance.

On the contrary, her behaviour is tinged with provocation, so that

> she did not scruple to appear in the most frequented streets in the company of her undesirable friends, being thus quite neglectful of her own reputation; while, on the other hand, she disdained no means of deception, no excuses and no lies that would make meetings with her possible and cover them.[23]

The relationship remained platonic, however. The young girl never ceased to proclaim 'the purity of her love' and 'her physical repulsion against the idea of sexual intercourse'.

> One day it happened, indeed, as was sooner or later inevitable in these circumstances, that the father met his daughter in the company of the lady, about whom he had come to know. He passed by them with an angry glance which boded no good. [*Er ging mit einem zornigen Blick der nichts Gutes ankündigte*] Immediately afterwards the girl rushed off and flung herself off a wall down the side of a cutting onto the suburban railway line which ran close by. [p. 148]
>
> The explanation she gave of the immediate reasons determining her decision sounded quite plausible. She had confessed to the lady that the man who had given them such an irate glance was her father, and that he had absolutely forbidden their friendship. The lady became incensed at this and ordered the girl to her then and there ... [p. 162]

In this 'acting out'[24] the girl was only injured, but Freud would take this suicide attempt entirely seriously. Six months later, the relationship with her love object had scarcely changed. Indeed, the Lady, sensitive to the event that had endangered the girl's life, shows her more consideration than before, and their relationship resumes with greater intensity. The father, exasperated and unable to accept his daughter's behaviour, leaves the matter in the hands of Freud and the psychoanalytic treatment. Through it he hopes his daughter will be able to return to the straight and narrow, the path of heterosexuality and marriage.

Freud's analysis

Freud emphasises above all the narcissistic problem the girl is suffering from. She cannot free herself from primary homosexuality.[25] It remains frozen and fixed to the exclusive, intense, and passionate relationship with the primary love object, the *Mutterbindung*.[26] Thus, in 1920 Freud writes: '[...] a homosexual stream [...] was probably the direct and unchanged continuation of an infantile mother-fixation'.[27]

Without going into Freud's in-depth analysis, it is worth noting that he also makes the link with the daughter's unresolved Oedipal 'crisis'. The (young and beautiful) woman coveted by the adolescent girl represents the mother, who, Freud says, is 'still a youngish woman' who was 'evidently unwilling to give up her own claims to attractivenesss'. He goes so far as to argue that for this woman 'still youthful herself, saw in her rapidly developing daughter an inconvenient competitor' and it follows that she 'kept an especially strict watch against any close relation between the girl and the father'. This is why she was not as strict as the father about his daughter's homophilic inclination. Freud also points out that this woman 'treated her children in quite different ways, being decidedly harsh towards her daughter and over-indulgent to her three sons, the youngest of whom had been born after a long interval and was then not yet three years old'.[28]

In an unexpected summary, Freud observes what ensues: '[The young girl] changed into a man and took her mother in place of her father as the object of her love'. Let us recall that, by all accounts, this adolescent girl, around the age of thirteen or fourteen, showed considerable affection and benevolence for a little boy who was not yet three years old, and whom she saw frequently in a kindergarten. The girl even befriended his parents. At that time she experienced, *a priori*, a real and strong maternal desire.

However, this starting position is then completely reversed. She grew indifferent to the boy, and she began to fall in love with 'mature, but still youthful, women', a series of women that culminates in her love for the 'lady', and who are all 'mother substitutes', as revealed, Freud tells us, in material from dreams. Disappointed, 'she turned away from her father and from men altogether. After this first great reverse she forswore her womanhood and sought another goal for her libido'; she then experiences a fervent love for this Lady, a '*coquette*' and brushes aside her Oedipal desire to have a child from the father. Freud makes the connection with the disillusionment through the father, from which follows a whole chain of sacrifices: father, maternity, femininity, beauty (the adolescent becomes insensitive to compliments about her own beauty). What happens next is the extreme case: 'She changed into a man and took her mother in place of her father as the object of her love. ...'[29]

Freud sees here one of the particular factors that would push the young girl towards homosexuality. He warns, however:

> We do not mean to maintain that every girl who experiences a disappointment such as this of the longing for love that springs from the Oedipus attitude at puberty will necessarily on that account fall a victim to homosexuality. On the contrary, other kinds of reaction to this trauma are undoubtedly commoner.[30]

Lacan's position

In his analysis of this *case of female homosexuality*, Freud rightly believes that the young homosexual's unseemly behaviour masks the buried and unacknowledged desire to have a child from the father, in her powerful phantastical representation of the phallus. What does the girl, the woman, want? The phallus.[31] According to the Lacanian approach, in his analytical development Freud neglected to address the 'enigmatic' question of women.[32]

Taking up this case, Lacan thinks that the girl, through her outrageous behaviour, is sending a cryptic message to the father about the way in which she loves: this is what Lacan will call *acting out*, that is, any demonstrative attitude directed towards the Other, a disguised display of a desire concealed from an Other. Acting out is a language that 'says' something other than what we think it 'says'. It makes visible something other than what it is; but 'what *it* is, no one knows, but that it is *other* no one doubts'.[33] Thus, the suicide attempt, the *passage à l'acte* for Lacan, discovers the desire at stake in the 'acting out'.

The *passage à l'acte* is the leap into the void which accomplishes 'at the very moment that there is conjoined … this conjunction between desire and the law'.[34] In the *passage à l'acte*, the subject is offstage, out of the game. Conversely, in *acting out*, the subject remains on the stage and, unbeknown to him, we could say in a 'game' of signifiers, he 'plays the I', he 'plays his I'. As we know, 'I is an Other' in the sense of the Other in the scene of the unconscious. It is the scene of the big Other that is exposed in particular in intersubjective dialogue. The scene is opposed to the real.

When the adolescent throws herself on to the rails, it is a '*passage à l'acte*', because the harsh sentence received in the violent gaze of the father dislodges her from her position as the object cause of her desire.[35] When she has an affair with the Lady, it is an *acting out* because nothing that happens between her and the Lady has expelled her from this subjective position.

Falling from the parapet, 'meant the attainment of [...] the wish to have a child by her father, for now she "fell" through her father's fault'. The verb *niederkommen*, literally 'to come low', means at the same time 'to fall' and 'to give birth' (*mettre bas* in French).[36] Lacan, in his seminar on anxiety, supports Freud's reasoning by completing the amphibological expression of *laisser tomber* [letting drop][37] which is in play in the *passage à l'acte*.[38]

The girl, identifying with the father, as Lacan says in 'The Object Relation',[39] would thus be transvestite, psychically male, loving women in a platonic and courtly way.[40]

Aesthetic encounter

The young girl falls in love with more than the woman, but with the image of femininity and beauty, or female beauty. She is dazzled by the beautiful. It is her criterion for love, if not for passion. Beauty and love come as a defence against the repulsion of sex. The adolescent girl is an allegory of beauty. It is the Lady's general appearance that has seduced her: her beauty, her gestures, her refinement, her grace. The girl's love for the Lady at first sight is dominated by her extreme sensitivity to the image of a beautiful woman. She represents the mother who possesses all aesthetic qualities, the beautiful, the feminine ideal. The daughter is fascinated by this woman-mother. She is quite probably under the influence of the narcissistic traits attributed to her mother, who offered all guarantees of femininity: not only her beauty, which she has retained, but also her relative youth – the mother had just had a new child – and a propensity in her character to please men.

In a biographical work, Freud's young patient, who lived to almost a hundred, confirms that beauty was an 'aphrodisiac' for her from an early age and throughout her life.[41] In it, Sidonie Csillag is presented as one of the most beautiful women in Vienna, with a pure and radiant charm. Of the family beauty, Sidonie states that 'the Csillag children have inherited some of Mother's good looks, that's the sum of it. All their human qualities are thanks to Father, even though he is small and rather corpulent and not at all handsome'. This description of the father by the daughter does not at all correspond to the one given by Freud. He describes the young patient through her father: 'Beautiful, well-built, the girl was tall like her father with pronounced features...'. The dazzling beauty of the mother is blinding for the daughter. Several decades later, the daughter is extremely affected, so much so that she cries when she talks about her mother: 'I think my mother is so beautiful, and I do everything for her, but she only loves my brothers ...'. When the mother is with the boys, Sidonie no longer exists. The mother gives them almost everything, while with the daughter she appears harsh and unfair. Sidonie brings her presents, spoils her with flowers... nothing helps. Her mother remains distant and cold... she has never hugged her daughter, who so desires it. Sidonie explains why she was driven to love women's beauty this way: it is '... because of my mother... Every woman was her enemy ...' Only beauty – her mother's, her own and that of many other women – has moved her and brought out her strongest feelings. 'I have always been in love with beauty. A beautiful woman is still a pleasure for me, and this will be true until I'll die'.

This fascination with the beautiful mother, with her idealised face, probably finds its source in early childhood, in the primary homosexual relationship.[42]

The mirror, the mother's face, is the primary aesthetic object of cathexis. It is a fundamental image of beauty, which is part of a primordial aesthetic encounter as the primary care object.[43]

The feminine as legacy

If the masculine seems to play an essential role in the construction of the feminine and femininity, what is really going on with these two concepts? How do they come about? 'How does femininity come to woman'?

The birth of the feminine in a woman is first inscribed in the female relationship of mother–daughter filiation. The mother passes on her own femininity to her

34 The feminine and castration

daughter. This transmission is generally troubled. It does not take place without a conflictual identification with the mother and femininity.

Lacan,[44] the first to employ the term 'ravage', uses it to define the singular and complex character of the mother–daughter relationship.[45]

To be a girl or a boy is the result of a form of assignment by the environment. Being cannot be separated from the past and from what is to come. The gendered subject is forged by its history and determined for its future. Gendering is an eminently dynamic process. One is not born a woman, nor *is* one, one becomes a woman. To be a woman is, in a way, to 'act like' a woman.[46] The feminine only exists in relation to the masculine and *vice versa*. It is a question of asserting oneself as woman by bearing female identity characteristics. These are mainly related to secondary identifications: identification with the mother, inevitably, but also with the father. The structuring of the feminine and femininity cannot be freed from the masculine.

Being or becoming 'woman' depends on natural, biological, and physical specificities (anatomy is fate), but also on attributes and assignations (in the sense of attributing or assigning a gendered form to) that are deeply rooted in culture.

The cultural (secondary) feminine is grafted on to a natural (primary) feminine that is established in the 'hollow' female body, by identifying with the mother of origins. From the very beginning, the child – regardless of the sex – is impregnated with the feminine. The orificial *infans* is penetrated with the feminine by an adult. The seduced child is a cavity child, a receptacle child.

There exists a primordial feminine. In the archaic period, the child depends on the object. Very early on, the child is subjected to the infringement (*impingement* in Winnicott's sense) of the object.

Continuing the work of Jean Laplanche on the theory of generalised seduction and the 'fundamental anthropological situation', Jacques André[47] extends the Freudian theory on original seduction, clearly developing its phantastical and metapsychological consequences. He develops the idea of a repressed original femininity. The 'fundamental anthropological situation' brings together an *infans* in need of tenderness and attachment and an adult who, with their unconscious, unknowingly transmits 'feelings issued from their sexual life' (Freud). This is an original situation of passivity, because primordial sexual experiences are certainly lived in a passive way. It feminises the one who is *subjected* to it, seduced and dominated: the original and 'orificial' child.

The first child is an 'orificial' child, seized by the torment of the sexual received as an enigmatic language and marked by passivation.

Anxiety that is feminine – or from the feminine – seems to be rooted in this primitive period. The first body is of the feminine 'type' long before the difference of the sexes.

The position of the *infans* is feminine in type, dominated by passivity and especially by passivation.

The passive feminine position cannot be equated with the entire feminine, which is not solely constituted of the feminine. Femininity is defined by 'active receptivity', which is quite distinct from the 'passivity' described by Freud. This notion of active receptivity is traversed by psychic bisexuality. It contains the two gendered poles: the feminine (receptivity) and the masculine (activity). In this way, the pure feminine – like the pure masculine – does not exist.

The mother also carries the masculine within her. From the outset, she also transmits the masculine element that she inherited very early on from her own father. The girl's access to femininity does not take place without conflict with the mother. In the primary homosexual relationship, fascination and unconditional love are the girl's dominant feelings for the mother. This period of the early inter-sexed relationship is fundamental in the process of secondary identification with the feminine and the balanced development of femininity.

However, the risk of maternal feminine suffocation, of an adhesive identification with the mother, requires the saving intervention of the father as a separating third party. The mother's love is completed by the daughter's love for the father. This heterosexual love is important. It intervenes in relation to the primary homosexual love. The presence of the man, the father or the father figure, the relationship to the masculine, is therefore indispensable in the construction of femininity. The little girl feels an intense love for her idealised father. Normally, it is the advent of puberty that will separate the father–daughter protagonists. However, the quest for the father's masculinity is constantly sought. The father figure is paradoxically even more desired after the father has been damaging or too 'exciting' with regard to his daughter.[48]

Natacha

Natacha, a twenty-year-old student, comes for consultation because she regularly feels afraid without really knowing why she is afraid. She says she is 'anxious, lost, dreading the future'. She complains of 'destroying everything she builds'. She adds that she sometimes has 'feelings of a tight throat', as if she has 'a knife to her throat'. Throughout the sessions, she constantly talks about the difficult and particularly unpleasant relationship she has with her mother. Very early on Natacha felt 'rejected and abandoned'. It should be noted that she was born after her mother had had an abortion. In order to be accepted, the girl says she 'did everything to please her mother'. The girl's discourse is dominated by the expression of a 'need for recognition' and elements of 'depressiveness'. For example, Natasha thinks that she is 'not made for living on this earth'. Similarly, there is a feeling of devaluation and negative judgement towards her. She believes that she is the target of constant reproaches from her family and friends. 'They reject me; they expel me; they resent me'. Furthermore, she is 'very afraid of committing suicide' like her idealised paternal grandmother[49] who died 'of a bullet in the head' at the age of fifty. Very preoccupied by this grandmother's suicide, Natacha searches in vain for the reasons that led her to kill herself.

During a session of psychotherapy, and without really dwelling on it, Natacha reveals to me that she had had an abortion about a year and a half earlier. She didn't feel ready and didn't want to have a child with one of her former friends.

She remembers some most unpleasant moments from her childhood, moments of great sadness and distress, notably when her mother left her in her 'room in the

36 The feminine and castration

dark', or when she locked her in the house to go shopping, or when her parents 'forgot' her at the school gate several times, at the end of the day.

The mother is described by her own daughter as 'hysterical and selfish'. The father, a company director, is portrayed as weak with his wife. Natacha, who has a younger brother, is regularly asked to ally herself both with the mother and the father. The parents are, in fact, in violent and permanent conflict. They live separately in the same big house. 'I have always seen my parents tear each other apart,' says Natacha. She is more sensitive and benevolent towards her father, who is 'helpless' in the face of his wife: 'I am disappointed in my father. I put him on a pedestal. He doesn't know how to defend himself against his wife.' Natacha is much more vehement about her mother. She mainly reproaches her for her 'coldness, her individualism, her interfering and her immodesty'. On this subject, Natacha's parents are keen nudists. They raised their children according to this ideology and practice. 'We are familiar with each other naked,' says Natacha. However, from the age of puberty, she has absolutely refused to go with her parents to private holiday camps. Since that time, she says she has been repulsed to see her mother and father's naked bodies. She is, she says, 'disgusted', adding: 'Anything that is not healthy disturbs me'. In particular, she describes a 'revolting' scene in which her 'mother is naked and the cat was sucking at her hand'. She forcefully expresses her wish to 'experience healthy things', situations that are simple and non-conflicting. In this regard, she is sometimes troubled and overwhelmed by homoerotic and homosexual impulses, especially at the sight of a young and exciting bare female body. She has the fantasy of touching and caressing this body. This inclination causes Natasha a mixture of excitement and anxiety. She also talks in detail about a feeling of shame about this desire, which is reprehensible to her morals. Consequently, she experiences anxiety due to her identification with the potentially desiring boy in this instance. Moreover, in a *lapsus linguae*, she strangely uses the expression 'opposite sex' when it is a question of the sex of a girl, like her. This homosexual tendency – or rather temptation – is probably rationalised by Natacha. She associates it with her mother's almost constant nudity. And yet she says she hates to touch her mother's body, even lightly. The daughter's refusal to brush against or touch the maternal body recalls the prohibition of incest, a reactionary self-defence that responds to the absence of a parental ban of the other.

In this way, the incestuousness of the parent–child relationships and the lack of limits within the family around the intimacy of bodies probably favoured Natacha's precocious sexuality and her quest for symbolic paternal protection. 'At thirteen, I was dating a twenty-year-old boy who was in his final year of high school, and at nineteen I was dating a thirty-three-year-old guy,' she says bitterly.

Pauline

Pauline is nineteen years old. She is an art student. She has come to start psychotherapy because she 'feels a bit lost'. She has 'bouts of anxiety'. She talks about her dissatisfaction and disappointment with life. She endures her life. She feels as though she is in a 'dead end'. She says she is the victim of a family tragedy.

Her maternal aunt committed suicide. Her maternal grandfather also killed himself. Similarly, her grandmother's father killed himself after the loss of his wife. Pauline's mother, who witnessed their suicides, feels responsible for their deaths.

The adolescent wants to rid herself of a 'conflicting and painful family past'. She now wants to stop suffering from this family 'legacy'. She feels 'quite bewildered about choosing a profession'. She does not know what she is going to do with herself, with the impression of being lost and abandoned, when in particular 'there is no longer any concern for her'. She is looking for a 'context' and warns that she cannot bear the idea of being left to herself.

She feels she knows how to 'analyse the suffering but cannot overcome it'. Pauline makes clear that in daily life, she is often invaded by 'fears, anxieties that paralyse her'. She is afraid of 'getting a little lost in her anxieties'. Sometimes she has 'real suicidal urges' but often she feels absorbed by a significant depressiveness, 'a tendency to melancholy'.

Pauline is the last of five children, and has three brothers and a sister. She explains that she has lived almost exclusively with her mother, as an 'only daughter without a father'. This specific mother–daughter relationship has led her to be 'an anxious witness to her mother's ageing'. Her mother was particularly saddened and disturbed by her divorce. A 'dirty' divorce, says Pauline. The breakdown of the parental couple had begun when Pauline was about eighteen months old. The mother suffered a lot from this separation.

In this regard, the adolescent talks about her fear of her mother dying. The mother's 'fears' have been transferred to the daughter. 'I have always been afraid of something happening to her.'

At birth, Pauline says she and her mother almost died of pneumonia. 'It was a matter of hours.' They both came close to death. She thinks they both should have died, but they were saved 'by some miracle'.

However, Pauline observes that 'her birth broke and destroyed her mother's life as a woman'.

She recalls that she was born by caesarean section. The large scar on her mother's stomach is an enduring reminder. In Pauline's speech, the scar – 'rupture, claw marks everywhere' – the daughter's mark on the mother's body, displays the early violence of Pauline's life.

The adolescent feels invested with an enormous 'responsibility' for her mother's depressive state. 'Whenever she is suffering, I feel responsible.' Pauline even feels a responsibility for her mother's life. She thinks that 'the fact that she has managed to live is because of her daughter'. Indeed, with distress, Pauline thinks that her mother would have preferred death.

'It was you who saved me', the mother reportedly told her daughter. She says she is 'tired' and can no longer bear this heavy involvement in her mother's life. In a defensive and rationalising move, she thinks that this guilt was probably bequeathed to her or instigated in her by her mother.

The mother is described as depressive. Later on, she will remember that the diagnosis made by the psychiatrist was, she says, that of 'manic depressive'. In addition

38   The feminine and castration

to this flawed diagnosis, it is of particular note that the mother presented with anorexia when her husband left. Feeling jilted and abandoned by her husband, she was treated for her depression in a specialist institution for about three years. During this time, the children were placed elsewhere. The older sister also showed signs of depression. Pauline suffered a lot from this separation. She was 'placed and shuffled' between her mother and her mother's cousin. She has in particular the bad memory of losing all her hair while with this childminder and godmother. She must have been two or three years old.

Pauline reports that her mother complains all the time. There is nothing right with her. She often uses the notion of sacrifice to define her life, especially her life as a woman. The mother says that the only pleasure she can feel is for her children.

As for her father, Pauline admits to not knowing him. She bears his name but 'it's as though he's a ghost'. Generally, she even says she 'doesn't have a father'. And yet, having rebuilt his life, he actually only lives a few kilometres from the family home.

To escape the unpleasantness of her young life, the adolescent sometimes manages to sublimate her affects in artistic creation. On this subject, she declares: 'I have a lot of fun with sculpture'. Pauline shapes and creates mainly female figures in the foetal position. She calls them *Femmes foetales*, 'Foetal Women'. They are, she says, 'very fat women. Very round lines. I draw mostly round women. Perhaps because I had a model in front of me, that of my mother'. Note the phonetic proximity to 'femme fatale'. Moreover, does this representation not involve the image of a woman in gestation, of a woman to be born (or not to be?); the image of the mother who never became a woman, or of herself unable to become a woman-mother? Did her mother not experience pleasure only with her children, keeping Pauline in this state of perpetual child? A fascinating 'game of mirrors' in which the mother becomes a foetus again – and Pauline, feeling responsible for her mother, constantly 'carries' her within herself.

The cases of both Natacha and Pauline highlight narcissistic frustrations and anxieties about object loss. The feeling of abandonment and insecurity resonates in the lives of the two adolescents. Periods of mourning and separation follow one another. Violence is predominant, particularly through the act of suicide in the family history. Both have a life imbued with pain, dissatisfaction, and lack. A life dominated by the disease of ideality and guilt. Suffering from not being what you should be. Not meeting parental expectations, especially those of the mother. To be in the unbearable and intolerable impossibility of satisfying the illusory wish of the mother. 'Too much' mother. A mother left to her own devices. A mother whose excessive or depressive functioning dramatically impairs the daughter's capacity for subjectivation and fulfilment.

In addition, we find this unvarying characteristic in ill-treatment, a pathology of excessive or bad treatment, the absence or the deficiency of the paternal character, a strong, protective, separating and mediating father. The father is as though 'dead' or 'playing dead', leaving the child and the adolescent under the catastrophic hold of the mother. Natacha confided that her father 'is afraid of his wife, a weak man dominated by his wife. He can't stand it. One day, like his mother, he will kill himself'.

Notes

1 Freud (1930a).
2 This fantastical idea of the merging of the two sexes is even more prevalent in the adolescent (see Maïdi, 2012). In this respect, the myth of Narcissus has an analogy with that of Hermaphrodite. The androgynous desire-fantasy intrinsic to adolescence seeks to produce, through a form of *coincidentia oppositorum*, the satisfaction and realisation of coitus with oneself, the achievement of a merging or reunification of the two sexes.
3 Hermaphrodite (Ancient Greek Ἑρμαφρόδιτος/*Hermaphróditos*) is a character from Greek mythology. The son of Hermes and Aphrodite, as his name suggests, he inherits the beauty of both his parents at his birth on Mount Ida in Troadia. While bathing in the lake of Caria, inhabited by the naiad Salmacis, the naiad falls in love with the handsome adolescent. As he rejects her advances, she embraces him by force and begs Hermes, his father, to be united with him forever. The wish is granted and they become a single bisexual being, both male and female. Hermaphrodite then makes a vow, that any man bathing in the nymph's lake would find himself endowed with female attributes.
4 In antiquity, the androgyne or hermaphrodite (union of the two sexes) represented a monstrosity, but with magical healing power. See the sequence (in the style of Boccaccio) in *Fellini Satyricon* (1969).
5 Freud used this expression in his correspondence with Groddeck, whom he reproached for depreciating these sexual specificities 'in favour of the seductions of unity'. Ernst, L. (1961), Letter of 5 June 1917.
6 Freud (1913j).
7 The 'instinct' is a borderline concept between psychological and biological conception.
8 *Ibid*
9 Author's emphasis.
10 Freud (1905d), p. 160.
11 Nunberg & Federn (1962), p. 232.
12 Freud (1913j).
13 Freud (1920a).
14 Freud (1933a), p. 114.
15 Freud (1940a). 'An example of psychoanalytical work', in *An Outline of Psychoanalysis*.
16 Groddeck (1923).
17 He is a married man with a family, who has done well in life.
18 Winnicott (1971b), pp. 98–99.
19 Freud (1933a), p. 132.
20 Rousseau (1734).
21 This reminds us of the androgynous, even feminised, portrait of Bacchus as a young, handsome ephebe, by the Italian painter Caravaggio.
22 Freud (1920a).
23 *Ibid.*, p. 148.
24 The phrase used in French here is *passage à l'acte* and is a common translation of the English 'acting out'. In their *Vocabulaire de la psychanalyse* (1967), Laplanche and Pontalis translate the German term *Agieren*, regularly used by Freud, into French as *mise en acte*, insisting on the transitive form of substitution of the drive into an act.
25 Évelyne Kestemberg gives a very fine description of primary homosexuality as follows: 'It consists of the *first exchanges of love* between a subject and their mother through a series of bodily contacts involving the whole body, notably the skin, the gaze, the voice'. (See Kestemberg [1984].)
26 Freud coined this neologism, which is the counterpart of *Vaterbindung*, in Female Sexuality (1931b).
27 Freud (1920a), p. 146.
28 *Ibid.*, p. 149.

40 The feminine and castration

29 *Ibid.*, p. 158.
30 *Ibid.*, p. 168.
31 Lacan (1962–1963).
32 *Ibid.*
33 *Ibid.*, p. 110, author's emphasis.
34 *Ibid.*, p. 98.
35 Freud had already pointed out the importance of the 'penetrating' gaze of which a young hysteric may feel herself the victim. Indeed, as early as *Studies on Hysteria* (1895a, pp. 179–180), he relates:

The following is one of the best, and relates once more to Frau Cäcilie. When a girl of fifteen, she was lying in bed, under the watchful eye of her strict grandmother. The girl suddenly gave a cry; she had felt a penetrating pain in her forehead between her eyes, which lasted for weeks. During the analysis of this pain, which was reproduced after nearly thirty years, she told me that her grandmother had given her a look so 'piercing' that it had gone right into her brain. (She had been afraid that the old woman was viewing her with suspicion.) As she told me this thought she broke into a loud laugh, and the pain once more disappeared.

36 Freud (1920a), p. 162.
37 The object a is that which lets itself fall (Lacan, 1962–63, p. 103).
38 *Ibid.*, 'The *letting drop*, the *niederkommen lassen*'; and p. 99:

Confrontation with this desire of the father upon which all her behavior is constructed, with this law which is presentified in the look of the father, and it is through this that she feels herself identified and at the same moment, rejected, ejected off the stage. Only the 'letting fall', the 'letting oneself fall' can realise it.

The force of the father's gaze is the element that caused the girl to act out. *Niederkommen* = act of giving birth (Lacan largely took up this interpretation in his seminar of 9 January 1957, 'The primacy of the phallus and the young homosexual'. The adolescent girl is thought to reveal her desire to replace the mother, to give a child to the father according to the oedipal theory, the gaze symbolising the fertilising element).

39 Lacan (1956–1957). In this seminar, Lacan points out the difficulty of understanding the notion of identification.
40 Lacan understands courtly love ('bundling') as a conception of the love relationship between man and woman in which the woman is partly inaccessible.
41 Rieder and Voigt (2021).) Sidonie Csillag is an assumed name. She is Freud's famous young patient. She lived to be almost a hundred years old. Born in 1900, she died in 1999.
42 As I tried to show in my book *Clinique du narcissisme* (Maïdi, 2012), the gaze – drawing its source from early childhood – occupies a predominant function in the psychic functioning of the adolescent. At this stage of development, the need to see and to see oneself through the other is crucial. One cannot but note the impact and importance of the 'scopic drive', and its singularly intimate relationship with the problem of narcissism in adolescence. The adolescent is attracted by beauty and seeks to be loved as the mother once loved them. Narcissism is, in fact, confused with the extreme beauty that originates in the fundamental aesthetic encounter of early childhood. Beauty, the reunion of the original aesthetic object, is the supreme ideal of the adolescent. On the contrary, the failure to bring the narcissistic ideals closer together is a factor in great shame.
43 See Meltzer (1988).
44 In 1972, in 'L'étourdit' p. 21, Lacan states:

... the Freudian elucubration of the Oedipus complex, which makes the woman a fish in the water, because castration is in her from the start (*dixit* Freud), contrasts painfully with the fact of the devastation that is in the woman, for the most part, the relationship to her mother, from whom she seems to expect as a woman more sustenance than she does from her father. ...

The feminine and castration   41

45 'The little girl is in a state of reproach, of disharmony with her [her mother]. I have enough analytical experience [says Lacan] to know how devastating the mother–daughter relationship can be. If Freud chooses to accentuate this, to build a whole construction around it, it is not for nothing.' Lacan (1975).
46 See Joan Rivière's famous text (1929) on 'Womanliness as a Masquerade' which states her thesis from the outset: 'Women who aspire to a certain masculinity may put on the mask of femininity in order to ward off the anguish and avoid the revenge they fear from men'.
47 André (1995).
48 One can therefore wonder about the children of female homosexual couples.
49 In contrast to the maternal grandmother who is described as 'horrible'. As abject and detestable as the mother, since both are compared early on to the character of 'Folcoche' by Hervé Bazin (*Viper in the Fist*).

Chapter 3

From the guilt of being feminine to the feminine being of guilt

Clinical work dealing specifically with the feminine often reveals psychic preoccupations that are linked to guilt, negativity, and mortifying, destructive repetition. It is also quite common to find a particular family constellation that is dominated by the confusion of roles, generations, and sometimes even identities. As a result, attitudes towards parenting and intra-family relationships are commonly marked by excess, by 'too much', or even a surfeit of 'too much' in the case of violent behaviour, which is the characteristic mode of communication in these families. Conversely, they may be marked by lack, by an excess of 'not enough', for example where there is maternal depression, a form of 'cold' violence. In these instances, there is invariably a situation of severe emotional and narcissistic deficiency, a lack of parental reassurance towards the child. These opposing excesses, generally supported by one or other of the parents, can be produced[1] jointly by them both, particularly in the case of 'acted' violence, when, for example, the authority of a parental or guardian figure is disproportionate and abusive, and the child is subjected to significant and arbitrary frustration.

Note that this excess, initially external and environmental, generates and develops an internal type of excess symbolised by a severe and austere superego. In fact, the child's superego imitates the parent superego. This is how the feeling of guilt, which is a form of 'psychically bound' anguish, can be transformed into autosadism and moral masochism. It should be remembered that moral masochism is the expression of a 'need for punishment', the partial role of which is to relieve what Freud called the 'anguish of conscience' (*Gewissensangst*)[2] or moral conscience (*das Gewissen*). However, it should not be forgotten that, in a circular fashion, identification with the feminine victim object and the person's confrontation with recursive situations of failure, encourage the moral reaction and the feeling of guilt.[3] Thus, guilt induces the 'negative', which in turn creates guilt.

The 'victim' subject, passivised and feminised, is in fact imprisoned and immersed in a frightening circle where guilt both precedes and succeeds social behaviour that is sometimes quite harmless. The repetition compulsion, which lies beyond the pleasure principle, certainly seems essential in the compulsive act of

DOI: 10.4324/9781003414247-4

From the guilt of being feminine to the feminine being of guilt   43

failure. This negative, mortifying act, while temporarily relieving the sufferer, secondarily makes them feel guilty. It was in this sense that Freud (1932) wrote:

> There are people in whose lives the same reactions are perpetually being repeated uncorrected, to their own detriment or others who seem to be pursued by a relentless fate, though closer investigation teaches us that they are unwittingly bringing this fate on themselves. In such cases we attribute a 'daemonic' character to the compulsion to repeat.[4]

Thus, in everyday life, the repetition of the negative is fraught with setbacks and disappointments. However, the person, who is, usually unwittingly, placed in the position of victim, tries not to be sensitive to the afflictions imposed by 'fate', and seeks compensatory and prosthetic aid through potentially addictive behaviours. These defensive measures, designed to 'stun' and soften lack, are themselves marked by repetition, regression, and substitution.[5] Addictive action serves in effect as a defensive mechanism for escaping suffering. In this way, it also allows the reality principle to be changed through a search for jouissance.

These addictive actions embody forms of self-calming processes, that is to say defensive behaviours by the ego that seek to restore calm, but without procuring soothing satisfaction. The addictive behaviours describe a failure of repression and obey a constraint of repetition, an identical behaviour. Along with Claude Smadja,[6] Gérard Szwec[7] put forward the idea that certain motor behaviours aim to bring calm through the iterative quest for arousal. Self-calming processes are understood as defences that attempt to suppress a distressing situation, generally of traumatic formation, which is renewed by external conditions. Subjects are in a state of psychic survival. They cling to their hypermotor behaviour and find themselves unable to use the external object. They choose this system of defence for 'anti-traumatic' purposes.

For Smadja, the use of self-calming processes can be explained by the subject's *lack of passivity* in the primary relationship. This does not mean a refusal of passivity in both sexes. Thus, he writes:

> No doubt the experience of mutual passivity between mother and baby was not encountered very early on, plunging the child into a state of suffering, without the possibility of erotic withdrawal, support of representations, and forcing him into an endlessly progressing process, the urgent aim of which is a return to calm.[8]

This hypermotor behaviour is like a perpetual rush forward.

These behaviours testify to fixations on early traumas.

In this situation, we could say with Smadja (1994) that self-calming systems have taken precedence over representational systems, resulting in control processes rather than symbolisation and phantasmatisation processes. In these people, there is a search for self-excitement, which gives them a sense of existence and, at the same time, suppresses representation and phantasmatisation.

Michel Fain (Kreisler et al., 1974) also observes that self-calming processes are at the same time self-exciting processes. Above all, he suggests that the repetitive production of excitation through motor agitation could be interpreted as a therapeutic attempt to suppress an over-excitement that the mother had induced, by producing an excitation that cancels out her illusory resurgence.

Based on certain behavioural disorders in children, Fain (*ibid.*, 1974) analysed self-calming processes as 'an excitation capable of putting an end to a traumatic state'. He goes on to say that it is 'a disorganising energy that follows the impossibility of carrying out the primary investment, or that appears when this investment cannot be maintained'.[9]

According to Fain, the death instinct is called upon to produce excitation protection systems that attest to the relationship with a reality governed by trauma.

'The failure that can affect these (self-calming) processes cannot, therefore, be seen as a break with the repression, but as a return from within of the traumatic reality that they had hitherto contained.'[10]

Note that Jean Cournut[11] (2002) has also studied this type of psychic functioning, dominated by self-calming processes, in patients he calls *désertiques et défoncés* ['empty (desert-like) and stoned']. These patients are characterised by having had a 'badly bereaved' mother, from whom they have 'borrowed' unconscious feeling of guilt.

To illustrate my point, I'll present three observations that are fairly typical of this 'victim compulsion'. It is a compulsion dominated by the mechanism of negative iteration, moral masochism and that which concerns the feminine: guilt, the cruelty of the superego, as well as the feeling of an exceptionally invalidating existence. Psychoanalytic treatment, which is, in essence, 'anti-traumatic', aims to modify the subject's psycho-affective configuration, with a view to alleviating suffering and better distributing their investments. It is a question, then, of avoiding sterile and unfortunate repetition; in other words, making the symptoms disappear and tempering the ferocity of the superego. Ultimately, as Freud put it, analysis simply seeks to restore a person's ability to *love* and to *work*.

Julie: 'As though it's my fault for being born!'

Julie is a thirty-six-year-old sales assistant in a banking firm. She has been married for around seven years to a former colleague, now a regional manager in the same company; she has two children, a six-year-old girl and a four-year-old boy.

Julie requested a consultation almost as a matter of urgency, because she was 'fed up' with her situation. When she asked for a consultation, a certain excitement could be heard in her voice over the phone. However, she sounded coherent. Exceptionally, I saw her late in the afternoon of the same day.

In this first interview, Julie appears a little drunk. After briefly introducing herself, she complains of having too many family responsibilities, including caring for

From the guilt of being feminine to the feminine being of guilt   45

her father, who has been suffering from cancer for three years. She wonders why she alone, and not her brothers, must somehow bear her father's illness. Indeed, we find out that she has, she says, 'two little brothers', who are two years and one year younger than her. The eldest, an engineer, works abroad, and the second, according to his sister, seems rather unconcerned about her life and that of her parents. Julie says she has suffered from a lack of attention and being heard, and that she's had to 'suffer in silence'. She feels, in a sense, attacked on all sides within her family. By her brothers as well as her parents. She says she can't take it any more, doesn't know what to do to get out of it, declaring that something has to 'break'. She has to get out of this demonic loop that is engulfing her.

Describing her life, she claims, metaphorically, to have received a 'slap in the face' from her mother at the age of nineteen, when she asked Julie to announce the death of her maternal grandmother to the whole family. This event, which was *a priori* traumatic, is brought up at the very first session, without any further details. It is only close to three months into the analytical work that she tells me what is 'still torturing her' and 'giving her nightmares'. Julie was very close to her maternal grandmother, and spent a night with her when she was in hospital. Following an allergic reaction to some medicine, the grandmother could not be resuscitated and died. In the early hours of the morning, when her aunt arrived, a little late, Julie 'felt as though she was taking her place', because 'she, the aunt, should have been there'. Julie felt responsible for her grandmother's tragic and 'accidental' death, that she had 'killed her'. Ever since, she has felt an intense guilt. Especially as, since her grandmother's death, the already fragile family has fallen apart. Julie also tells me that the siblings on her mother's side have been 'depressive'. On antidepressants herself, she came to see me, she says, because at times of 'feeling blue', 'anxiety attacks' and loneliness – especially when she's at home and not working outside the home – she tends to drink up to a bottle and a half of wine during the day. She drinks, she claims, to 'get rid of dark thoughts, the misfortunes of others'. She warns me that she doesn't miss alcohol, but she says she can't stop once she has one glass. With alcohol, she also says she can 'do more things when things aren't going well, that she feels a helping hand, a defence'.

Julie associates this dipsomania with the onset of her father's illness. When weakened by his illness, he became impotent and helpless. At the same time, she states that some psoriasis broke out again that had appeared on her back before, around the time of puberty. It should be noted that this somatopsychic condition, which is difficult to resolve, is also present in her son. Since weaning, he has suffered from 'eczema from head to toe', says his mother.

In different sessions, Julie talks about her 'devastating' and painful relationship with her mother, tinged with passion and rejection. Her mother is described as 'depressive', but above all particularly intrusive in her daughter's life. She calls her three or four times a day at work, and comes with her husband every evening to visit her, as the two homes are only a few dozen metres apart. Julie literally feels invaded by her parents. 'We built a house close to my parents because I thought I could help them,' she says. She regrets it a little today, but doesn't dare admit it to her conscience. She may even be confronted with an unconscious desire for her parents' death. This desire, more or less well repressed, gives rise to terrible guilt, especially as the father's illness could have an irremediable outcome.

In day-to-day reality, the mother, unable to bear the emptiness and dissatisfied with her daughter's lack of availability, goes to see a neighbour who has the same first name as Julie and is the same age. This relationship contains a real bond and place of substitution, since with this 'other Julie', presented ideally and defensively as 'better', the mother continues to dwell on her complaints and other annoyances. The double is quickly exchanged. The mother isn't looking for her daughter Julie for herself, but to fill her 'hole'.

As a result, the mother's intrusion into her daughter's life now seems to be a determining factor in her daughter's unease and malaise. I was able to see for myself the mother's excessive intervention and unrestrained interference. Right from the start of the analysis, the mother, who, unbeknown to her daughter, had taken down my telephone number, called to 'make me aware' of the seriousness and 'recklessness' of her daughter's behaviour, as well as the danger of alcohol, noting, however, that she had 'inherited' this problem from her father's side of the family. As for Julie's mother, she states that she only drinks water. Citing the risk to her grandchildren, she also informed me of her daughter's 'marital discord'. Frustrated, having had no response from me, the mother called me again a few months after the start of the psychotherapeutic analysis undertaken with her daughter and left a courteous message on the answering machine, asking for details of the 'treatment given to her daughter'. As we can see, this is a mother who wants to know everything about her daughter. Paranoid, she complains: 'It's too easy, you're going to say it's my fault again.' From the outset, it's clear that the mother completely 'confuses' herself with her daughter. Moreover, they look physically very much alike. The identification is very strong. On the other hand, 'de-subjectivised', Julie suffers from not being herself. She suffers from not being able to express her own identity, her singularity, living *her own* life, not her mother's.

It should be noted that Julie was her mother's confidante from a very early age. She was her double. A form of complicity united the two women. They had to tell each other everything. Today, however, the daughter 'doesn't want to know everything'. She has to proclaim and forcefully demand her autonomy. She has to loudly and clearly assert her dis-identification from the mother who, dissatisfied in her marital relationship, projects her affects on her daughter, as if in an 'inverted' or rather 'reversed' Oedipal moment, signalling a major reverse identification. The complicity was made all the more possible by the fact that there is only a twenty-year gap between mother and daughter, who are, as I have emphasised, a perfect copy of the other. The relatively small difference in age bothered Julie a great deal, especially, she says, during her teenage years. At that time, the mother, more of a woman than a mother, 'wanted to live life to the full for herself, without taking sufficient care of her children'. The 'confusion' of generations was followed by a 'confusion' of people and roles, since Julie's status as the daughter and eldest sibling meant that she often replaced her mother in looking after her brothers.

This inconsistency in status and 'identity' is also evident when Julie, exasperated, declares, for example, that her daughter 'confuses Granny and Mummy', that she has 'the impression of being her parents' mother', or that her 'husband is like a child, an only child who was spoiled for too long, especially by his mother'. With these few elements, the Oedipal and 'incestual' problem, in Paul-Claude Racamier's sense of the term, seems to be salient in the complex emotional bond uniting mother and daughter.

In the same way, in an explicitly Oedipal triangle, Julie, who at the age of seventeen still had her mother as a confidante, met a married man twenty years older than her – that is to say, within a year of her father's age. This passionate love affair, which lasted six years, left a deep impression on Julie, as many years later these moments continue to haunt her dreams.

Explicitly and directly, Julie says she's ashamed of her mother, who flaunts her life without restraint or moderation. Shameless in her complaints, 'she'll tell anything to anyone': a 'rival' mother who is also disqualifying and 'guilt-inducing'. She calls her daughter negligent and a 'bad mother'. Julie believes that if her mother resents her, sometimes harshly, it's also because she's a girl and because she has chosen her own education and profession, contrary to the life and wishes of her parents.

Guilt is an almost constant theme in Julie's speech. She feels constantly criticised, that she is 'always being blamed for something'. As a result, she no longer wants to feel 'responsible for other people's misfortunes', and particularly those of her parents. She also says that a lot is expected of her, and that people are mainly demanding of her. She even goes so far as to express guilt about being and existing: 'As though it's my fault for being born!', she says with bitterness.

In one of her sessions, Julie tells me about a recurring, distressing dream. The dream is about failing to obtain a Master's degree. However, in reality, she does actually hold this degree, awarded on completion of the second level of higher education. While this exam was very important to her at the time of her studies, I have the feeling today that the anxiety-provoking, dream-like iteration of this theme reflects a real need for Julie to 'master' her life. She seems, in fact, particularly concerned with controlling her relationship with her parents, especially her mother, and preserving the 'identity' of her existence. Julie's parents, young retirees, have found in her a kind of prosthesis that she is refusing. The father's illness has somehow accentuated the incestuous promiscuity that has now become unbearable.

Julie's parents do not get on well. They married young, when the mother was only nineteen. At the time she was not yet of age, so she had to pretend to be pregnant (with Julie) in order to leave her own family. So, from the outset, Julie's conception was linked to the notion of fault and failure. But it was also a way of gaining autonomy and detaching herself from her own parents, hence, perhaps, an ambivalent image of this baby as both forbidden fruit and saviour. Julie's expression 'as if it's my fault for being born' expresses this ambiguity quite well. In this respect, it would have been interesting to know about her mother's relationship with her own mother, whom Julie has somehow 'made die'. She's never in the

48 From the guilt of being feminine to the feminine being of guilt

'right place', by virtue of her birth, by virtue of her presence in hospital, by virtue of her presence in analysis perhaps?

The depressive mother is also, as I indicated, excessive. 'She exaggerates everything,' says Julie. 'She has buried my father a hundred times.' Each time, she says: 'There's nothing to be done.'

The descriptions of the mother, provided by the daughter, reveal, over and above the sometimes acted out depressive elements, a symptomatology in the hysterical register. This is a woman who makes her intra-psychic conflicts visible and audible, sometimes in the crudest terms. In one of her sessions, Julie relates the following fact: the mother, who is apparently tormented by her daughter's condition, asks her if she is feeling better, specifically whether she is better 'in all areas'. Her implication, according to her daughter, was whether her habit of drinking alcohol had disappeared. Profiting from this questioning, the mother told her that on one occasion, a friend of theirs, in great distress, had phoned for help, after apparently taking some medication. When she arrived at the home of this depressive and suicidal friend, the mother had immediately slapped him, instantly waking up the 'desperate' man. The mother's conclusion was clear and brutal. Addressing her daughter, she immediately said, 'I should have done the same to you, to get your head straight.' This episode of the slap is, of course, reminiscent of the 'slap in the face' she received from her mother. It is worth noting that the mother herself was allegedly a victim of dizzy spells at work, while claiming to be surrounded by 'nasty' and ill-intentioned people. I don't know if she was revived by the same process.

Beyond the notion of guilt, there seems to be a major problem of differentiation, an impossibility of leaving the world of the mother. There are, in fact, several elements that imply the confusion of identities, generations, and roles: her mother's intrusive, excessive, and invasive words versus Julie's silence and lack of being heard. In this sense, repetition doesn't just seem to be limited to the mechanism of individual repetition, but to a kind of intergenerational circularity. From generation to generation, no one seems able to make up for the other's lack, hence this veritable transgenerational depression. Evolving time seems to be cancelled out by the impossibility for each of them to create their own space. The mother goes so far as to present herself as a therapist, who is, what's more, effective in her own way: the mother's slap of the desperate man is reminiscent of the salutary slap given to someone who has fainted or an oxygen-deprived baby.

Julie's 'superego' seems to be, 'I'm taking it all on myself'; she is perhaps called upon to carry a heavy and overwhelming phylogenetic guilt that spans several generations.

Today, Julie continues her therapy. Although she remains psychologically fragile, at the time of writing she seems to be regaining an interest in artistic and cultural activities. She paints watercolours and is interested in architecture. She seems to be better able to control her tendency to drink to excess. 'Before,' she says, 'it was hell. My husband used to watch me with regard to alcohol. I don't need it any more. There's no alcohol in the house. Especially as when I drank, I felt guilty.

It was a vicious circle. I wonder how I did it. It doesn't occur to me now.' Likewise, she wants to move on in her work, because she's bored there, and resume her studies so she can practise the profession she's secretly cherished for a long time, that of teaching children: a job that involves passing on from one generation to the next a discourse that also implies listening to the child, unlike the mother who 'knows' but doesn't listen.

Nadia: 'You can't do anything for me'

Nadia is a thirty-three-year-old woman, who leads activities at a social centre, and is also a painter with a passion for *art brut*. She has two children with two different men, a girl of twelve and a boy of ten months. She came to see me because, she says, she's 'the kind of person who goes round in circles'. She also suffers from a kind of social phobia, manifested by discomfort in public places, and a susceptibility to tiredness and anxiety when using public transport, which she is forced to do regularly because she does not have a driver's licence. She feels suffocated in enclosed spaces and shops, where she is particularly keen to find 'emergency exits for escaping in the event of a disaster or accident'. When we first met, all I knew was that her problems began with her first pregnancy.

Seeking to be 'understood' and 'overcome her discomfort', she explains that she chose me as her therapist mainly for cultural reasons, which she assumes I share, but also for practical convenience, as her home is not far from my consulting room.

In the first session, Nadia appears depressed. Many tears accompany the telling of her life story. At this point, I learn that she comes from a large family of eleven children, and that she has a twin brother. Her father, a former soldier, is said to have instilled 'mistrust' and predicted there would be suffering in his family. One day, in a conflation of generations and identities, he bluntly announced to his children, like an oracle: 'I have suffered, you will suffer too.' The father is extremely hot-tempered and violent, and even spent several months in a psychiatric hospital. The mother is described as a 'depressive' who, through weakness or conviction, does her husband's bidding. In any case, she seems to be united with her husband in the rather rough and crude upbringing of the children. The violence of the father, a former alcoholic and expert in corporal punishment if not sadistic 'torture' – a legacy from the war – was so ferocious and cruel that at around the age of eighteen and a half, Nadia and her sister, a year younger, left the family home. But while the family allowed her younger sister to reconnect with her parents, they never wanted to see Nadia again, who felt harshly rejected and abandoned. Nadia, the 'bad one', the 'traitor' even, is repudiated by her parents. With this idea of treachery, the parents display a projective type of defence. The betrayal experienced or denounced by the other is here projected on the daughter, all the more so as she has chosen young men from different cultures as successive companions. So, the feelings of hatred are genuine on both sides. But Nadia seems to be suffering this unbearable, psychologically terrifying situation to a much greater degree.

At the third session, Nadia tells me she's afraid when she ought to be happy. She doubts the peaceful, serene moments. She doesn't find it 'normal'. As though 'being normal' for her is the equivalent to 'being sore', or 'being in pain'.

It also suggests that, at times, it is she herself who does not consider herself 'normal', or who fears that she no longer is. This concern about not being like everyone else is paramount here. As she says: 'I'm in danger. I don't want people to think I'm crazy. There's nothing you can do for me.' Nadia is absorbed by the idea of 'madness' because of her own history. Indeed, apart from her childhood, which was marked by the mythical and magical beliefs of her highly superstitious mother, her elder brother, after a short stint in the army as a conscript, developed mental problems that have since required hospitalisation in a specialist facility. This brother has lost touch with reality, but also with his family. Nadia doesn't even know where he is 'interned'. As we shall see, being alive and 'disappeared' is also one of the peculiarities that torment the patient. Likewise, not being like everyone else, being original and non-conformist, not joining the ranks (of the army?) are also the conditions she is consciously or unconsciously looking for.

She adds that it is as if there were 'two Nadias inside her, one good and one evil'. She associates evil with death. She goes on to tell me that she 'carries with her a heavy burden, a feeling of death'. Tearfully, Nadia tells me that she was born after the death of a sister, on the same day and month, and has the same first name as the deceased. She confesses that on her birthday, she has already thought about suicide, and that only death could 'deliver' her. In her discourse, the feeling of not being herself appears very frequently. Completely absorbed by the evil identity that her parents, especially her mother, had instilled in her, she finds it hard to assert her true self. I later learn that this sister had died mysteriously around the age of six months. This led me, later in the analysis, to use the hypothesis of 'shaken baby' syndrome.[12] Indeed, Nadia's mother, who complains of being abandoned by her husband, oscillates between 'depressive' and despondent moments, and excessive, brutal reactions. She is also said to have fainted on several occasions.

Three months later, in the course of the work, Nadia brings a dream with few details that principally involves the image of a 'café owner' being merged with that of a 'gynaecologist'. At my request to link this content, she reveals that she has 'had several terminations' and is not able to talk about them at present. The session ends with these painful memories. When we next meet, she says that the work we've done together is too difficult for her, and that it was particularly testing to talk about her various abortions. She says she is thinking about death again, and really blames herself. At this point, she says she feels as though she is 'confessing and admitting faults'. Similarly, feeling 'profoundly negative', she wonders whether she was made to have children. Indeed motherhood, for her, represents either death or suffering.

Nadia says she gets worried about every little thing. She would like to feel nothing, or nothing but indifference. She admits that in the past, she regularly used cannabis to forget the bad times and be 'dynamic'. Hashish helped her to relax and calm down in the moment. Now, to combat her inhibiting anxieties, she doesn't take any toxic products or molecules, but she retains a certain nostalgia for that period of her life, which she paradoxically characterises as 'free'.

From the guilt of being feminine to the feminine being of guilt 51

In Nadia, feelings of guilt and self-reproach are omnipresent. For example, she blames herself for having failed at everything and 'trailing' her way through life. The patient often uses this term *traîner*, to trail or drag. It is a contrite reminder of the delay in the unfolding of her life, but also, in a disparaging way, the feeling – probably assimilated – of being a bad woman, one who 'trails around' after men. Similarly, from a 'melancholic' point of view, Nadia says she carries the other dead Nadia with her, like Schreber dragging the other leprous corpse behind him. Guilt affects her sense of being, since she wonders why she exists. Why is she living this life? Why does she follow this demonic destiny? Here, the sense of injustice is at its most acute. Here again, we find that painful existential preoccupation, if not the 'trouble', in Cioran's sense,[13] then the 'fault' of being born.

In addition to the guilt of being, which is, moreover, in total contradiction with the desire of the parents, Nadia often uses notions when she talks that are linked to shame,[14] cowardice, and betrayal, fault and mistrust. Her psychic life reveals itself to be totally disturbed by these representations, which are connoted by negativity and destructiveness.

Confronted from an early age by senseless violence, Nadia's very identity seems disturbed. As she puts it: 'We children don't know where to position ourselves.' These difficulties in life are rooted in Nadia's early relationship with the maternal imago. Indeed, the first identifications, which ought to be reassuring, were not successful, and did not help the patient to structure her personality in a tempered neurotic mode. Another form of preoccupation with identity arises when she talks about her weeping in some of the early sessions of her treatment. In this regard, she announces: 'You had to not cry in that family. You had to be a man. I would have preferred to be a man.' This assertion, which probably has an echo in the transference process, masks the fact that the mother preferred the twin brother. The boy would have been more valued than the girl. In her internal reality, Nadia seems to remember that she was an early victim, because she was neither wanted nor expected as a girl. So she believes her mother would have nurtured her less and not loved her from an early age.

On several occasions Nadia also expresses her anxiety about what she believes are recurring premonitory dreams[15] and, at the same time, reveals her attraction to clairvoyance. When we delve deeper into this concern, we discover that these are by no means predictive dream productions. She does, however, have the feeling that, in her nocturnal imaginary activity, when someone's face gradually occupies the whole dream screen, some unfortunate event is in store for that person. This anxiety suggests that Nadia sees herself as potentially evil and harmful to others. She is the embodiment of evil. On this subject, she said *ex abrupto*: 'I'm sure my mother was afraid of me... She *saw* me as a witch.' There is, in effect, a kind of mirror game between the two women. The 'witch' is here and there, on both sides. In this identifying chiasmus, the 'evil' figure of one is perceived in the face of the other.

On the whole, the analysis shows that, beyond certain hystero-phobic elements at play, most of the latent economic data could be related to borderline depressive mechanisms. The deep anxiety that is to be fought against clearly appears as a

52 From the guilt of being feminine to the feminine being of guilt

fear of object loss. This anxiety is also linked to actual separations experienced in early childhood. Nadia, for example, was placed in foster care when she was eighteen months old, when her mother suffered a bout of depression. Today, it is for Nadia to resist this massive phobic anxiety and to 'de-connect'. To achieve this, the counterphobic figure would essentially be the patient's pre-adolescent daughter or partner, in a reversed or paradoxical substitution for the narcissistically all-powerful but threatening parental figures. Sometimes, food is used as a compulsive defence strategy against the feeling of incompleteness, emptiness, and insecurity.

My patient also exhibits a constant oscillation between the reassuring ideal and the dangerous reality she may have been confronted with as a child. The other is always potentially bad, and therefore to be distrusted. But danger also lies within. It now comes from oneself or from the other within oneself. So, in the absence of successful elaboration and repression, unease and dread of 'falling' into a 'fear of collapse' terrify and worry. However, the terror is archaic: when Nadia says she scares her mother, for example.[16] Is this not an early identification with the toxic and harmful maternal imago, and a reversal after the fact of deeply hostile feelings? Nadia adopts and makes her own the mother's resentments towards her daughter, who has become totally confused with the dead sister. The hatred of the lost object is obvious. And Nadia, despite her mother's best efforts, will never be able to replace it. Frustration is a mirror image. It is on both sides. This intensifies the relationship of hatred between the two women. Hate and aggression towards the combined parental couple are accompanied by shame. But the aversion and loathing experienced and confessed produce a great deal of guilt, creating a never-ending cycle that forces the patient to 'go round in circles', to use her expression.

Nadia, now in her third year of treatment, seems entirely burdened by her past. A weighty past that forces her to compulsively repeat the negative. It is like an infantile fixation with the violence of primary objects, with a mortifying experience. The analytical work involves helping her to free herself from the imprints and memories, from her first violent encounters with an environment represented by a depressive, devouring, and destructive mother, and a sadistic, paranoid father. Now Nadia has to overcome the feeling of persecution that absorbs her, the distrust of others and of herself; to be more at peace with the other in herself, and finally regain an identity of her own, a kind of 'birth body' that is loved, secure, and narcissistic.

As a consequence, the analysis has allowed her to put into words, to find the words to say what she authentically is, to take greater ownership of her own life, her body, her emotions, her difference. It is a question of helping her understand what she's going through, find her true identity, and, ultimately, 'find' the pleasure of living.

Olga: 'I fail at everything I do'

Olga phoned to tell me that it was advice from her doctor that led her to ask for a rather urgent appointment for her son. But she didn't know whether he would agree to come to see me. A few days after our telephone conversation, I met Olga alone. Curiously, in this first meeting, she barely mentions her son, but essentially blames her husband. She testifies that there is regular conflict with him. The relationship is virtually non-existent. The couple co-exists: they are separated but share the same house. This is a broken couple that has had no emotional ties for several years. In this first conversation, Olga describes herself as undervalued and belittled, and blames her husband for being highly critical and rejecting of her. 'He's ashamed of his wife,' she adds.

Olga is thirty-eight years old; she lives in a region where she feels alone, far from her family, without friends; she works part-time in a retirement home. She got married when she was about twenty-four. She was five months pregnant at the time. Her husband works as an IT specialist in a large company. The couple have two children, a son of twelve and a daughter of fourteen. She tells me that she had an abortion at the age of twenty. Her partner at the time, whom she had known since the age of seventeen, did not want the child. In the course of the treatment, she sometimes says that she's 'unlucky with men'. Quite often, in fact, she presents herself as an abandoned woman, forced to live on her own, left to her own harsh fate. An extramarital relationship that lasted seven years failed to fill her emotional void. She sheds tears about this relationship, which left its mark on her. Feeling guilty, she nonetheless believes she was exploited.

The second time we meet, she reveals that she's having trouble with her son, who is rebellious towards her. But very quickly the 'difficult' relationship with her son shifts to the troubled relationship with her husband. For Olga, it is clear that the reason her son doesn't listen to her is down to her husband who, unlike her, is lax and permissive. Clearly, however, the son's 'symptoms' seem to be an extension of the mother's emotional difficulties. At this point, Olga says she has suffered from her parents' silence and has been called a 'schizophrenic' since she was a teenager by one of her sisters, who is a doctor. This sister, who I'll call Nathalie, is five years older. This sister is of capital importance, as she acted as a parental substitute.

The session ends with the recounting of a 'dream of being pursued', the content of which is not detailed. Olga had simply remembered that in this dream, she was 'pursued and in danger'.

The fourth appointment starts with Olga talking about the problems with her son, who spends a lot of his time playing computer games or watching TV, to the detriment of his schoolwork. But here again, Olga dwells only on herself, on her feeling of personal depreciation, 'the lack of recognition, contempt, and indifference' to which she is subjected. She also talks about her husband, who is often absent because of his work and hobbies. She says he has a rich social life, whereas hers is dull and uninteresting.

She says of her husband: 'He says some terrible things. He finds fault with me all the time. I feel as though I owe him something.' Abandoned and unfulfilled at home, Olga appears equally unfulfilled outside it. She is frustrated in all areas of her life. She says, for example, that colleagues at work feel she is incapable because they know that she has failed and take advantage of this to diminish her. At work, people tend to reproach her for being incompetent and 'blame her for mistakes' she didn't make. Olga's complaints are many and express quite clearly her position as an abused and defenceless victim. As she states throughout the analysis: 'I'm not recognised. I'm a bit lost. I don't know how to say what I think, I don't know how to defend myself. I let things happen to me. I hold back. I'm afraid of being badly thought of. I'm afraid it'll turn against me. That people will use my weakness to put me down again. I put up with it. I'm often faced with people who speak like they're "high and mighty", but I don't know how. In front of the people I work with, I crumble. With my family, it's the opposite, I'm very aggressive. My problem is that I don't know how to assert myself. I'm afraid of not being up to it. I think my size is wrong. I'm small. My looks don't do it. I have a height complex. I'm not proud of myself. Because others can do it and I can't... ultimately it's my fault. I feel scorned by some people. It's hard to be there and not have people take an interest in me. They reject me. This isn't a passing thought. I'm afraid of failing. I need to hurt myself. It's the infernal spiral of failure that engulfs me, my youth is going to hell. I'm close to dead and buried. It's going to take a lot of effort to pull myself out of this. I feel like I'm taking and not receiving. I'd really like to get my optimism back, that strength to think that I can succeed. I give in to it because morally I have no resources to overcome this misfortune. I play the martyred woman. I don't finish what I start. I have the impression that I won't make it. But I have to. I'm terribly lacking in self-confidence because my nerves are fragile. I feel like a loser, a failure.'

These few fragments of speech, reported here in a scattered fashion, show the dereliction and depression that is being more or less successfully combated. Olga admits that in difficult times, she would find comfort in toxic substances. She said she smoked 'dope', usually with her husband. Sometimes, she drank alcohol – wine – 'several glasses until [she's] plastered'.

In everyday life, Olga feels attacked. She's defenceless, passive, an object of attack. She thinks she's unworthy of interest. She's afraid of being judged negatively, but puts herself down. Narcissistic concerns are important. Superego and ego ideal are amalgamated here. Their severity finds an alliance with a feminine masochistic ego. The 'need to hurt oneself' is a masochistic expression that expresses the unconscious desire to live in pain and unhappiness. Guilt and the automatic need for condemnation and punishment are also omnipresent in the patient's discourse. Frozen in the status of a negative exception, she feels rejected, abandoned, and 'without resources'. The melancholisation of affects is evident.

After several months of treatment, Olga brought me her family tree on two photocopied sheets. Olga's parents divorced when she was eleven, the second youngest of her siblings. The mother was depressed. She attempted suicide several times. Indeed, this is how she died at the age of sixty-six. Olga was pregnant with her son.

The father is described as very authoritarian, 'dictatorial' as his daughter calls him. Headteacher of a secondary school, he left at the age of fifty (Olga was eight or nine), with a twenty-five-year-old teacher. He married a second time, to 'a woman who could have been his daughter', says Olga.

It was her sister, Nathalie, who took on the role of parental substitute, due to the mother's depression and the father's absence. She was the spokesperson. She is, however, described by Olga as 'selfish, controlling, and infantilising'. Olga suffers from having a patient–doctor relationship with her sister. Faced with her sister, she feels diminished, 'scorned', says Olga, who adds: 'She's a doctor, not a sister in front of me. She enters into my intimacy, my private life. I don't have a sisterly relationship with Nathalie... I don't want to be her friend either. Right from the start, we didn't have a good relationship. She was above us. She was the boss. She was my mother's pet, the confidante, the go-between. With her, there are no barriers. She mixes up her private life and flaunts it in front of me. She tells me everything. She acts like the father. She lectures us. She's in charge of our upbringing. Maybe she was ashamed of me.' Disparaged, this sister has long been secretly a 'male' role model who was difficult to identify with. This explains the frustration and aggression towards this double who possesses the 'phallic' complement lacking in her.

Olga feels that from a very early age she was 'broken', castrated, and diminished. Consequently, she proclaims her innocence in relation to the unpleasant life she leads, recalling that she was an 'unwanted child'. What is also striking in the patient's discourse is the distinctive appeal to the question of 'knowing'. She says: 'I'm more interested in improving my mind, in being captivated. Eager to learn, I know nothing! Can't compete. I know only a tenth of what others know, my family, my husband, my sisters. …' The complex linked to knowing reflects the unbearable castration of which she feels victim. Here, knowing and having are one and the same. Doesn't she herself say that she *has* no one to help her, no one to love her? Of course, this 'quest' to know has a transference dimension. Let's not forget that the analyst is 'supposed to know'. This paternal substitute, is probably – for the father was endowed with knowledge [*savoir/s'avoir*] – immediately placed in the position of being the one who knows.

In this perspective, a love transference became clear as the treatment developed, with the patient imploring the analyst: 'I need love. I'm not a nun. It's not easy taking things on by myself. I'm attracted to you. I'd like to stop the treatment. I've understood, I want to continue working on my own. I have the impression that you don't like me. I'm afraid of being rejected. You don't want to talk to me. …' We're on the verge of *acting in*, since, for Olga, expressing love affects in the context of analysis 'is like acting out' in the present. Acting and speaking are barely differentiated. In a way, saying is doing, or more precisely, saying cannot resist doing. Word takes on the value of an act.

This episode made it possible to analyse the transference and, at the same time, make progress. The positive love transference, clearly composed of erotic elements, enabled the patient to try to discover and seize what was going on inside her. Thus, she demonstrated her ability to admit that the absence of a response is not a refusal to respond, but a failure to respond to her desire. Fortunately, her hope did not turn into disappointment, but into a capacity for understanding and improvement. It is perhaps in this sense that she expresses her evolution:

'Therapy helps me distance myself from situations in which I'm helpless, violent and distraught. However you can't constantly be influencing[17] me.' Olga is entering her fourth year of treatment and is becoming increasingly independent. In her

56 From the guilt of being feminine to the feminine being of guilt

personal life, she is divorced and takes care of her two children, while pursuing professional training that could lead to a job in administration.

Olga's case, like Nadia's, is clinically and psychopathologically reminiscent of Kretschmer's former 'sensory paranoia', also known as sensitive delusion of relation.[18] Although there is no delusional experience in my patients, Kretschmer's pathogenic hypothesis seems highly relevant here. In this symptomatology, the subject, engaged in dramatic daily relationships, seems to be crushed under the intolerable weight of unpleasant circumstances. The person seems, in effect, to be undergoing a multitude of distressing events, an accumulation of failures and conflicts. In each case, we can identify a different situation of abasement and weakening, a 'lived experience' of inferiority and persecution, failure and dissatisfaction, humiliation and guilt, as well as extreme sensitivity to the other's gaze, which risks 'impregnating' them. The other is always potentially dangerous, the one to be wary of. You have to be on your guard. We also find this same invariable characteristic of the contrasted qualities of being and acting in the parents: authoritarian father–depressive mother. This opposing and pathogenic parental duality hinders vital expansion and encourages guilt. This neurotic symptom, linked to a feeling of inferiority, is expressed by a supposed devaluation by the person themselves under the gaze of the other. Inferiority, literally 'placed below', that is, to be lower, to be 'smaller', can only be envisaged in relation to the other or to the image of the other considered as superior, as 'dominant'. The victim often feels unloved, rejected, and challenged by the other, who prevents them from realising their own value.

Furthermore, there is another constant in the notion of the child who was not chosen, the child who was not wanted, or who should not have been. Therefore, placed in a position of passivation, the person has the feeling of not being accepted, of not being 'recognised' by those around him. On the one hand, they don't feel 'identified' as such, and, on the other, they feel that others have an obligation towards them. In this respect, the question of duty and debt is often at the heart of internal and external conflicts. In this respect, the defensive mechanism of projection is fully at work. All the grievances made against the subject are, in fact, *their* own reproaches that come back to them from the outside.

Within this perspective, we can easily say that both male and female personalities with an exacerbation of 'feminine' psychic functioning suffer precisely from a narcissistic and identity-related pathology. In fact, their problematic lies particularly in the violent conflict between the ego ideal and the ego reality. These people genuinely find it painfully impossible to satisfy the illusory wish of the parents: to be what they are not. Thus, the 'deficient' ego, lacking the ability to fulfil the desire of the other, unable to match parental expectations, finds itself, despite its defence and resistance, severely judged and subjected to the attacks of the superego.

As a result, the fragile narcissistic and identity foundations of these people require external support, constant and repeated reassurance, as these subjects are also prey to anxieties about object loss. These few elements elicit a tone of self-deprecation, or a pejorative aassessment of insufficiency. These subjects are certainly caught up and absorbed in particularly unpleasant feelings of dissatisfaction, frustration, and

From the guilt of being feminine to the feminine being of guilt   57

lack. In them, something is fundamentally missing. From this point of view, the condition of pain-sufferer highlights a kind of depressive manifestation that comes close to the liminal type of depression as defined by Jean Bergeret.

Finally, the 'mortifying' repetition compulsion seems to have its origins in the initial suffocation of the ego, which now demands intense narcissistic reparation for early harm. It is worth noting that early damage is essentially located on the axis of having. In this way, the person feels they have been 'deprived' of an advantage they were entitled to receive (love, food, care...). This advantage has a phallic sexual value. They believe they were 'wronged' and made to feel inferior very early on, hence their 'endless' compulsion to repeat the negative, the failure, the lack.

In a way, the negative and 'commemorative'[19] repetition of a subject justifies their original situation of being a victim, perpetuating an *a priori* unpleasant status of exception that is not, however, devoid of 'a pleasure … of which he himself was unaware'.[20] Jouissance, where pleasure and pain are combined, lies in effect 'beyond the pleasure principle'. It affects desire, and, more specifically, unconscious desire.

Notes

1 In some of my clinical observations, it was the father who behaved violently, and the mother was often depressed. But certain parents, who are in fact in opposition, can just as easily appear to be in coalition (without being in collusion): one, for example the mother, adopts the violence of the other, the father, as in the case of the Schreber parents (cf. *infra* Chapter 9).
2 Freud (1912–1913).
3 *Ibid.*
4 Freud (1933a), pp. 106–107.
5 This defensive form of substitution, essentially libidinal in nature, is mentioned by Freud in his letter to Karl Abraham dated 7 June 1908. In this correspondence, he writes: 'all our intoxicating liquors and stimulating alkaloids are merely a substitute for the unique, still looked for toxin of the libido that rouses the ecstasy of love.' Freud & Abraham (1907–1925), p. 45.
6 Smadja (1993).
7 Szwec (1993).
8 Smadja (1994) p. 1075.
9 Kreisler, Fain, & Soulé (1974), p. 93.
10 Fain, M. (1993), p. 59.
11 Cournut, J. (1991).
12 This is a singular form of abuse. Shaken Baby Syndrome, first described in 1971 by A. N. Guthkelch, concerns children under one year of age who are violently shaken. The consequences are generally serious. The shaking can damage the brain, leading to permanent disabilities such as loss of sight or paralysis, and even death.
13 See Cioran (2020)[1973].
14 Shame is most often linked to one's parents, and therefore to one's very self-identity. Here, hatred and shame, of the other and of oneself combined, coalesce.
15 Remember that, according to Freud, a premonitory dream is a dream after the fact that the dreamer is convinced was before the event. This temporal displacement serves to thwart the censorship that prevents a repressed desire. Cf. Freud (1899).
16 It should be noted that in some families, the first name given to the child has a meaning, even a predictive value on destiny. In this respect, Nadia, whose first name is fictitious

58 From the guilt of being feminine to the feminine being of guilt

for this work, seems to carry with her the 'negative'. According to this animistic notion, she is 'possessed' by a sick spirit, the literal meaning of 'having the devil in your belly'.

17 She uses the verb *imprégner* here, which, as in English, can also mean to pervade, or to fertilise, but also has this additional meaning of 'to influence deeply'.

18 Kretschmer, E. (1918).

19 I refer here to the work of Janin (1996). This author differentiates and contrasts two types of repetition: *representative repetition,* which is a 'reel game' type of repetition, an example reported by Freud (1920g) in *Beyond the Pleasure Principle*; it presupposes the recollection of moments of separation from the mother, and is part of the elaboration of an *organising* trauma. *Commemorative repetition*, on the other hand, is linked to the death instinct, and is part of the composition of a *disorganising* trauma.

20 Freud (1909d) uses this expression in his analysis of 'Rat Man'.

Chapter 4

The feminine victim

Feminam victimam: the *victima* is undoubtedly feminine in gender, unlike the *victimarius* and *victimator*[1] of antiquity that represent masculinity and virility. Whatever the person's sex, the position of victim is feminine. It is feminising. It evokes passivity and weakening. It is interesting to note that in certain languages (Latin, French, Arabic...)[2] the word victim is only used in the feminine form, something that merits deeper reflection and analysis from a theological and anthropological point of view. In any case, this characteristic of the female gender is in line with Freud's understanding that activity is masculine and passivity feminine. With this in mind, Freud (1933a)[3] asserts in his *New Introductory Lectures* that: '... sadism has a more intimate relationship with masculinity and masochism with femininity. ...' However, in the lecture on 'Femininity', Freud revises the masculine–feminine and active–passive parallel. He points out that women's 'passivity' is, in a way, culturally 'educated' through their environment, arguing: 'The suppression of women's aggressiveness which is prescribed for them constitutionally and imposed on them socially favours the development of powerful masochistic impulses, which succeed, as we known, in binding erotically the destructive trends which have been diverted inwards'.[4]

It is worth remembering that in human sacrifice, with the exception of children, women and their representation of castration ('severed' sex, menstruation, etc.) were among the most coveted victims. Indeed, it is the feminine aspect of woman that seems to evoke and symbolise the sacrificial victim. They were sometimes immolated, or else a 'willing victim', offering themselves masochistically and narcissistically as a sacrifice for the salvation of others.

In ancient Greece, the sacrifice of the feminine can be represented by the immolation of Agamemnon's daughter, Iphigenia. It was for her that Lucretius wrote: 'This chaste princess, trembling at the foot of the altars, was cruelly immolated there in the prime of life, by order of her own father'.

Similarly, according to Pausanias, every year inhabitants offered a virgin girl as a sacrifice to the spirit of one of Ulysses' companions, whom they had stoned to death. Such sacrifices were gradually denounced. According to Plutarch, an oracle ordered the Lacedemonians to sacrifice a virgin, and when the lot fell on a young

DOI: 10.4324/9781003414247-5

60 The feminine victim

girl called Helen, an eagle took the sacred knife and placed it on the head of a heifer, which was sacrificed instead.

The same Plutarch reported that Pelopidas, leader of the Thebans, had been warned in a dream on the eve of a battle against the Spartans, to immolate a blond virgin to the spirits of the daughters of Scedasus, who had been raped and massacred in the same place, and this command seemed cruel and barbaric to him. Most of the army officers were in agreement, arguing that such an oblation could not be pleasing to the father of gods and men, and that if there were intelligent beings that took pleasure in the shedding of human blood, they were evil spirits who deserved no consideration. A young red-haired runaway then offered herself to them, and the soothsayer Theocritus decided that this was the host the gods were asking for. She was immolated, and the sacrifice was followed, it is said, by a total victory. So, according to this age-old myth, the blood of an innocent girl was necessary for the departure of a fleet and the success of a war![5]

There are countless examples that highlight the female–victim relationship. One example is the famous 'witch hunt' that raged in the 16th century. Persecuted female victims, mainly hysterical patients, prompted Freud (1897) to consult the *Malleus Maleficarum* to examine the fate of these unfortunate women. In this collection, the woman labelled as a witch was described in all manner of negative ways. It said she went as far as trying to 'steal' and 'deprive the man of his virile member', or symbolically deny him a virile attribute. Indeed, Freud saw a phallic representation in the 'theft' of the witches: '... the broomstick they ride is probably the great lord Penis'.[6] These women, who were usually hysterical and ill, became the martyrs of the widespread fear of witchcraft at that time, but above all they were victims of male fear faced with the 'jouissive' sexuality and castration of the woman ('*Horror feminae*').[7]

Remember that in the name of the 'witch-hunt' – women were the main target of this elimination – thousands of women were murdered and tortured. Hysterical and masochistic, they accepted their ordeal with 'passion'. Frightened out of their wits, they were pricked with a needle all over their bodies to look for areas of insensitivity, presumed to be demonic clues attesting to bewitchment and maleficence. In a letter to Fliess, Freud recalls the ordeal of these women. He writes: 'The pins which make their appearance in the oddest ways; the sewing needles on account of which the poor things let their breasts be mutilated...'[8] By this time, Freud was already linking the unbridled masochism of these hysterical women to a traumatic seduction suffered in childhood. These women were probably already victims during the period of their infancy. It is an iteration, then, of their 'same cruel stories'.

Other examples combine victimhood and female masochism. Take, for example, the renowned 'Society of Victims', a secret community, founded by Amélie Brohon (1770–1778), of women who claimed to be victims in atonement for the acts inflicted on Jesus Christ in the Eucharist, subjecting themselves to daily punishments in a spirit of sacrifice. But is it not a question, here, of women who were previously ravaged and 'traumatised' (in reality or in an unsurpassed fantasy) and who now identify masochistically with the scapegoat victim figure of Christ?

Trauma and seduction

Trauma is a painful event in a person's life. It is defined by its intensity, the person's inability to respond adequately to it, and the upheaval and lasting pathogenic effects it provokes in the psychic organisation. On a psychological level, trauma generally involves three closely related elements: an excessive shock, a penetrating wound, and a backlash on the whole of the psychic life.

In his '*Introductory Lectures on Psycho-Analysis*' (1916–1917), Freud begins by pointing out that the concept of trauma is essentially an economic one:

> We apply it to an experience which within a short period of time presents the mind with an increase of stimulus too powerful to be dealt with or worked off in the normal way, and this must result in permanent disturbances of the manner in which the energy operates.[9]

In this pathogenic traumatic situation, there is, therefore, a violent and intolerable overexcitement of the psychic apparatus. In *Beyond the Pleasure Principle*, Freud gives a rudimentary image of this state of overexcitement, envisaging it at the level of a simple relationship between an organism and its environment. Thus, the living vesicle shelters beneath a protective filtering layer that acts as an excitation barrier, allowing only tolerable quantities of excitation to pass through, and the trauma occurs when this layer is subjected to a large and brutal breach. Consequently, the task of the psychic apparatus is then to mobilise counter-investments, while re-establishing the conditions for the operation of the pleasure principle.

The theory that trauma is essentially sexual took hold in the years 1895–1897. In this same period, original trauma was discovered in prepubertal, presexual life. The action of trauma is thus divided into several elements, and always presupposes the existence of at least two events: in a primal scene, known as the seduction scene and called by Freud their *neurotica*, the child undergoes a sexual attempt on the part of the adult, without this giving rise to sexual arousal; a second scene, often seemingly innocuous and arising after puberty, recalls the first by association.

It is, therefore, the memory of the first seduction sequence that triggers a sum of sexual excitations that overwhelm the ego's defences. It is only as reminiscence that the primal scene becomes pathogenic *après-coup*, in so far as it provokes a surge of internal excitation. 'Here,' notes Freud, 'we have the unique possibility of seeing a memory produce an effect far more considerable than the incident itself'.[10]

Such a theory gives full meaning to the famous phrase in *Studies on Hysteria*[11] '… the hysteric suffers mainly from reminiscences'. Consequently, the second scene does not act through its own energy, but only in so far as it awakens a lively excitation of endogenous origin. In adolescence, there is an important feature: the return of this excitation coincides with the rebirth of sexuality in a new form, marked by maturation and the advent of puberty and genitality.

In his critical analysis of the case of Katharina, the adolescent victim of an attempted seduction by her own father, Freud states that 'impressions from the pre-sexual period which produced no effect on the child attain traumatic power at a later date as memories, when the girl or married woman has acquired an understanding of sexual life'.[12]

Trauma theory is, therefore, closely linked to seduction theory. The latter is an essentially clinical discovery: in the course of treatment, patients come to evoke experiences of sexual seduction, that's to say, 'scenes' in which the subject has been the involuntary auditory or visual witness (sexual relations between parents, between adults), or sexual experiences in which the initiative lies with the other person (generally an adult), ranging from simple verbal or gestural advances to a more or less characterised sexual attack, which the subject submits to passively, with terror (*Schreck*). It is an automatic anxiety, a reaction to a situation of danger or to intense external stimuli that surprises the subject in a state of unpreparedness and incomprehension, such that they are unable to protect themselves from them or control them.

In the period 1887–1902, in several texts and notably his letters to Fliess, Freud tends to explain how, instead of the normal defences habitually used against a distressing event, the primordial traumatic event triggers, on the part of the ego, a 'pathological defence' operating in the sense of the original repression by 'inscribing' the traumatic representation in the unconscious.

Freud first approached the second stage of trauma, the *après-coup*, at the clinical level through the case of Emma, presented in 'Project for a Scientific Psychology' (1895). Emma's fear of going into a shop alone was linked to a memory dating back to the age of thirteen. At that time, after entering a shop, she had noticed that the two sales assistants were laughing and mocking her clothes, and she had been sexually attracted to one of them. Further analysis brings to light another memory where, at the age of eight, she had entered a grocer's to buy sweets, and the shopkeeper had laid a hand on her genitals. Because of her young age, the little girl couldn't integrate the meaning of this sexual touching, which she had repressed. However, the memory of this presexual-sexual experience will give rise to painful emotions during puberty, because at this time the remembered events acquire a new understanding.

With this in mind, Freud writes:

> We never fail to discover that a repressed memory is only transformed into a trauma after the fact. The reason for this is to be found in the late period of puberty compared with the rest of an individual's evolution.[13]

The same *après-coup* process is also widely invoked in the analysis of the 'Wolf Man' (1918b). Having witnessed parental coitus at the age of one and a half, he did not understand it until he was four, 'owing to his development, his sexual excitations and his sexual researches'.[14] So it was only at this relatively early age that the '*avant-coup*' of the 'primal scene' took on its full determining psychic efficacy in his fantasy and his symptom.

To summarise, seduction concerns first and foremost a 'scene' before being theorised by Freud and abandoned. It is above all a real or phantastical[15] 'scene' in

The feminine victim   63

which a child is passively subjected to a traumatic 'sexual' seduction by an adult. We can, therefore, assume that the adolescent or adult victim has been an early victim in childhood. Thus, we are in the presence of a fixation on the trauma and a compulsion to repeat the trauma. As a result, a young girl who has been the object of seduction in her early childhood may arrange her subsequent sexual life in such a way as to always provoke aggressions of this kind[16] (Maïdi, 1996).

Here, I also agree with Jean Laplanche's 'theory of generalised seduction'[17] in its close relationship with masochism and the position of victim. Indeed, the idea of 'co-excitation' retains all its value in masochism. And victimhood as a clinical form of masochism can be apprehended through 'masochistic fantasy' ('feminine masochism' according to Freud), of which the beating scene, developed below (cf. Chapter 10), is a fundamental example.

Feminam hostia

From the Latin *victima*, the notion of victim belongs, according to various etymologists, to the same family as the verb *vincere*, to conquer, literally to bind, and would thus precisely designate the victim as the *bound* animal. This word has also been considered as a superlative formed with the suffix *imus, ima, imum* from the radical in *vigor* (vigour, strength), and *vigere* (to be strong). According to ancestral mythology, the *victima* was sacrificed on the return from victory, while the *hostia* was sacrificed on the way to the enemy.[18] Ovid asserts that the word *victime* indicates that the throat was cut only after a victory over enemies, while *hostie* makes it known that hostilities had gone before.

In the history of religions, it refers to the animal or person being sacrificed to the deity. Human sacrifices were also made to the gods to please or appease them.

The notion of victim is, therefore, intimately linked to human sacrificial practices that date back to earliest antiquity. Pagan religions gave great prominence to sacrifice in their liturgy. Human victims were offered to Baal, and the Canaanites immolated first-born royal offspring. More often than not, in ritual offerings to the divinity, characterised by the destruction of a person, the 'castrated', weakened, and feminised victims were slaves, children, or foreigners. And while the human sacrifices of polytheistic peoples were reproved by the biblical and monotheistic prophets, being transmuted into bloody animal sacrifices, the fact remains that religious sacrifice is not absent from the Holy Scriptures. There is the sacrifice of the patriarch Abraham who, in obedience to God, had to immolate his son Isaac (or Ishmael according to Islamic tradition), the sacrifice of the Jews or the original sacrifice of Jesus, the 'voluntary victim' or 'scapegoat victim'. Finally, the essence of the sacrificial victim can be found in the prehistory of humanity, with its myths and rites, religious practices, and beliefs.[19]

In the idea of sacrifice, which has a close association with mystical ceremony, we enter the realm of profanation, since what is ordered on certain occasions is precisely what is ordinarily banned. This no doubt explains why, as Catherine Parat points out, '... the emergence of unconscious elements is often equated with the

64 The feminine victim

emergence of the forbidden, hence the anguish and guilt that can accompany the experience of the sacred'.[20]

Drawing on the ethnological work of his time, Freud elaborated the initial myth of the murder of the original father, his devouring by the sons – the cannibalistic incorporation of his power – the resurgent guilt and the pact of brothers that this murder inaugurates. The elimination of the father, original sin, is humanity's 'primal scene', a renewed, displaced scene (Moses, Christ) around which fantasies of desire and guilt are elaborated.

The sacredness of all myths and rites is, therefore, founded on primordial human sacrifice. Just as ritual sacrifice substitutes the *original* victim for a sacrificial victim who becomes *ritual*,[21] upon whom purifying violence is assuaged. At the same time, this expiatory and propitiatory victim concentrates on themselves all the evil that is destroyed by their own destruction.

As Freud points out, a crime had been committed against God, and only death could redeem it.[22] According to the law of an eye for an eye, which is deeply ingrained in the human soul, 'a murder can be atoned only by the sacrifice of another life; self-sacrifice points back to blood-guilt'.[23]

While human sacrifice is probably determined by the initial myth of the murder of the original father, and of the subsequent guilt, it seems legitimate to me to question, from a psychodynamic point of view, the profound motivations that push one individual, among others, to sacrifice themselves, more than others, for others, and at the same time, perhaps (above all) against themselves (deadly narcissism). Consequently, self-sacrifice and the feeling of being the 'unwitting' victim of designated sacrificers and persecutors can certainly not be separated from the complex issue of female masochism and its paradoxical manifestations in the psychic economy.

While the victim has existed in all places and at all times, and attracted the attention and identification of the masses – there have even been famous and heroic victims – recent years have seen a keen interest in the place of new martyrs. Today, this 'cult' of the victim appears to be a return to original myths, in which the victim's sacrifice, through their blood, brings redemption for the community, which has always believed that the innocent, through their *devotion*, could pay for the guilty. However, guilt, which goes back to the 'primal scene' of the murder of the father, engenders sacrifice, which in turn creates guilt. In this way, the victim of Antiquity is still very much relevant today. Likewise, today there is an 'enigmatic and incomprehensible' pleasure, to use Freud's[24] expression for masochism, in seeing oneself and being seen as a victim. Displaying one's innocence has become an individual and collective necessity. Thus, as a psychic compulsion driven by the forces of the unconscious, this 'temptation of innocence' dominates interpersonal relations. So, by exhibiting their victimhood, everyone thinks they've found their victimiser.[25] In a way, the victim has once again become the hero of yesteryear, the hero of the great ancient tragedies. Indeed, we should remember that in Antiquity, the tragic offence someone was accused of belonged to the entire crowd, and they had to be accused of that office in order to save the city. The scapegoat victim is, thus, a heroic figure (cf. 'Dionysus's goat').

But before we go any further, we need to ask ourselves a few questions: what is a victim? What about their innocence? Is the victim their own executioner? These essential questions quickly became apparent to me in the context of my consultations, where I frequently come across patients who express their suffering as victims, and are particularly keen to highlight their innocence. That is why I've used the clinical experience of these people trapped in a victim position to try and describe a 'victimhood syndrome' marked by the repetition of painful situations, the feminine, complaint, the demand for reparation, and the status of negative exceptionality.

The victim and the law

The notion of victim, which dates back to the end of the fifteenth century, is nonetheless still poorly defined. In civil law and the welfare system: for example, a person is recognised as a victim when they have suffered personal injury caused by a third party. This victim may claim compensation or reparation in line with what jurists mysteriously call the *pretium doloris* (price of pain).[26] As though pain could, in effect, have a price. 'You cannot put a price on tears' recalls an old French aphorism.

In this respect, it should be noted that society has always had a myth of reparation through the price to be paid, confusing reparation (making reparation to someone, not repairing something), indemnity, and 'compensation'. Reparation is, in fact, quite illusory, since we can never remake what has been undone. What has been 'broken' can barely be replicated. How can the irreparable be repaired? Morally, reparation is represented by the condemnation of the offender. As for financial indemnity, this is simply 'compensation' that corresponds to an entirely relative 'satisfaction' on the part of the victim.

In psychoanalysis, the notion of 'reparation' is essentially Kleinian. The concept is generally accepted. It refers to 'repairing something' as well as 'making reparations to someone'. For Melanie Klein, it is a way of combating the child's guilt, a tendency to make amends for 'the disaster created by their early sadism' that is linked to the depressive position. The latter is marked by the triggering, in relation to the primary object, of phantasies of destruction (*Zerstörung*), of being torn to pieces (*Ausschneiden*; *Zerschneiden*), of devouring (*fressen*), and so on.

In his text 'Réparation et rétribution pénales', Jean Laplanche (1970)[27] exposes the 'aporia of reparation', pointing out that 'what has been destroyed will never be repaired, but reinstated in a new way' because, he adds, 'the act is unique'. Referring to the myth of the horde: the sons who killed the Father thereby determine the incarnation of a society based on equality and fraternity, Laplanche asserts that: 'The need to pay, and *therefore to quantify*, is only justified in intersubjectivity'. The need for justice is also the need for equality. Finally, this author 're-examines' the notion of forgiveness, which is addressed *to* someone – to an other, of course, but also to oneself – for let's not forget that, as Freud put it, the human being has within him a 'plurality of psychic persons'.

Beyond forgiveness and reparation, Guy Rosolato,[28] drawing inspiration from the great and generous commandments of the Holy Scriptures, adds two other

The sacrificial feminine and the sacred

There are hardly any peoples in the world for whom religion has not been inhuman and bloody. 'The Germans in their manners resembled the Gauls, for they sacrificed human victims …' wrote Voltaire in 1759. Long sacrificed in the history of humanity, the human scapegoat victim was gradually replaced by an animal ritual victim. In his book *Sur les sacrifices*, Joseph de Maistre[29] recalled that animals were always chosen from among those 'most precious for their usefulness, the gentlest, the most innocent, the most in tune with man for their instincts and habits. Unable to immolate man to save man, the most human victims were chosen from among the animal species'. So, while de Maistre still sees the ritual victim as an 'innocent' creature, 'atoning' for some 'guilty' act, for René Girard[30] the relationship between the potential victim and the actual victim must not be defined in terms of guilt and innocence. In his view, society simply seeks to divert violence that could strike its own members, those it is determined to protect, to a relatively indifferent, 'expendable' victim. Sacrifice, thus, has a *catharsis* effect. Its function is to 'purify' violence, that is to say, according to Girard, to 'deceive' it and dissipate it on victims who are unlikely to be avenged, scapegoats in the form of *Katharma* and *Pharmakos*, which would have given these two therapeutic types *catharsis* (evacuation) and *Pharmakon* (poison and remedy).

In ancient Greece, the notion of *Katharma* referred to the victim, or scapegoat, object. *Katharma* was the name given to the evil object, the harmful and 'impure' 'foreign body' that had to be extracted and expelled during ritual operations comparable to shamanistic procedures. *Katharsis* is the benefit to the person or city of destroying the object or killing the evil person (human *Katharma).* This is a variant of *Pharmakos* (plural *Pharmakoï*, equivalent to *homo sacer* in Rome). It represents the victim or scapegoat. *Pharmakon* is simply a derivative of *Pharmakos*. Like *sacer*, it has a dual and antagonistic meaning (august and accursed).[31]

For René Girard (1972): 'Sacrifice protects the entire community from *its* own violence; sacrifice diverts the entire community towards victims outside it. Sacrifice polarises onto the victim the seeds of dissension spread everywhere, and dissipates them by offering a partial satisfaction.'[32] This 'psychological' theory, which uses *violence* as the key word to *explain* the phenomenon of sacrifice – considered as real or symbolic and virtual murder – and also sets out the function of all rituals, fails to take account of all anthropological differences. From this perspective, Luc de Heusch (1986)[33] rightly points out that 'violence never appears as such in the sacrifice of the ox that the Nuer of East Africa perform on an individual basis'. Quoting Evans-Pritchard, Luc de Heusch asserts that violence appears even less in collective sacrifices, the main function of which is to

> confirm, to establish, or to add strength to, a change in social status – boy to man, maiden to wife, living man to ghost – or a new relationship between social

groups – the coming into being of a new age-set, the uniting of kin groups by ties of affinity, the ending of a blood-feud – by making God and the ghosts, who are directly concerned with the change taking place, witnesses of it.[34]

However, when there is 'too much' violence, massive and excessive, this can also be 'purified', purged, and evacuated through the sacredness of chance. Thus, when a victim minority can no longer find enough traits to distinguish its scapegoats, it institutes ordeals to decide the fate of its fellow creatures. I am thinking, for example, of certain particularly wretched prisons, where, in order to escape over-crowding and poor prison conditions – sources of crisis and violence – inmates regularly resort to a trial by ordeal through which a victim is chosen and sacrificed. Here again, sacrifice is a way of deceiving or regulating violence through violence. Beyond this particular practice, which is in a certain sense self-sacrificial, since it kills the 'same' while distinguishing it in its alleged negativity, 'legal killings', as Rosolato points out, 'should also be understood as secular sacrifices in which the victim, *though guilty*, is nonetheless strictly determined by unconscious motives that make them the plaything of *destiny*, and therefore excusing them, the law find-ing in this way its transcendence'.[35]

Oedipus the scapegoat victim?

In a movement of collective narcissism and atonement, every society finds its scapegoats, designated by certain 'victim characteristics'. In Greek mythology, as Rosolato[36] reminds us in *Le sacrifice*, Oedipus, the scapegoat victim, possessed a number of signs that concurred with and suited his fate: he was infirm, he was lame, he appeared to the Thebans as unknown, he was a foreigner; he knew he was the son of a king, even if he was mistaken as to his ancestry; finally, he was an only child. In this sense, Moses also had the characteristics of a scapegoat: he was Egyptian, so, for the Jews, he was a foreigner who was moreover innocent and a saviour, of royal origin, and also marked by an infirmity, in this case of expression.

Myth that implies a given rite or behavioural determinism is not devoid of mean-ing. The function of myth can be to illustrate human 'drama', to make sense of it. Although the mythic and psychodynamic levels of access and discernment are dif-ferent, myth allows a certain understanding of the problem at hand. The 'field' of myth can, in fact, shed light on the psychopathological field, without the two being confused. Let us not forget that Oedipus did not have an 'Oedipus complex'. He actually experienced a human drama.

Oedipus's destiny was unquestionably that of a victim. Indeed, from birth, he was abandoned and exposed as a scapegoat. Neither should we forget that Oedi-pus's crime was not the murder of his father, but his incestuous relationship with his mother. This is the 'tragic fault'. Although unintentional, it was the attempt, through incest, to drastically reduce the disparities. Freud saw in the Oedipus Tyrannus 'a tragedy of fate; its tragic effect is said to be found in the opposition

68 The feminine victim

between the powerful will of the gods and the vain resistance of the human beings who are threatened with destruction'.[37]

Note, however, that in Sophocles's *Oedipus Rex*, the son of Laïos is no more or less guilty than Tiresias or Creon, gradually exaggerating his guilt during the course of the action to end up, like a scapegoat, delivering the city from the plague that had befallen it, that of mutual and fraternal violence.

In a metapsychological understanding in which antagonistic doubles meet and unite (sadism–masochism, love–hate, activity–passivity, life instinct–death instinct ...), Oedipus can be said to be both victim and culprit, but more victim (*Pharmakos*, according to Jean-Pierre Vernant, 1965) than culprit. He is a victim because all the Thebans conspire against him. He becomes the repository of the evil forces besieging the city of Thebes. In this way, Oedipus is not guilty, but responsible for the city's misfortunes. His role is that of a genuine human scapegoat. In the city of Thebes, inter-individual antagonism gives way to an alliance of all against a designated target, the scapegoat. On a collective level, the scapegoat plays the role of the object that miracle workers claim to extract from the bodies of their patients, and which they then hold up as the source of all evil. The 'culprit', the harmful element, is found.

In spite of this, and paradoxically, the victim ends up becoming a 'hero', just as a hero can turn into a victim,[38] specifically in the case of Oedipus. While he was essentially a dangerous, terrifying object of evil (incest, parricide, plague, etc.), he also became *sacer* (sacred and damned) and very precious. Indeed, his future corpse is a kind of talisman that Colonus and Thebes fiercely dispute. The victim is a hero because he concentrates *all* forces against him. His sacrifice unquestionably has a noble and even more heroic dimension. What is more, the victim may unconsciously provoke their own position. In this way, they demonstrate their unfulfilled and unsatisfied need for punishment. The victim may transform themselves into a hero out of narcissistic ambition, and from this perspective seek to be recognised, distinct and distinguished. Being persecuted can lead to mass identification with the 'victim', making them a potential leader. As a result, we see that masochism and narcissism are in perfect coalescence. Similarly, in contrast to our statement above, a wounded and negative narcissism can give rise to masochism, which finds its significant expression in victim-like behaviour. In this sense, we can say that the victim's personality is structured above all in narcissistic mode. The other is merely an 'alibi'. In a sense, it 'satisfies', favours, and assists an already long-standing feminine and moral masochism. The victim's narcissism is, in a way, 'on display' and easy to perceive, since the person, like the hysteric, 'reveals' their suffering and their jouissance. In this sense, there may be a link between neurotic organisation and victim-like behaviour.

Victimology and organisation of the personality

The personality of victims has been of particular interest to criminologists, who, in the 1950s, created their own branch of research: victimology. Victimology seeks to study the specific role of victims within the overall criminal act. Considered the founder of victimology, Hans von Hentig[39] in his well-known book, *The Criminal and His Victim* (1948), highlighted three essential concepts: the 'victim criminal', the 'potential victim', and the 'specific criminal–victim relationship' (*subject–object relationship*). Going beyond this author, the fundamental structural character of the victim's personality has been the subject of much research, all of which has led to the same result: chance plays an infinitely less important role than it first appears. Sophie de Mijolla-Mellor (1998) offers a particularly interesting definition of the clinical condition of subjective victim. She writes:

> To be a victim implies having been recognised, even chosen, as such, and not having to suffer *at random* the unconsciousness of the other who annihilates you even before having met you and collided with you, because he neither anticipated nor imagined either your existence or your presence.[40]

We can see that personal characteristics play a decisive role in the choice of victims, unconsciously favouring victimogenic situations. Thus, some people appear to be driven and guided by a kind of victimophilic and traumatophilic impulse. They are more often than not described as neurotics suffering from a guilt complex that makes them seek punishment inflicted by themselves or in the form of 'victimisation'. In this conception, we can say, with de Mijolla-Mellor: 'that no victim is a stranger, consciously or unconsciously, to the damage they suffer and in which they play an active part in the couple they form with the perpetrator of the violence done to them'. Sometimes, this is a genuinely unconscious pact, or what Masud Khan (1973) calls *the perverse alliance*, that is, the form of implicit collusion born of 'the meeting of the "active" will and the "passive" will in (two) separate and autonomous beings, and yet marked by a symbiotic empathy, which allows this set of factors to come to fruition in experience'.[41]

With reference to biblical mythology, the term 'Abel syndrome' has been coined to describe those people who suffer principally from a guilt complex and unwittingly seek out distressing situations. These are individuals who have been favoured by fate, but who feel a certain amount of guilt and attract jealousy and hatred, making them obvious victims. Chronic depressives also belong to this group, as do subjects whose vital drive is clearly weakened, expressing itself in the form of moral masochism and *spleen*, particularly well rendered by the 'cursed' victimophile poet Charles Baudelaire in 'Héautontimorouménos'.[42]

Feminine masochism in Baudelaire

While Baudelaire's sadism has been the focus of much attention, the poet's feminine masochism[43] is indisputable. Evident in a number of texts, the cruelty turned against the self is particularly on display in 'Héautontimorouménos'. Here are the last four stanzas of the piece, in which pain is inflicted on the self:

> *Am I not a discord*
> *In the heavenly symphony,*

70   The feminine victim

Thanks to voracious Irony
Who shakes me and who bites me?

She's in my voice, the termagant!
All my blood is her black poison!
I am the sinister mirror
In which the vixen looks.

I am the wound and the dagger!
I am the blow and the cheek!
I am the members and the wheel,
Victim and executioner!

I'm the vampire of my own heart
— One of those utter derelicts
Condemned to eternal laughter,
But who can no longer smile!

The masochism at the end of the poem is undeniable. The suffering prescribed to the self is unmistakable. Through the juxtaposition of antagonistic predicates (wound and knife, blow and cheek, etc.), the author assumes the dual role of persecuted and persecutor, 'victim and executioner'. In this way, the ferocious and reversed inclinations confirm the Freudian thesis that sadism and masochism are two opposing entities that act in a complementary way in certain people. The pair of opposites (*Flowers of Evil, Spleen and Ideal*), the two antinomic 'postulations', as the author himself calls them, dominate the poet's work. This is evidenced by the importance of antithetical formulations that tend towards oxymoron. Indeed, oxymoron is a characteristic device in Baudelaire's rhetoric. There is a profusion of juxtapositions of words with opposite meanings: 'pleasant horror', 'delicious pain', 'funereal gaiety', 'abject grandeur', 'sublime ignominy', 'gloomy and clear', 'horror and ecstasy', etc. The contrasting and complementary duality of sadism and masochism runs through several of Baudelaire's texts. Without producing a metapsychological reading of the different poems, we can note that the author himself asserts the antithetical dualist postures of his behaviour and existence. 'I am but one,' says Baudelaire, 'both victim and executioner'. Poet, expiatory victim, scapegoat of a persecuting God,[44] sacrificial victim on the altar of convention, his sense of guilt combines with the punishment of an offence he did not commit. Self-punishment and masochistic identification with the victim's suffering are characteristic of several poems. In 'The Irremediable', for example, the masochistic ego is tortured by a cruel superego force, 'the conscience in Evil'.

An unfortunate, enchanted,
Outstretched hands groping futilely,
Looking for the light and the key,
To flee a place filled with reptiles;

A damned soul descending endless stairs
Without banisters, without light,

On the edge of a gulf of which
The odor reveals the humid depth,

Where slimy monsters are watching,
Whose eyes, wide and phosphorescent,
Make the darkness darker still
And make visible naught but themselves;

The identification with the victim is likewise particularly salient in 'The Old Showman': '... the old poet without friends, without family, without children, brought down by misery and public ingratitude, into whose booth the forgetful world no longer wishes to enter!'[45]

The creator's martyrdom is even more ferocious in 'An Heroic Death'. In this 'Little Poem in Prose',[46] the buffoon Fancioule succumbs to the sadistic misdeeds and reprisals of his prince, who is compared to Nero. The poet's masochistic expression also culminates in 'Knock Down the Poor!' In this ode in prose, the narrator encounters a beggar who hands him his hat 'with one of those looks that would throw down thrones if mind moved matter, and if the magnetizers could really ripen grapes'. Enlightened by his 'good Demon', he pounces on the pauper and nearly beats him to death after hearing his Demon whisper to him: 'One is equal to another only if he can prove it, and worthy of liberty only if he can win it'. As he whacks the wretch with a large branch from a tree, he sees 'that antique carcass flip over and rise up' and 'with a look of hatred that appeared to me *good augury*' launch himself at him, brutally beating him and hitting him over and over again 'near to jelly'. The persecutor, who has in turn become a victim, is pleased with the result ('By my active medication, I had restored to him his pride and his life'). He tells the poor man that their 'discussion' is over, and that in future he is his equivalent, distributes half his money and proclaims to him: 'You must render to all your colleagues, when they go to begging, the theory that I just had the *pain of* trying on your back'. Here the poet suggests his struggle against the pain symbolised by the beggar. However, though defied, pain sometimes seems necessary to Being and existing. It is in this sense that the expression of masochism is patent.

Pain is allegorised, particularly in his prose, his studies in art criticism and his correspondence. Some authors have spoken of a melancholic type of pain,[47] but melancholy in its generic, 'romantic' sense. Thus in 'The Swan', a great poem about suffering, lament, exile, and outcasts,[48] the author describes his experience of *spleen* ('melancholic mood'), particularly in the first stanza of the second part:

Paris changes! but naught in my melancholy
Has stirred! New palaces, scaffolding, blocks of stone,
Old quarters, all become for me an allegory,
And my dear memories are heavier than rocks.

In 'The Swan', the poet proudly proclaims his dereliction. The swan in exile has become the *measure* of the beaten and defeated, of whom the poet feels as much a

72 The feminine victim

part as the 'negress, emaciated and phthisic', the captives, the dispossessed or the orphans. The poet experiences the same suffering as the banished, and feels a sense of solidarity with the community of victims.

Freud and the notion of victim

Although Freud's work doesn't really include a clear and detailed study of the victim position, the correlates of this concept, such as female masochism and the death instinct, the compulsion to repeat and the need for punishment, as well as conscious and unconscious guilt, are discussed throughout. The Germanic signifier *Opfer*, which also has the meaning 'sacrifice', is essentially used as a state or replaced by the synonymous word *unschuldig* (innocent) or *schuldlos* (not guilty).

Freud[49] analysed this type of victim very early on, first through the dream productions of 'punishment dreams', encountered mainly in men who had risen rapidly to an important social position. In the conflict between the arrogance and insolence of the upstart and self-criticism, the dream takes the side of self-criticism and seeks its substance in a relatively moderate admonition, rather than in the illicit realisation of a desire. It is a question here of the return of an unpleasant experience in the dream, a return of the 'negative'. In this way, the excessive fantasy of ambition in the dream is blocked and transformed into degradation and debasement. These punishment dreams vividly reveal the failures and painful or unpleasant trials we try to erase and overcome in our daytime life. The pride of the daytime alternates with punishment in the dream life.

It is also worth looking again at Baudelaire's famous lines from his sixteenth poem in *Fleurs du Mal*, entitled 'Punishment for Pride'.[50] This tale describes the offence and sin of pride, for which the author is severely punished. In the first part, a holy man who was a 'learned doctor' and had 'clambered too high' in theological ideals, is suddenly 'panic-stricken' and 'carried away by a satanic pride', and launches his sacrilegious attack against God:

> *Jesus, little jesus! I raised you very high!*
> *But had I wished to attack you through the defect*
> *In your armor, your shame would equal your glory,*
> *And you would be no more than a despised fetus!*

The sin of arrogance and demonic self-importance, the serious transgression of the sacred, is immediately followed by chaos, night, silence, and a demented abyss. Subjected to a swift and radical punishment (*sanctio*) that doesn't even allow the feeling of guilt to develop, the possessed 'victim' finds himself in a place 'like a cellar to which the key is lost'.

In a different style, Freud addresses the question of the scapegoat victim in *Moses and Monotheism*,[51] particularly in Chapter III, entitled 'The Latency Period and Tradition'. Here, he draws an analogy between traumatic neuroses and Jewish monotheism, through the latency that characterises them. According to Freud's premise, there is 'in Jewish history a long period after the abandonment of the Mosaic religion'. Within this context he puts forward the idea that Egyptian Moses was murdered by the Jews, and that the religion he had introduced (that of Akhenaton, the religion of Atenism) was abandoned. This fate of Moses as victim can be compared to traumatic neuroses, through precisely this common characteristic of latency or 'incubation period' between the traumatic event and the return of its repression, the *après-coup*.

In the same text, *Moses and Monotheism*, Freud recalls the hypotheses put forward over twenty-five years earlier in *Totem and Taboo*, which is that the powerful male was the master and father of the entire horde; he was not limited in his power, which he used brutally. Then the hunted sons, living in community, joined forces, defeated the father and devoured him raw according to the custom of the time. The cannibalism of this act was an attempt to identify with him by incorporating a piece of him. This first scapegoat victim, later replaced by ritual victims (animal sacrifices, for example), undoubtedly led to the existence of guilt that was repressed or projected on others, thus creating new guilty victims. The victim can, in effect, be a repressed guilty person.

Thus, according to Freud, 'original sin' was nothing other than a crime against God that could only be atoned for by the death of a son. 'It had to be a son, because the murder had been committed against the father'. But the 'Redeemer' could be none other than the main culprit, the leader of the band of brothers who had struck down the father. In this original crime, the unconscious feeling of guilt becomes a consciousness of guilt in which no one is innocent, including, perhaps even and above all, the scapegoat victim.

The original murder and identification with the devoured and incorporated father was replaced in the liturgy by that of the son through the host. It should be remembered that the host, originally a victim offered to the divinity as a sacrifice, underwent transubstantiation in Christian religious dogma through the real presence of Christ in the host. Everyone becomes a victim through a process of identification. Victim, yet also guilty, if we refer to Freud's analysis of the *Guilty Redeemer*.[52] In this respect, it is worth noting the importance of amphibology in the act of incorporating the host, which denotes destruction (of the victim) and identification with that same victim. To incorporate, then, is to destroy and identify at the same time, to kill and resemble the victim. To kill (in French *tuer*, pronounced the same as *tu es*, 'you are'), to destroy and to be: to be what one destroys through identification. The victim is certainly not indifferent. Just as the sadist identifies with the masochist in the perverse relationship that unites them, the executioner identifies with the victim in the act of victimisation. It was in *Totem and Taboo* that Freud showed the analogy between the paranoiac in their relationship to the persecutor and, referring to the work of evolutionist James George Frazer,[53] between the primitive and his king. Both, writes Freud, have the infantile attitude of the son towards the father, with the son's unconscious desire to kill the father. The paranoiac, through their persecution, reproduces the relationship between the child and the father. The child attributes, in effect, an omnipotence to the father or to his imago, but also

74   The feminine victim

shows a distrust with regard to this father that is directly related to the degree of power they have attributed to him.

So when a paranoiac recognises his 'persecutor' in someone close to them, they have, writes Freud, thereby promoted that person to the rank of father: they have placed the person in conditions that allow the paranoiac to make them responsible for all the imaginary misfortunes of which they are the victim.[54]

The victim and their innocence

The victim thinks they have 'paid enough' for others, but their unconscious debt is too great, seeming definitively impossible to settle. And yet, repeating the (conscious) complaint does not stop the mortifying repetition of negative compulsive behaviours. Indeed, the victim is unconsciously guilty because, as Laplanche rightly points out,[55] there is 'no innocence in the unconscious'. In this sense, the victim is unconscious rather than innocent.

We can take, for example, the case of a woman of forty-five, who does not appear to be in good health (smoking and alcoholism). She explains that she comes from a well-off family, but she is the only one to have been struck by this cruel fate. Alone with her children, who were eventually taken away from her and placed in the care of children's social services, she sought help after being questioned by the police and the courts about a rape she had allegedly suffered. What is striking about her speech is the iterative use of defence expressing denial: 'You're not going to tell me that I'm guilty... that it's all my fault ...'. In the myth of innocence, victims need to be cleared of any presumption of guilt.

It is also interesting to note the element of victimhood displayed by this woman who, although not of the Jewish faith, visibly wears a chain with a six-pointed star (seal of Solomon or shield of David), the emblem of Judaism sadly used for the victims sacrificed by Nazi barbarism. It is also worth remembering that many people see the star (in the sky or descending from the sky) as a symbol of the angel, of purity and innocence, but also of good luck: the 'lucky star'.

The feeling of guilt, in its broad and polysemous sense, can very often have unconscious motivations. Clinical analysis reveals that it lies at the root of failure behaviours, delinquency, self-inflicted suffering, and other profound existential negativities. It is guilt that, sometimes *from* birth (or even *as a result of* birth), the subject must carry and bear. This woman, for example, has to come to terms with the fact that she was born after a sister who died, and specifically 'celebrates' the same birthday (the day and month are identical) and bears the same first name as this sister. Here is a victim condition, one could say, from the moment of conception, who must defend herself against this harmful feminine destiny, but sometimes 'act out' her guilt through self-calming processes, negative and mortifying behaviours (multiple addictions, repeated abortions, risky behaviour...). In this situation, the moral suffering is cruel and the guilt intense, and other elements in the person's life generally develop and support it.

The victim is a martyr of the unconscious

While the victim's moral masochism expresses the sadism they suffer from within, from the outside, in the intersubjectivity of opposites – sadism and masochism – there is a completeness, even a complacency, between the two protagonist objects. Jacques Lacan[56] was the first to approach the problem of aggression from the angle of intersubjectivity. In 'Aggressivity in Psychoanalysis', he writes in his Thesis I: 'Aggression manifests itself in an experience that is subjective in its very constitution'.

Daniel Lagache[57] has also pointed out the sadomasochistic aspect of the victim who, according to the author, presents a 'split interiority' playing the roles of both executioner and victim. The victim, thus, finds an external superego alliance. In a way, it is a reversal of aggression against the self mediated by others. The 'executioner' is an ally of circumstance, fulfilling the victim's masochistic need for punishment.

As a result, the victim maintains an almost totemic relationship with the executioner, who is now both sanctified and feared. Moreover, the degree of power that the victim attributes to their persecutor and executioner sometimes seems surreal and magical. Take, for example, the case of a woman of forty-nine[58] who complains about her husband. She gives a strange detail about him that is very important to her: his eyes. 'He has,' she says, 'peculiar, supernatural eyes, which enable him to know my every thought even from a distance.'[59] Note that the theme of the eye is predominant in the intersubjective victim–executioner dynamic. Does this interest in the scopic drive have anything to do with the original scene? It is legitimate to think so, for, just as in paranoia, there is a connection between the victim position and the primal scene,[60] as well as a very close link between masochism and sexual drive in the fustigation scene developed in Freud's text 'A Child is Being Beaten' (1919e). Let's remember that this phantasy is charged with a strong excitation that is undoubtedly sexual, and, as such, leads to onanistic satisfaction through incestuous love. In this phantastical production, the consciousness of guilt, combined with eroticism, no longer merely brings punishment for the forbidden genital relationship, but triggers the libidinal excitement inherent in a regressive stage and discharges it in onanistic acts.

The scopophilic impulse underlies the scene of fustigation (see Chapter 10, 'Feminine Masochism'). For this reason, and in this sense, it is perfectly complementary to the primal scene, a 'spectacle' that evokes an aggressive duality in the representation of the child, and elicits identification with the feminine victim.

Notes

1 The *victimarius* was the one who prepared the sacrifice, and the *victimator* the one who struck the victims.
2 However, in Hebrew, for example, victim, which is *Karbane*, is masculine. Perhaps because *Karbane*, like the neutral Germanic concept *Opfer*, also means both victim *and* sacrifice. With this in mind, it's worth remembering that the victim was most often

76 The feminine victim

either female or of a 'neutral' gender, or one without a dominant sexual identifier, i.e. a hermaphroditic type.

3 Freud (1933a), p. 104.
4 *Id.*, Lecture on 'Femininity' in 1933a, p. 116.
5 De Maistre (1796–1797).
6 Freud (1897), p. 227.
7 Even relatively close to home, in the second half of the 19th century, so-called 'hysterical' women were mutilated and subjected, in the name of so-called scientific knowledge, to barbaric surgical procedures, either a clitoridectomy (excision of the clitoris) or, more often, an ovariotomy (ovarian ablation).
8 Freud (1897), p. 224.
9 Freud (1931). Introductory Lectures on Psycho-analysis (Lecture XVIII) (J. Strachey, Ed. & Trans.) *The Standard Edition of the Complete Psychological Works of Sigmund Freud*, Vol. XVI (1916–17). Hogarth Press, London, 1953–1974.
10 Freud (1894a).
11 Freud (1895d).
12 *Id.*, p. 133.
13 Freud (1895a)[1954], p. 413.
14 Freud (1918b).
15 External trauma or internal factors? Reality or fantasy? What is the reality of fantasy? Is it psychic reality (conflicts, fantasies, drives) or what Freud calls *Wirkliches* (effectivity)?

In his correspondence with Fliess and even later in his writings, Freud developed two successive aetiological models: the trauma model and the drive model.

The trauma model, for example, focuses on visibly external factors, while the drive model concentrates on internal, invisible factors, always evading our perception.

In the famous letter of September 1897, renouncing his *neurotica*, the paternal aetiology of traumatic seduction, Freud concluded that: 'The certain notion that in the unconscious there is no hint of reality, so that one cannot distinguish truth from a fiction invested with affect'. It is, in fact, particularly difficult to disentangle unconscious memories from unconscious phantasies.

However, it could be said that a kind of 'compromise' was reached. Thus, in *The Interpretation of Dreams* (1900a), Freud writes: 'It is not to the memories themselves, but to the fantasies constructed on the basis of the memories, that hysterical symptoms are first attached' (*Standard Edition*, Vol. V). So, there is always a basis of reality.

Ultimately, the trauma model, as a theory of seduction, presupposes a complex causal ensemble in which external and internal realities, social, psychic, and somatic factors are interwoven in multiple networks. In this way, the trauma model and the drive model are genuinely coupled in the aetiological approach to trauma.
16 Cf. Freud, S. (1895d). 'Katharina ...' pp. 125–134.
17 Jean Laplanche's 'theory of generalised seduction' is made up of the 'early seduction' inherent in the bodily care provided by the adult to the child, the 'infantile seduction' marked by sexual abuse, and the 'originary seduction' that underpins the first two. Cf. Laplanche (1987), pp. 119–120, and the article 'Masochisme et théorie de la séduction généralisée' (1992).
18 As Joseph de Maistre (1796–1797) reminds us, *Hostis* in Latin meant *enemy* and *stranger*, and, in this double respect, subject to sacrifice. See 'Eclaircissements sur les sacrifices', in *Les sacrifices* (1994), pp. 19–67.
19 On the *function* of sacrifice in myths, rituals, and religious practices, we cannot avoid mentioning the famous and indispensable 'Essai sur la nature et les fonctions du sacrifice' [Essay on the nature and functions of sacrifice] that Henri Hubert and Marcel Mauss wrote together at the end of the nineteenth century (1899), Mauss M. (1968), *Œuvres*, I, Paris. I also recommend Luc de Heusch's (1986) fascinating work *Le sacrifice dans*

les religions africaines [Sacrifice in African religions]. This author attempts to go beyond the anthropological interpretation outlined by Hubert and Mauss, and attacks the 'scapegoat ideology' developed by René Girard. Luc de Heusch offers new explanations for the reason behind the sacrificer's gesture. He examines the choice of animal victims observed in various African societies, as well as man as a sacrificial victim when the fate of society is at stake. He takes as an example the king, 'a formidable symbolic machine', at the centre of the ritual scene in Swaziland as in ancient Rwanda. The author studies his sacrificial fate in the renewed spirit of Frazer, which leads him to question the killing of gods.

20 Parat (1988), p. 16.
21 Hubert and Mauss (1968), p. 205, give a generic formal definition of sacrifice: 'Sacrifice is a religious act which, through the consecration of a victim, modifies the state of the moral person who performs it or of certain objects in which it takes an interest'. These authors intend to use the words *sacrifice* and *consecration* in their etymological sense, 'to make sacred'. Consecration, *con-sacré,* means establishing communication between the profane and sacred worlds.
22 Freud (1939a).
23 Freud (1912–1913), p. 154.
24 Freud (1924c).
25 Over the past fifteen years, a number of victim support associations have been set up. By law, they have a special mission to protect the interests of certain victims 'who feel their rights have been infringed …'
26 A circular issued by the Ministry of Justice on 15 September, 1977 recommends calling *pretium doloris* 'compensation for suffering', which corresponds to the damages awarded by the courts as reparation for the harm suffered by the victim. Common civil liability law affirms 'the right to full compensation for injury', i.e., the right 'to be placed in a situation as close as possible to that which would have existed had the harmful event not occurred' (Council of Europe Resolution of 1975, a formula consistently affirmed by the Cour de Cassation).
27 Laplanche (1970). In *Vie et mort en psychanalyse* and in *Psychanalyse à l'Université.* 1983, 30, p. 211–24.
28 Rosolato (1987).
29 De Maistre, J. (1796–1797).
30 Girard (1972) and (1982).
31 In *La violence et le sacré,* René Girard uses these different notions to explain the drainage and expurgation of violence in the city, as well as the role of the tragic genre and the *Kathartic* virtue of tragedy. Thus, he writes of the fate of Laios's son: 'As we have seen, the tragic Oedipus is one with ancient *Katharma.* Instead of replacing the original collective violence with a temple and an altar on which to immolate a victim, we now have a theatre and a stage on which the fate of this *Katharma*, mimed by an actor, *will purge* the spectators of their *passions*, provoking a new individual and collective *Katharsis*, also salutary for the community.' (p. 434–5).
32 Girard (1972), p. 22.
33 De Heusch (1986), pp. 35–37.
34 Evans-Pritchard (1956). *Nuer religions.* London, Oxford University Press, p. 199.
35 Rosolato (1987), pp. 126, 142.
36 *Id.*, p. 45. See also Girard. (1972), Chapter III, pp. 105–134.
37 Freud (1900a).
38 Here we are close to the notion of 'militant masochism' defended by D. Lagache. This expression illustrates a behavioural tendency in which the subject relentlessly manufactures new opportunities to seize the heroic role of innocent victim. (Cf. Lagache, 1960, 1961.)
39 Von Hentig, H. (1948).

78 The feminine victim

40 De Mijolla-Mellor (1998), p. 148.
41 Khan (1973).
42 Title borrowed from a comedy by Terence: 'The self-tormentor', probably via J. de Maistre (3rd Interview of the Soirées de Saint-Pétersbourg): 'Tout méchant est un *Héautontimorouménos'* [Every villain is a *Heautontimorumenos*].
43 Maïdi, H. (2003b).
44 Was Baudelaire paranoid?
45 Baudelaire (2012).
46 *Ibid.*
47 I'm thinking in particular of Jean Starobinski (1989) and Ross Chambers (1987), pp. 131–187.
48 The dedication 'To Victor Hugo', then in exile, immediately makes this clear. A copy of this poem was sent to the dedicatee on 7 December, 1859:

> What was important for me was to say all that an accident, an image, can contain of suggestions, and how the sight of a suffering animal pushes the spirit towards all the beings we love, who are absent and who suffer, towards all those who are deprived of something irretrievable.

> Hugo replied on 18 December, acknowledging that the swan 'is an idea' with 'depths', 'abysses', that we 'glimpse in your verses full of shivers and thrills. The immense wall of fog, the pain like a good she-wolf, that says it all, and more than anything else'. (Letter published by V. and Cl. Pichois in *Lettres à Charles Baudelaire*, Neuchâtel, La Baconnière, 1973, pp. 189–190).

49 Freud (1900). *The interpretation of dreams.*
50 English translation from Fleursdumal.org/poem/115.
51 Freud (1939a).
52 In this sense, Freud (1912–1913, p. 154) writes in *Totem and Taboo*: 'In the Christian doctrine, therefore, men were acknowledging in the most undisguised manner the guilty primaeval deed, since they found the fullest atonement for it in the sacrifice of this one son'.
53 Cf. Frazer (1911).
54 Freud (1912–1913).
55 Laplanche (1981), p. 282.
56 Lacan (1948), p. 11.
57 Lagache (1960).
58 Cf. *infra* Chapter 6, 'Can you be innocent when in love with someone guilty?'
59 This evokes God's guilt-ridden gaze on Cain in Victor Hugo's famous line: 'The eye was in the tomb, looking at Cain'. The accusing eye that pierces the walls (see also the piercing gaze).
60 Cf. *infra* Chapter 9, 'Feminine or "*Sacrifixion*"''. See also Rosolato (1969).

Chapter 5

The melancholic feminine

The melancholic impulse expresses the extreme state of failed, disappointed or bitter love. This state leads to unbeing (*désêtre*), mortification, desubjectivation, even disobjectalisation and pathological narcissism.

Melancholy shows the omnipotence and tyranny of pain over pleasure, and is an affection, a disease, of passion. Here, passion is characterised by its dark and negative aspect. The passionate subject 'suffers', endures, goes through agonies. Pain manifests itself 'in its purest form'; the subject, plunged into endless grief, suffers inconsolable loss. They feel that the lost object (*verlorenes Objekt*) is the 'Whole' object. The one they truly and fully desired, because it illusorily filled the 'whole' of their *lack* (hole).

Consequently, in the existential drama of melancholy, the investment of this Whole-object is, in fact, the ideal, mythical self, 'complete' and flawless. This is how the coveted love object – in this case narcissistic in type (oneself fully realised) – beyond its desire, is 'wholly' transmuted, simply and radically, into *need*. Without this now lost imperative object, the abandoned, helpless and powerless subject, torn apart by lack, lets themselves die. Their psyche is as though anaesthetised, and their internal and external investments are severely altered. The libido, disobjectalised by constraint, is uncoupled and withdrawn from the objects that were previously desired and sought.

Forsaken by their narcissistic love object, the subject feels lost, ruined. Abandoned, they are now 'nothing', empty and useless. It is understood here that this horrifying weakening that the subject undergoes, a kind of forced psychic anaemia, nevertheless remains closely linked to anal eroticism and the function of the pleasure principle.[1]

In the same way that the melancholic subject, victim of an external, irreparable loss, is marked by an open wound, it is also the object of a permanent endogenous depletion, an 'internal haemorrhage' (*innere Verblutung*), a 'hollowing out of the self' in the sense aptly evoked by the figurative and trivial expression, 'Everything's falling apart'. Nothing holds. Everything escapes the subject, who, in fact, manifests their powerlessness, their lack of control, their loss of connection and relationship with others.

80   The melancholic feminine

This emptying and impoverishment of the now pierced ego, generates in the patient, who is plunged into total confusion, a sharp pain that declares itself in the form of a heart-rending complaint: 'I don't want to give any more. I don't want to suffer any more.'[2]

Indeed, for this subject, to give is precisely to risk losing and losing oneself. This is all the more interesting given that, as Lacan puts it: 'To love is to give what you don't have'. In this case, the subject cannot accept castration, because they are subject to incompleteness, to the horror of lack-of-being.

Generally, the melancholic expression conveys the state of being nothing, of being *worth* nothing: 'I'm worthless. I'm just a piece of rubbish'; and the state of no longer *having* anything, or even of no longer *being* anything: 'I have(am) nothing' (*Je n'ai(est) rien*). The subject feels, in effect, the powerless victim of total dispossession, of a cascading loss of all possessions and energy.

This idea of painful, indefinite loss clearly reveals narcissistic trauma and intolerable castration (cruelty of lack). Pathological melancholic mourning, like insurmountable mourning of love, also expresses significant self-deprecation and *inverted sadism*.

As has been demonstrated in the clinical setting, this is genuine 'unworthiness syndrome', a 'delusion of inferiority' (*Kleinheitswahn*). Here, the pitiful self[3] is fascinated by martyrdom, negation, and mortification. However, it should be noted from the outset that the conscious expression of this hypotrophic self obviously masks the 'enormity' of a megalomaniac ego.

As loss is a source of hatred, melancholia is also characterised by the violence of ambivalent affects, an infatuation towards this lost object love. Clinically and meta-psychologically, this infatuation appears to be intrasubjective and intersystemic, according to the Second Topic. Indeed, it signifies the expression of a profound aversion of the subject towards its own ego, identified with the lost object.

In this situation of autosadism, the subject, who is both victim and executioner, *punishes themselves*. In so doing, they undergo a powerful attack from within (superego violence). Here, the mortifying destructive drive that dominates the ferocious superego is in full effect.

So, while destroying the incorporated love object, now confused with the ego, the subject ends up destroying themselves. In this way, the pleasurable self-torment of melancholia, like self-punishment from the repetition of constraint, signifies the satisfaction of sadistic and hateful tendencies that initially concern an object, but which are now reflected and turned against the person themselves. In this way, the subject is transformed, so to speak, into the object-thing of their own hatred.

In line with this elaboration, Freud writes:

> The shadow of the object fell upon the ego, and the latter could henceforth be judged by a special agency, as though it were an object, the forsaken object. In this way an object-loss was transformed into an ego-loss and the conflict between the ego and the loved person into a cleavage between the critical activity of the ego and the ego as altered by identification.[4]

The melancholic feminine 81

Rendered insignificant, the ego is indistinguishable from the hated object which, in this duality, seems to altogether dominate. The subject is now nothing. It is but the shadow of the coveted lost and triumphant other, who is presented as responsible for its own evil and loss.

Pathological grief and the pain of a bitter mother

Mrs S. came to see me following the tragic accident[5] of her daughter, a young teacher in her twenties. She did so with an impulse to complain (*klagen*), while wanting to 'lodge a complaint' (*Anklage*), and having met with several people (carers) from whom she was essentially and desperately looking for comfort.

Likewise, she went to associations and even political representatives to ask for help in finding subsidies to erect a stele at the site of the accident, in memory of her daughter.

In this type of organisation of the melancholic feminine, in order to admit the reality of the loss and overcome their grief, it may be necessary, if not vital, for the subject to erect a stele – with a phallic symbolic valency – that recalls the deceased at the place they died, rather like the *Kolossos*, representing the link with the dead, in which the Greeks saw 'nothing more than a simple *mnema*, a sign intended to evoke memories of a deceased person in the minds of the living'.[6]

The *Kolossos* as a substitute for the absent corpse is not an image, but a double, just as the dead are themselves a double of the living. This ancient method of memorialising the dead is certainly elementary, and while it may not 'heal' the negative psychic mode of functioning, it can, nonetheless, prove essential. It can, in effect, help immortalise mortals in some way, while accepting loss and avoiding death.

Often tearful, this patient wears 'the mask of pain'. Forty-eight years old at the time, and seen on about ten occasions, she began by expressing a kind of irremediable 'negative' personal destiny. Long before the death of her daughter, she said, all attempts at therapeutic help and support that might have helped her had been in vain.

So, at the same time as asking for help, she believes that nothing and no one can 'mend' what she has suffered. Which, of course, is not entirely unreasonable. Turning to me, she warns, 'I'm seeing a psychiatrist, but there's nothing to be done.'

This clearly stated[7] fatalism nevertheless seems antagonistic and discordant. For behind this melancholic defeatism,[8] the patient is clearly aiming for the interlocutor's 'compassion' in a kind of urgent purging of dark affects: 'I need to do a lot of talking …', she says.

Mrs S begins introducing herself with a form of self-diagnosis: 'I tend to be quite depressive. I've attempted suicide by taking alcohol and pills (medication). After these attempts, I stay asleep for two days. I'd like not to wake up for eight days, to stay in a deep coma.'

In search of *la petite mort*, of jouissance, she seeks to be suspended [*sus-pendue*] from life (in time). Iterative bouts of melancholy have consequently led to several

82 The melancholic feminine

serious suicidal acts. 'I've hanged myself,' [*Je me suis pendue*] she says, while announcing: 'If I do it again, I'm sure I won't fail.' And as though to remove the slightest doubt as to the effectiveness of her real desire for death, through the use of infallible and uncommon means, she adds: 'I feel like buying a revolver ...'

From the few elements of her history that I have, the most important thing to note is that Mrs S could be characterised as an unwanted, unexpected child. She was, in fact, the fruit of a relationship she describes as 'illegitimate' and 'illegal': an encounter between 'a German a prisoner of war during the Second World War, and a modest Catholic farm girl'. Placed in an uncomfortable situation between the two, the affair led to her being repudiated by her own family and rejected by her companion's family at the end of the war.

Exiled and stuck in the desert of her solitude, Mrs S's mother was a 'foreigner' everywhere. In France, she was criticised for having had a relationship with a German; in Germany, she was criticised for being French.

As for Mrs S, an unwanted, 'unexpected' child, she too claims to have been severely deprived emotionally: 'I never had any affection.' Like her own mother, she married at the age of twenty-one because she was almost six months pregnant with her eldest daughter. The latter, now twenty-seven, spent a brief period in a psychotherapeutic clinic. The mother of a small child, she didn't cope well with the separation from her partner. As for Mrs S's only son: 'He's taking his baccalauréat for the third time', says his mother, with a contrite, desperate air.

In a clearly incestuous position, Mrs S cultivates and suggests confusion of roles – 'I'm more married to my children than to my husband' – and of generations: 'I'm like a sister to my children.'

The husband, who had often been absent due to the demands of a job that involved travelling all around the country, is described as passive since his retirement. He appears mournful and extinguished, and his wife insists that 'he has no appetite for anything any more'. Note that the husband's retirement coincided with the tragic death of his daughter in an accident (Mr S retired two months after her death).

Steeped in melancholic mourning, Mrs S said she was living like a 'living corpse', probably through identification with the lost object. For her, this is a masochistic way of continuing to love her daughter narcissistically and to exist. A masochistic relationship with the dead daughter results in playing dead and identifying with the dead.

She is, in fact, a 'melancholic' mother steeped in death. A graveyard mother. She says herself, 'I convey death', as if to say, 'I am a graveyard.' A mother who contains a tomb within her, who feels herself to be a waste object.

As a consequence, the heroisation and mythologisation of the daughter as a genuine projection of infantile megalomania produce the impossible task of mourning. In my opinion, the grief is deep-rooted and clearly ancient. Unprocessed and unsurpassed, in reality it is simply the present-day reawakening of an archaic traumatic tear.

Thus, pathological mourning is a form of melancholic mourning that is based on a primary, unresolved mourning that is revived and reactivated by a present-day traumatic loss. In this unhappy and painful experience, the infantile depressive

The melancholic feminine 83

position is resurrected. This has never really been overcome, because there has been a 'failure' in the internalisation of 'good' parents perceived exclusively as 'bad'. The subject's tragedy is that she finds not the objects she loved and lost (gratifying parental imagos), but the 'bad and dangerous' ones that she especially hated.

Melancholia and primary narcissistic trauma

Is melancholy the expression of a fundamental narcissistic 'illness'? The question may be justified. Indeed, if the ego allows itself to be totally submerged by the lost object, it is probably because it was based on fragile narcissistic strata. The wound is, in fact, ancient. The loss is archaic, historical, even possibly intergenerational, through a process of close identification with the parent who may have been the victim of rejection in the past. It seems this is an ancient process of identification with the victim, in this case the passive, impotent, inconsistent mother, herself dominated by a cruelly melancholic feminine.

As Karl Abraham puts it, the damaging event can only be experienced as pathogenic in so far as it recalls and renews an original painful and unsurpassable lack that the subject is desperately trying to fill. This fundamental, genuine lack may also be coupled with a primitive identification with the primordial object, an insecure, unsatisfying, and depressogenic maternal imago.

It is basically the loss and absence of the object, or the early confrontation with the depressive or *bad mother*, deficient and incapable of empathy and love for her child,[9] that has inscribed this fundamental traumatic defect, and, through ancient identification, provoked an *après-coup* of the suffering of the maternal parent (primary caring object), who is herself abandoned and depressive.

Thus, *pathological mourning appears to be the retrospective expression of an original 'victim position' suffered by the subject.*

It is from this perspective that Abraham[10] states in a 1911 monograph on Giovanni Segantini (p. 263), that:

Melancholic states very regularly follow an event which the subject's psychic constitution cannot face up to: a loss which has shaken the very foundations of their psychic life, appearing absolutely intolerable and insurmountable to them, and for which they feel they will never again be able to find any substitute or remedy.

The author adds (pp. 263–264):

However, a current event of this kind is not in itself sufficient to trigger such a serious disturbance of psychic equilibrium [...] The violence of the affect associated with this experience is largely explained by previous impressions of the same kind, which have already caused a similar upheaval in their own time. Based on our experience with humans, it is always the mother who, at this early stage of life, has caused such a disappointment.

84 The melancholic feminine

Giovanni Segantini (1858–1899) made a name for himself as a great painter. Born into a poor family in Arco, near Lake Garda in the Tyrol, Segantini lost his parents at an early age: his mother at the age of five, and his father a year later. Young Giovanni's father left his native country, abandoning his child, who spent time in reformatory schools. Segantini struggled with his many difficulties, and found a kind of sublimating impulse, a narcissistic revolt, through his passion for artistic creation and painting. Segantini's entire body of work, from his paintings entitled My Mountains to his dysphoric, Christ-like self-portraits, seems imbued with 'nostalgia for the mother [...] who made him live and die'.

Dominated by melancholic thinking[11] and necrophilia,[12] the painter's artistic universe is characterised by the permanence of the primitive mother–child dyadic relationship, either brought together in a symbiotic collage or directly associated with death. In particular, the figure of maternal feminine dolorism, based on the model of the pietà.

As the artist himself acknowledged, these paintings were inspired by his childhood history, which was shaped by a series of traumatic situations: an intense emotional relationship with a 'dead' mother afflicted by the loss of her first child; the premature death of this love object, followed by abandonment by the father, uprooted from his native country that he was never to see again.

In the depiction of the painful mother–child couple, united in 'hopelessness without recourse', in which the figure of death is prominent, two paintings in particular reveal a poignant image: the first – *L'Enfer des femmes voluptueuses* ['The hell of voluptuous women'] – depicts female bodies asleep, frozen, floating like corpses above a great desert-like field of snow, and the second – *Les Mauvaises mères* ['Bad Mothers'] – presents a female body floating like a 'suicide', with a naked, chilled breast, at which can be seen the upturned, pleading head of the child, abandoned to death, without protection or help.

Yet, it is in the nature of the primordial object to be lost, as Lacan reminds us: 'It will never be found... at most as a regret. Something is there waiting for better, or waiting for worse, but waiting'.[13] To be in *waiting*, in suspense, is an intolerable and mortifying condition specifically of the melancholic subject, abandoned and passivated.

As a result, the subject, in their present misfortune, is unaware that they are continuing to yield to the damage caused by the original catastrophe resulting from the primary homosexual relationship. With this in mind, I believe in the same way that, if 'the discovery of the object is really a rediscovery', *the lost object, which generates pathological mourning, is in fact re-lost* (whether this initial loss is real or fantastical), in the process of compensatory psychic work.

Thus, the subject is once again deprived of gratifying cathexis. The deobjectalisation (relational and social breakdown) is therefore a kind of 'negative' response[14] to archaic deprivation.

Moreover, melancholy, in the sense that it can be defined as a *disease of the double*, a disease of annihilated identity and emptiness – 'I am (have) nothing [*Je n'est(ai) rien*]'[15] – is linked to a flaw in the mirror and in the original identification.

The unwanted, uninvested child cannot identify positively with a lacklustre, inexpressive mother, or one who, because of her narcissistic depression, acts as though dead.

Indeed, the pathology of lack that we might say arises *après-coup*, is linked to a deficiency that is harmful to the subject in their primordial relationship with the primary cathexis. It is in this sense that Freud puts forward the idea that the melancholic knows *who* they have lost, and not *what* they have lost in the person. In this way, in dramas of passion, the pathetic subject, proclaiming their innocence, also does not 'know' why they have been cut off from the love object they miss so much and who, they believe, really loved them.

Pathological grief and melancholic organisation

While Freud and Abraham were the first to clearly highlight the relationships linking depression and the loss of the object, in France it was Daniel Lagache who, as early as 1937,[16] carried out an original and detailed study of the problem of pathological mourning, through the analysis of a woman given the name Marie. At the age of forty-four, she was presenting pathological mourning following the death of her only son, aged twenty, in an accident.

After this sudden and dramatic death, the author noted that nothing and nobody interested this woman, who lived like a 'living corpse'. The only living, violent link with others was hatred, especially hatred of young people. Consequently, in a projective gesture, she had begun accusing others of her son's death ('They killed him for you'), before accusing herself ('You killed him').

In a position of *negative exception*, she felt that she was the only one to have lost her son, that only she was unhappy, even that she was simply not made like other people.

She blamed herself, reproaching herself for being a monster-mother, either because of the perversity and dangerousness of her repressed ideas, 'or because of their contradiction with what she owed her son'. Overwhelmed and stuck in a psychic death, she felt as though she had fallen into an abyss, a bottomless pit. She was self-critical and self-deprecating, saying that she was 'crazy', and only fit for an asylum. The sense of loss was general, with violent and profound desolation.

In fact, the madness seemed to be defensive for this woman, a way for her to temporarily escape death by suicide.

In this melancholy woman, the 'work of mourning' was completely inhibited. All her interest, all her love, tended to focus on her 'phallicised', idealised, and idolised son, who filled her emptiness and met her expectations. At this point, there is no need to stress the incestuous relationship between the two protagonists.

In the end, the insurmountable loss of her son led to her own radical loss. Suicide allowed this severely and pathologically grieving woman to free herself, outwardly, from her mother and, inwardly, from the sadism of the superego. Joining her son in death was her only way out. Lagache's analysis of the 'Marie case' provides a relevant insight into the survivor's ambivalent conflict with the dead person, which lies at the heart of the metapsychological work of mourning.

86   The melancholic feminine

In this conflict, the dead person plays the role of an 'anti-life' moral authority. The survivor is, in effect, under the permanent, heavy, and painful yoke of this categorical imperative: 'You must follow the dead person' or 'You cannot – indeed you must not – live without me'.

So, in order to separate from the dead once and for all, it is necessary to un-invest in them and symbolically kill them. Quite simply, they must die a second time in the mind of the subject.[17] For the dead person continues to haunt and psychically torment the living. The latter is also affected by a dual and conflicting feeling, a state of megalomania – 'I could have prevented his death' – and guilt: 'It's my fault. I did nothing to prevent his death'.

Identification with the dead person is an attempt to assuage the guilt of living and maintain the relationship with the dead, in a masochistic form, if not by dying, at least by being mortified. Consciousness is, thus, torn between duty to the dead, which prescribes dying, and the desire to live.[18] The meaning of the work of mourning is not only or essentially to detach oneself from an object of love on which acts of love can no longer be effected, it is the destruction of a persecuting and 'diabolical' moral omnipotence that demands that one should not live.

Melancholy of fate

Being inscribed within a negative, irrevocable destiny is expressed in no uncertain terms: 'I was born for things to go badly'. The body-ego is identified with the bad, the 'monstrous'. That is why, it seems to me, there exists an unconscious 'feminine' predisposition to melancholisation.

Through her 'illness' of despair, the patient affirms her impregnable castration, and her profound and primitive narcissistic wound that underpins, for example, the following statement: 'I've never been accepted... because I was the daughter of a German.' This expression denotes quite clearly the unconscious desire for death, and an indirect accusation against the guilty mother.

By deferring to *fate*, the subject of the melancholic feminine believes that fate has bequeathed them this lot of mortifying existence, thereby granting her a negative place outside the common order. Resigned to the power of fate, they moreover accept to take on the 'sin' of generations,[19] which ensures them their place as a tragic exception. This is why, for want of being ideal,[20] they seek out everything that can be lethal to them.

On the other hand, even a simple and familiar parental punishment in the banal adult–child, mother–daughter relationship is transformed into a prediction of misfortune, a maternal curse. As Mrs S points out: 'When I didn't listen to my mother's advice, she'd often say to me: "You'll be punished later".' This melancholic organisation, which could be characterised as 'predestined', perpetuates the manifestations of negative behaviour that express the unleashing of the destructive drive.

Trapped in an unpleasant position, the subject is the victim of successive defections and catastrophes. But, while they were originally a passive victim, they are now largely an actor in their misfortune. Unbeknown to them, they anticipate the rupture and its effects, and quite simply express a form of permanent illness of *loss* and *abandonment*, of lack and dereliction.

Loss and guilt

In melancholic functioning, the subject seems to introject and take on the guilt of the loss of the parental other. The feeling of guilt may, indeed, have a primary character (*primäre Schuldgefühle*), as Theodor Reik points out.[21]

This introjected guilt is rekindled by the painful and distressing separation, of which the subject finds themselves this time the object. But, in both cases, the narcissistic wound is cruel and the devastating hatred is turned against the self. Of course, this guilt seeks meaning in causality and rationality. The fault is, in effect, propelled outwards. It is pointed at the other, while at the same time blaming the I.[22] For example, Mrs S says, with ambivalence: 'I blame myself. I feel guilty.[23] I have a lot of remorse ...', while also expressing an unconscious responsibility for her daughter's tragic behaviour: 'Like it was my fault! Like I'd raised her badly! I didn't do anything to make her less reckless.[24] She couldn't see the danger.'

The daughter's 'suicidal' behaviour[25] is implicitly recognised by the mother, as though she had been at the source of an infection of 'evil' in her daughter, transmuting her into a kind of female victim by delegation.

As I pointed out earlier, the suffering of the melancholic feminine is rooted in the archaic narcissistic wound and traumatic castration. Consequently, in an illusion of control, the passivated subject loses herself in the loss of the 'phallicised', desired, and hyperinvested object.

Lacan gives a good summary of the 'experience' that follows irreparable deprivation when he says:

> It is a question of what I will call, not mourning, nor depression owing to the loss of an object, but remorse of a certain type triggered by a denouement that involves something along the lines of suicide on the part of the object. Remorse, thus, regarding an object that has entered in some way into the field of desire and that, owing to its own actions or some risk it took in a venture, has disappeared.[26]

Note that it is guilt that develops sadism directed against the self. In 'A Child is Being Beaten', Freud (1919e) asserts: 'a sense of guilt is invariably the factor that transforms sadism into masochism.' (p. 189).

In a melancholic disorder, this feeling of guilt is the result of a despotic superego which 'rages against the ego with merciless violence, as if it had taken possession of the whole of the sadism available in the person concerned'.[27]

Consequently, the guilt of the melancholic feminine, which generates ferocious self-deprecation, contributes to the advent of moral masochism and to the permanent and harassing, psychic and hallucinating presence of the love object that has escaped the subject.

88　The melancholic feminine

Indeed, through masochism there is a rediscovery of the object. Even if the object is, in fact, physically lost, it is psychically reappropriated. Similarly, in the melancholic experience, the experience of fault and guilt is prominent. The subject seeks supreme punishment in their own destruction, mercilessly confounding themselves with the forces of Evil. It's worth noting that Freud refers to the melancholic's suffering as 'torture', 'sadism', and 'hatred', adding that this self-object sadism is the basis of the melancholic's potentially realisable suicide.

Suicide, autosadism, and melancholia

There is undeniably a close link between melancholia and the interdependent and complementary opposing poles of sadism and masochism. Freud rightly emphasised the sadism of the superego that combines with the masochism of the ego in melancholia. It is this sadism of the dominant superego agency that is thought to play a major role in the mortifying negative form and the melancholic suicidal tendency.

Thus, the self-destructive inclination allows us to regressively search for earlier archaic states of original narcissistic sadism, that is to say, the primary masochism intrinsic to the death instinct (cf. Freud, 1915c).

It should also be noted that in this state of great pain, where the benefit of regression to the stage of primordial narcissistic is nonetheless indisputable, the melancholic feminine subject reveals their unhappiness and their pain.

Indeed, there is a real taste for staging the tragic in repeated suicide attempts. It is as though the person takes intense pleasure in playing out this morbid idea of annihilation and extreme self-dominance, a kind of jouissance in horrifying themselves. But above all, the subject, through their pathological scenario, tries to – and enjoys – terrifying others. It is the 'triumph of the victim'. We find here the hysterical feminine aspect of this position, which I develop further below.

The suicide of the melancholic, which can be understood as a kind of failure in the work of melancholia (Rosenberg, 1991), corresponds to a narcissistic disinvestment of the ego. Carried along by the momentum of the terrible death instinct, its desire is precisely to not-desire in the sense of nirvana. In this state, it is a question of the death of desire intertwined with the desire for death.

It should also be noted that self-punishing and self-murdering behaviours can equally be expressed in terms of redemptive suffering. In this respect, it is interesting to recall the famous patient that Pierre Janet studied for twenty-two years at the Salpetrière – Madeleine – who presented more or less eroticised delusions of sacrificial torture and the stigmata of crucifixion during those dark depressive periods that Janet categorised as melancholic episodes.[28] Undeniably, the problematic of the melancholic feminine often and essentially refers to the theme of fault, sin, and redemption. In line with this observation, the victim cannot be dissociated from the question of the sacrificial feminine, the sacred and atonement.

Maternal passion

As Nicole Loraux (1990) reminds us in her book *Les mères en deuil* ['Mothers in mourning'] feminine excess always threatens in a mother's grief. *Mater affectus animo*: being a mother is, in itself, a passion, a suffering (cf. *Mater dolorosa* or the *pietà*). Thus, the 'pleasure of tears', of pain, is often translated as characteristic of the female subject, and mourning as synonymous with castration, not only that which is linked directly to a real loss, of the object for example, but above all that which corresponds to making the subject effeminate. To be in pain would be equivalent, in a way, to being 'castrated', 'cut off from ...', impotent, and 'emasculated'.

In ancient Greece, Demeter, in mourning for her only daughter Persephone, the 'spring flower virgin', who was kidnapped by Hades (Pluto), King of the Dead and god of the Underworld, may be the mythological personification of the original melancholy belonging to the figure of the feminine.

With the initial violence of an essential loss, the loss of the phallic imaginary completeness offered by her daughter, the child–penis repairing her lack, Demeter, in her immense grief, lost a part of herself, her most precious possession, the fruit of her womb. Flying over the world in search of Persephone, refusing her blessings to the now barren earth, Demeter, still inconsolable over the 'lack' of her daughter, the 'phallic' object of her desire, 'beautiful among all maidens', wandered, aged, exhausted, and emptied by the hole bored into her by the unbearable and horrible absence.

As we can see, guilt rises and rages relentlessly in the powerless parent whose child has died. Piera Aulagnier has said that the desire for death in relation to a child transforms that child into a murderer of the child they will have when they in turn become a parent: it is their own childhood that they destroy by conforming in this way to the desires of the parents.[29]

Mrs S's exacerbation of love and mythologising of her dead daughter therefore reflect the reawakening of an unconscious desire for infanticide. We know, in fact, that an excess of positive affective expression very often masks a repressed opposite desire. Thus, the heroisation of the dead object paradoxically manifests the hatred the subject feels towards it. This hatred, which destroys and annihilates, is found through identification in the ego.

The loss of the child resurrects the censored desire for infanticide, which returns to them from outside. The child's non-desire determines a phantasy, a desire for infanticide.

With the tragic death of the child, of the beloved object, this repressed desire for infanticide returns to consciousness. This is why the subject, sometimes explicitly, blames themselves for the 'murder' of their child: 'You killed him'. Displaying herself as a guilty and evil mother, obsessed by feelings of maternal inadequacy, Mrs S insists on the idea of her responsibility for the death of her daughter, her mortifying conception and her monstrosity: 'I carry death inside me. An expectant mother carries life, but I carry death,' she asserts. Here, indignation has been transformed into self-abasement. The mother gives life, but she can also give death.

Grief, melancholic sacrifice, and the feminine

Mourning generally appears more complicated for the woman, as the loss seems in some way to be experienced in her own flesh. It is as though, through the loss of a loved one, there is a revival of another grief linked to the problem of fundamental castration that has not been overcome, or a revival of an original grief linked to birth, to childbirth experienced as the loss of a part of oneself.

From another perspective, the *sâti*, the melancholic sacrificial woman exalted by Indian tradition, reminds me of those mortifying states of mourning where radical self-destruction on the part of the bereaved appears to be the only way out. In this age-old practice, the living person, in infinite, unthinkable, and unsurmountable grief, 'torn' by the loss of the phallic object of their desire, will attempt to rejoin them in death, the ultimate place for realising completeness.[30]

Thus, women in mourning, 'consenting' sacrificial victims, participate 'willingly' in the act of their violent death by burning themselves alive on their husband's funeral pyre. Yet why, beyond the dead husband – for whom the virtuous wife 'dressed as though for the wedding day' – is she preparing to celebrate a marriage of ashes?[31]

Does the woman plunged into grief want to make a ritual spectacle of her absolute faithfulness by following her husband into death? Self-sacrifice as proof of her unconditional love?[32] Or is it precisely, as I see it, a pathological 'feminine' mourning of the melancholic type, which finds its perfect expression in the mythical behaviour of self-denial that specifically impedes the possible work of overcoming the loss of the male object in the circumstances.

It seems to me that what we are talking about here is a mourning that was originally sacrificial, the ultimate expression of a feminine melancholic state. A way, moreover, of seeking through suicide an archaic regressive position, an inorganic and 'asexual' zero state of primary narcissism.

The 'diabolical' feminine: hysteria and melancholia

From 1897, Freud showed that both hysteria and melancholia are manifestations of pathological grief following a more or less recent object loss. Particularly when the bereavement is unforeseeable, it can trigger a hypo-manic reaction of excitement and exaltation of the libido.

Indeed, both the melancholic and the hysteric are people who like to expose themselves to the gaze and make an exhibition of themselves.[33]

These two states, marked by a genuine jouissance of the feminine that comes from 'showing off', complement each other perfectly or follow one another alternately. In this sense, Mrs S's 'inappropriate' attire on the day of her daughter's funeral, her enigmatic, maladjusted smile, as well as her generally excitable manic behaviour that is greatly embarrassing to those around her, are highly hysterical in appearance.

For this reason, Lacan rightly points out that there is something 'diabolical' in the hysteria of the woman who is, as he puts it, 'without faith'. Karl Abraham

The melancholic feminine 91

(1911) remarked that in the depths of melancholic misery is a hidden source of feminine auto-jouissance.

As Freud wrote in 'Mourning and Melancholia' (1917e):

> The self-tormenting in melancholia, which is without doubt enjoyable, signifies, just like the corresponding phenomenon in obsessional neurosis, a satisfaction of trends of sadism and hate which relate to an object, and which have been turned round upon the subject's own self.[34]

It should be noted that melancholia is often confused with the female subject, specifically in their negativity and 'perversity'.

Lacan insisted on the 'Other' jouissance of the melancholic woman. Of course, it is not a question here of sexual jouissance, but of the 'Other' jouissance, of a state 'between two deaths', a state beyond the pleasure principle.

The melancholic tear: neither living nor dying

To relentlessly invest in the memory of the dead would be to experience death itself. In his book about melancholia, *La mélancolie*, Tellenbach (1961) shows that while the initial melancholic situation lies in despair (*Verzweiflung*), overcoming it can be defined by the abandonment of doubt (*Zweifel*), which is akin to a doubling (*Doppelung*) of reality. The hallmark of melancholic doubt is alternation: living torn 'between' possibilities, none of which has become a concrete reality.[35]

In this situation of 'neither living, nor dying',[36] there is clearly an unbearable sense of immortality, of cruel eternity, as described in Cotard's syndrome. This is the greatest punishment that can be inflicted on the living. The paroxysm of this desperate attempt to have to exist in two or more places at once is reached when the melancholic experiences the heartbreak of not being able to live or die. The melancholic, this 'being-between-two-deaths', as Lacan put it, no longer separates the lost object from themselves, or life from death. 'To live or to die, there is no difference' proclaims my patient, for whom 'living is dying' and 'dying is living'.

Double figures and narcissistic relationships

Melancholia is characterised by three features: object loss, ambivalence, and identification. In this last aspect appears a kind of fantasy of incorporation of the deceased. Hence, the importance of oral elements in the melancholic feminine. Psychically dead, the survivor has metamorphosed into a *double* of the deceased.

'Every day, I go to the cemetery, to *my* grave', says Mrs S. A deep reverse identification with the dead daughter whose picture is visibly displayed in a pendant worn by the mother.[37] A strange image of the dead girl 'hanging' around her mother's neck, which is all the more real given the mother's attempted hanging: the daughter is literally hung from her mother's neck.

Failing to be a living phallic substitute for her mother, the daughter has become the equivalent of her mother's fetish object. An abundance of desire for her

92   The melancholic feminine

daughter, this Erynia-mother, intensely close and passionate, incestuous in type, wanting to have everything from her child, to the point of losing herself in her and no longer being (loss of identity), which leads to dis-being (absence of the vital impulse and mortifying autosadism).

The need to erect a phallic stele in place of the empty hole is a form of fetishism that refuses loss, and rejects separation and lack. The veneration of the deceased implies, in effect, the denial of castration, and the subject's inability to experience ambivalent affects towards the disappeared object.

Mourning can only take place if the subject acknowledges and accepts the ambivalence of their feelings and regains their trust in external objects. They can then, as Melanie Klein (1940) puts it: 'again bear to realize that this object was not perfect, and yet not lose trust and love for him, nor fear his revenge'.[38]

Notes

1 Cf. Freud (1917e, p. 252) when he writes:
   '... one particular striking feature of melancholia ... the prominence of the fear of becoming poor, it seems plausible to suppose that it is derived from anal erotism which has been torn out of its context and altered in a regressive sense.'
2 It is interesting to observe that in this apparently pathetic expression (see the case of Mme S. below), the patient omits the *ne* in the original French: *Je veux plus donner. Je veux plus souffrir*. This could imply an amphibology in the subject's desire in the sense that *plus*, without the *ne* means 'more'.
3 In reference to Heinz Kohut's 'grandiose self'.
4 Freud (1917e), p. 249.
5 It involved a fatal fall from a mountain where the foolhardy girl was skiing 'off piste'.
6 Vernant, J.-P. (1980)[1965].
7 Fatalism sometimes resembles a challenge to treatment (negative therapeutic reaction).
8 It's important to specify that throughout this work, I use the notion of melancholia in a non-psychotic sense. Here, it refers to the expression of a deep pain, that can be neurotic, marked by depressive negativity: different from Jules Cotard's denial delusion – narcissistic catastrophe, the feminine, and the victim positioning of the subject.
9 I'm thinking here of André Green's 'La mère morte' [The dead mother], 1983a.
10 Abraham (1907–1914). In his study of the painter Segantini, follows in the painter's paintings the traces of his mother's death and his father's abandonment. 'Giovanni Segantini, essai psychanalytique', pp. 216–226. See also, *Segantini*, the magnificent book published by the Fondation Beyeler, on the occasion of the exhibition of the painter's work at the Beyeler Museum (January–April 2011), Riehen, Switzerland.
11 The painter Segantini described himself as 'drunk with deep melancholy'.
12 At the age of seven, Segantini spent several hours beside the corpse of a little girl to paint a final portrait.
13 Lacan (1959–1960).
14 The 'positive' response, on the other hand, manifests itself in an over-investment in reality, or pathological objectalisation through excessive and greedy relationships, addictive sexual behavior, delinquent acts, etc. These pathological behaviours can also be found in people with abandonment syndrome.
15 In a way, we could say that the subject, not sufficiently represented in the object's psyche, is swallowed up in its loss as in a 'black hole' that absorbs all energy and radiation, if we may venture this cosmic comparison.
16 Lagache, D. (1937). See also: Lagache (1956)[1982], pp. 1–28.

The melancholic feminine 93

17 'Let the dead bury the dead', says Jesus in the Gospel. How often do therapists find themselves confronted with this difficult task of mourning when people say: 'I should have gone with them.' Death calls to death, and therapeutic work effectively consists in symbolically killing this pestering dead person, sometimes through dreams. The therapist recommends that these people 'talk' to the dead person, asking him to 'leave them alone'.

18 The desire to live is sometimes so intense and violent that it flirts with death.

19 The question of psychic transmission and the 'transgenerational' unconscious is of great interest here.

20 Mrs S has a unique and envied half-sister, whom she describes as her ideal double.

21 Reik (1957).

22 In the knowledge that 'self-reproaches are reproaches against a loved object which have been shifted away from it on to the patient's own ego', as Freud wrote in 1917e, p. 248.

23 This moment of self-reproach and self-blame clearly signals the separation of the (unconscious) subject who accuses and the ego who suffers from being persecuted and incriminated.

24 In the original French, the expression used – *casse-cou* ['breakneck'] – is not neutral. It can, in fact, refer to the castration of the feminine, to the attempted suicide by hanging of the mother who finds here a kind of identification with her late daughter described as a '*casse-cou*/daredevil'.

25 Let's not forget that Karl Abraham (1911) classifies as unconscious suicides 'some of the most frequent accidents in the mountains'. Cf. *Œuvres complètes*, Vol. 1, p. 260.

26 Lacan (1960–1961), pp. 396–397.

27 Freud (1923b), p. 53.

28 Janet (1926–1928).

29 Aulagnier (1985). See also Freud (1900a). *The Interpretation of Dreams*, chapter IV, on women's dreams and infanticide. Likewise Monique Schneider (1992).

30 For some people, the narcissistic notion of a taste for death evokes the mythical idea of an intimate reunion with the dead person, and consequently the promise of a new lease on life. Death and love are two entities that are often brought together. The word 'cemetery' is etymologically *koimêtêrion*, meaning bridal chamber (cf. Jung, 1991). In the same vein, Antigone's death is depicted as a sweet nuptial ceremony: 'Tombeau, ma chambre nuptiale' [Tomb, my nuptial chamber].

31 But what ideology underlies this ritual? Perhaps that of 'becoming one with your husband', of 'con-fusing' with him, in line with a conception of nuptiality. What's astonishing is that the reverse doesn't exist: the bereaved husband doesn't sacrifice himself ... Isn't there an underlying phallocratic vision?

32 Weiberger-Thomas (1996). *Cendres d'immortalité – La crémation des veuves en Inde*, Paris, Seuil.

33 The association between hysteria and melancholy, and the idea of 'spectacle' that characterises these two states, can also be found in literature. For example, Henri Beyle (1783–1842) wrote: 'I passionately desired to be loved by a melancholy woman, thin and an actress' (*Diary*, 30 March, 1806).

34 Freud (1917e), p. 251.

35 We find something of this in passion: 'neither without you, nor with you', which can only be extinguished in death. Cf. *Belle du Seigneur* by Albert Cohen.

36 The situation where the person is separated from both the living and the dead is precisely that of the ghost (or zombie, or voodoo) – neither dead nor alive.

37 'Conveying death', as the patient put it, is not just a metaphor.

38 Klein (1940) p. 355.

Chapter 6

Can you be innocent if you love someone guilty?[1]

Derived from infantile sexual emotions, love is classically differentiated from desire, which may have a different object. The affect or feeling of attachment that one person has for another is also usually defined by the ambivalence of affects (attraction–repulsion, love–hate) and self-love (narcissism) in the object choice. Indeed, when the subject loves another person, it is more often than not about the subject. The subject frequently loves the other as a split image of the self, as a symmetrical and ideal representation of themselves. In the 'hypnotic' state of love, the object and the ego-ideal find themselves confusingly united. In fact, the loving subject divests themselves of their own qualities, projecting them on the lover, the overestimated Other, an object of 'psychic exaltation'. This was noted by Plato in his first dialogue, *Phaedrus* 'On the Beautiful', where he wrote: 'He (the eromenos) cannot tell the cause of his evil, and he does not realise that he sees himself in the erastes (lover) as in a mirror' (255b–256b). In this sense, the other is the reflected self. But Plato's phrase can also take on another meaning: the beloved object finally sees and recognises itself through the mirror gaze of its lover. Isn't this strangely reminiscent of the mirror stage? The eromenos sees himself as 'loved' and, quite simply, 'sees himself': 'Yes, it is me that he loves'. Love returns him to himself: 'This other that he loves is me'.

Furthermore, from a mythical, Aristophanic perspective, we can state that the body is divided; each one, in the drama of primordial castration, pursuing its half – its *sumbolon* – so as to be reunited with it. In this way, love 'attempts to recover our original condition, to remake the broken unity and thus re-establish human nature', says Aristophanes (cf. Plato's *The Banquet*, 191d). It could be said that this is a true regression to primordial narcissism.

It is also worth remembering that in 'Three Essays on the Theory of Sexuality' (1905d), Freud makes a distinction between *Liebe* (what he calls normal love) and *Verliebtheit* or amorous passion, 'enamoration',[2] a passionate and violent state in which the sexual objective is not the priority, but in abeyance.

Enamoration is characterised by the passion that determines hatred. Passion, which implies 'excess', 'too much of too much', lies between love and hate. The excess and extreme of love is not love. It is passion. This 'impossible love' requires fusion, the passivity of absolute love, mad love, and is only perfectly realised in the

DOI: 10.4324/9781003414247-7

narcissistic desire for death, in death. Passion is, therefore, pain in its purest form, affecting the ego in its psychic and bodily dimensions. But passion develops or adds to hatred. For, in the passionate love relationship, where the victim is *a priori* difficult to distinguish between the lover and the beloved, the loving subject wants and resents the other object, the object of passion, the source of pain. Indeed, while there is pleasure in love, in passion there is only pain.[3]

The libido becomes the actual agent of the conversion of tendencies through the theory of the sexual: the cruelty implanted in the libido transfigures love into hate, tender reactions into antagonistic ones.

Ten years later, in 'Instincts and their Vicissitudes' (1915c), Freud analysed the question of love metamorphosing into hate, where, through the defensive operation of reversal into the opposite (of the content), he highlighted ambivalent and alternative feelings as an expression of enamoration. In the same person, this reveals the existence of a mix of jouissance and suffering (self-hatred and moral masochism). In this strange and paradoxical situation, pain, although usually rejected by the conscience, appears necessary and soothing for the subject.

Narcissistic love was characterised by Freud (1914c) as 'feminine'. Women are therefore thought to be more narcissistic than men, because women's 'need', he writes, does not 'lie in the direction of loving, but of being loved; and the man who fulfils this condition is the one who finds favour with them'[4] (p. 89). Nevertheless, the self-image reflected in the specular other does not only bring pleasure and delight. On the contrary, the other can become the object source of sensations of displeasure and, by projection, the bearer of what is bad or lacking in oneself (fundamental paternal castration), and is, thus, unwittingly transformed into a frustrating object of hatred, the object of negative love in the sense of hostile, threatening loathing. Here, where 'self-love' (*Eigenliebe*) essentially predominates, love engenders hate. In this passionate and violent state (*Verliebtheit*), the aversion felt for the enamoured other appears identical to the ruthless love described by Winnicott.[5]

Hainamoration in the love relationship

Love that turns into hate is the only case where the instinct turns into its opposite. These two contrasting tendencies are, more often than not, intertwined in their path towards the coveted and invested object. So, the separation of Empedocles's two apparently opposite figures, *Philia* and *Neikos*, seems quite ephemeral. 'True love leads to hate', as Lacan put it, making the French word 'love' feminine [*la vraie amour*]. This writer, who, by playing with the ambiguity of the signifiers 'hates' and 'is' (homophones in French), allows me to formulate with him that, for man, 'the less he hates [*hait*], the less he is [*est*], in other words, the less he loves'.[6] In *Encore*, Lacan presents an apology for hatred, and even invents the neologism *hainamoration*, composed of the noun *haine* ('hate') and the adjective énamoré ('enamoured'), in which love, through its excess of 'too much', is transformed into its opposite. It is an experience of destruction and, thus, distinguished from aggressivity, whereas hatred, that love of the negation of the other, is a kind of meanness or what irremediably fails at a given moment in a loving relationship. From then on, the quality of the emotion is transformed into its opposite. The affects are reversed.

The reversal of affects and the ambivalence of feelings were studied by Freud in *The Interpretation of Dreams* (1900a) through gestures of hostility – or even desire for death – against others and, through identification, against oneself. Repressed hateful thoughts find their preferred expression in dreams. They sometimes express a desire for the death of someone close to us, but who, through identification, sometimes happens to be the subject themselves. Freud writes: 'the following rule will often be a guide: If in the dream the dreamer is not reminded that the dead person is dead, he sets himself on a par with the dead; he dreams of his own death'.[7]

Examples of ambivalent feelings can be found elsewhere in Freud's work. For example, Fräulein Elisabeth von R. (Freud, 1895d) and her hatred–rivalry towards her sister, or Dora (Freud, 1905e), whose every impulse, not only of tenderness but also of aversion, leads to animosity and ferocity.

But it is probably in *Notes Upon a Case of Obsessional Neurosis* (Freud, 1909d) that enamoration[8] is most unbridled, in the intense confrontation of two antinomic tendencies violently felt for the same person in the father (the wish and fear that he will die).

On the other hand, as in any relationship of ambivalent feelings, in the transferential affective bond of the treatment, the manifestation of the analysand's enamoration for the analyst is an indispensable factor in the evolution of the treatment. In this context, the analyst's enamoration will be all the stronger if, as Freud points out in 'The Dynamics of Transference' (1912b), reality does not fully satisfy the patient's need for love.[9]

Finally, the erotic component of transference-love (*Übertragungsliebe*) is discussed in 'Observations on Transference-love' (1915a), in which Freud develops just one sort of example, that of a female patient who becomes enamoured of the male doctor. For if the latter,

> refuses her love, as his duty and his understanding compel him to do, she can play the part of a woman scorned, and then withdraw from his therapeutic efforts out of revenge and resentment, exactly as she is now doing out of her ostensible love.[10]

In reality, this transferential state is a repetition of old events, a passionate compulsion integrated into a psychic series whose prototype is the parental imago, but whose dynamic is current. It is precisely the archaic libidinal investment of this imago that renders patent and present, in their interweaving, the buried and abandoned amorous tendencies (*Liebsregungen*) and hateful tendencies.

The love-hate connection in persecution

In Draft H, dated 24 January 1895, Freud (*Standard Edition, Volume 1*) believes that an original scene of seduction as primordial trauma is at the root of a paranoid defence, and in Draft K, dated 1 January 1896, he considers in turn the primary incident, which is certainly comparable to the one that gives rise to obsessional neurosis; the memory of this incident, the displeasure (as yet undetermined) that it provokes; the consecutive repression; the projection. Associated with the latter is the defensive process which is the withdrawal–disconnection of belief (*Versagen des Glaubens*), in other words, consciousness refuses to give credence to the self-reproach and, to this end, employs the defensive strategy of projection. This is a denial of negative feelings towards the subject itself. Internal attacks are momentarily released and propelled outwards. The Other within the self, projected on the other, is made responsible for the displeasure. Freud writes: '*The subject-matter remained unaffected*; what was altered was something in the *placing* (*Stellung*) of the whole thing. Earlier it had been an internal self-reproach, now it was an imputation coming from outside'.[11] More specifically, since repression takes place through the disavowal of belief, content and affects of the unpleasant idea are maintained, but find themselves projected outwards.

Thus, in projection, 'an internal perception is suppressed, and, instead, its content, after undergoing a certain kind of distortion, enters consciousness in the form of an external perception'.[12] Similarly, in the process of persecution, deformation consists in a transformation of affect: 'What should have been felt internally as love is perceived externally as hate' (*ibid.*).

The intolerable feeling repressed inside is propelled outside, or, more precisely: 'as we now see... what was abolished internally returns from without' (*ibid.*).

On the other hand, drawing on the work of James George Frazer (*Totemism and Exogamy*, 1910), Freud shows that the relationship between the paranoiac and their persecutor is analogous to that of the primitive and their king. Both, writes Freud, have a regressive-type attitude of the son towards the father, with the unconscious desire for parricide. Thus, the persecutor (of the paranoid delusion) is a previously loved person (real or phantasised). It is a return, then, to a situation in the past. For this reason, 'the one who is now hated and feared for being a persecutor was at one time loved and honoured' (*ibid.*). More often than not, however, it is persecution of a filial and/or phallic type. By turns active and passive, the paranoiac, through their persecution, but also through their seduction,[13] reproduces the relationship between the child and the parent in their phallic and omnipotent representation. Deified and feared at the same time, the victim (child) thus has a 'fetish' relationship with the executioner (father), a mixture of veneration and apprehension.

In *Moses and Monotheism* (1939a), Freud takes up the idea that there is a need for submission to a tyrannical paternal figure:

> We know that there exists in people a strong need for an authority which they can admire, to which they can submit, and which dominates and sometimes even ill-treats them. We have learned from the psychology of the individual whence comes this need of the masses. It is the longing for the father [*Vatersehnsucht*] that lives in each of us from his childhood days, for the same father whom the hero of legend boasts of having overcome.

(p. 140)

As a result, this same surpassed (real or imaginary) father is, through regression, in a masochistic economy, ceaselessly sought in an intersubjective relationship of the submission–domination type. But this situation is most often accompanied by the phantastical production of a family story and origins, particularly when these are unknown or enigmatic to the subject. It is worth noting the turning point in Freud's understanding of the paranoid process in his letter of 24 January 1897: 'In paranoia,' he writes, 'I compare the combination of megalomania with the creation of myths relating to the child's origin' (Freud, 1897, p. 168). In the process of persecution, the subject invents a romantic filiation in which they believe themselves to be a stranger in their family, rendering the latter illegitimate. In paranoid functioning and in the victim's position, there is therefore a drama of destiny against which the subject revolts, through a kind of defensive compensatory 'romanticisation' of the original, filial reality, particularly when this remains mysteriously protected by the inviolable seal of family secrecy.

As we shall see, the lack of patronymic filiation is cruelly felt. The absence of the father and the failure to transmit his Name (phallic symbol) are experienced as a mortifying narcissistic hole. This situation is particularly guilt-inducing for the subject, who feels they are a victim of their origins and destiny.

Mrs E: 'Loving hurts, because since the time of sin, it means being crucified for someone else.'

Mrs E, aged forty-nine, presents deep feelings of self-depreciation, genuine psychic suffering, and moral masochism. She lives with her mother, for whom she is the only child and sole support, in a role of 'parentification'. In her misfortune, this woman complains primarily of being 'terrorised' by her husband. Her husband is often absent, however, sometimes for months at a time, working on large-scale projects abroad. He is described as sadistic and perverse, demonstrating a need to dominate and control his wife's life. 'My husband,' says Mrs E, 'is so skilful that he manipulates appearances to his advantage, and it will still be him who is the victim and me who is guilty.'

In this way, Mrs E presents herself from the outset as an innocent victim. She protests against her husband's persecution. But she also claims to have suffered this painful situation since birth: 'I'm a bastard,' she announces bluntly, insisting on the aggressiveness and negativity of her destiny, the violence of her existence marked primarily and painfully by the primordial rift in identity and filiation. The above allegation is also coupled with a convincing message of external hostility and annihilation: '(He) hates me and wants to destroy me.' As far as the person is concerned, the other wants them dead. In the same way, the failure to conform to the moral rule integrated as an irreparable 'fault' committed by one's progenitors; this parental failure is felt as a personal slap in the face, expressed in a cursed destiny of compulsive repetition. It could be said here that the 'illegitimate' child suffers a double violence: that of the unconscious desire for their death, and that of the intensely lived guilt transmitted, unbeknown to them, by their mother.

This legacy of guilt, as we shall see, is all the more strongly 'acquired' in the sexual and masochistic identification of the daughter with her mother.

On dozens of preciously conserved typewritten sheets, Mrs E has attempted to retrace her history, which could be characterised as a *victim of destiny*. Thus, she writes in her own biography, her mother first married a nephew, her sister's only son. The latter died in a psychiatric centre 'after a few years of internment for early-onset *delirium tremens'*.

Yet, Mrs E's mother always kept the identity of her daughter's father a carefully preserved secret,[14] or constantly cultivated hateful or self-indulgent ambiguity about the individual. It remains a mystery to this day. A shadow continually hangs over the name of the father. It is worth noting here that, with this censorship, these words left unsaid, the daughter becomes a sort of hole-filler (*bouche-trou)* or stand-in, a jouissance-inducing phallus for the mother. Moreover, the child whose father is unknown seems to be confronted with an unbearable *double bind*, in the sense that this child can hear the following affirmation expressed by the mother: 'You are (his child)', but immediately followed by the negation: 'You are not (his child)', because it is implied that: 'You do not bear his name', and, hence, the paradoxical and disconcerting conclusion: 'You are someone who is not'.

Mrs E does speculate, however, that her father, some twenty years older than her, might be a former soldier in 'Pétain's army'. It should be noted that this hypothetical assertion reveals the patient's 'encysted' affects of *shame*, as the parental *fault* is introjected and made her own. This sense of shame is coupled with unconscious guilt, which determines the patient's attraction to punitive, redemptive, victimogenic, and sacrificial situations.

Referring to her autobiography, Mrs E says that when she was four or five years old, her mother sat her 'on the lap of a man' whom she introduced as her father. She describes this 'supposed' father as an alcoholic with no morals, and says of him: 'I was ashamed of this human trash... He died like a tramp.'

As a teenager, Mrs E also describes being harassed and seduced by her mother's boyfriend: 'My mother's boyfriend used to make passes at me when she wasn't home. He didn't work, and used to drink beer and bet on the racing, but my mother was into him.'[15] It is worth pointing out here that Freud, in his letters 46 and 52 to Fliess in 1896 (Freud, 1897[1986]), admits that on the basis of clinical observation, we can put forward the hypothesis that, in paranoia, traumatic scenes of seduction occur later, after the 'second set of teeth' (between the ages of eight and ten) or during puberty up to the age of fourteen or fifteen.

Mrs E also states that 'from the age of nine until adolescence', she was 'sent to a religious boarding school', stressing also that she was a young girl who was 'very supervised' [*sic*].[16]

Later, lack becomes lapse, as Mrs E.= – following the primordial 'fault' of the parents – repeats the same 'error' by becoming pregnant and forced to marry because the 'family didn't want another bastard'. Yet, the man who was to become her husband refused to acknowledge the child's paternity from the outset. When I meet her, Mrs E says she is primarily a victim of her husband's persecution, and secondarily of her destiny as a woman, desperately trying to atone for a deeply ingrained guilt. The question of fault and guilt is prevalent in Mrs E's preoccupations. Indeed, she continually demonstrates her need to plead her innocence, and denounces her position as a sacrificial wife.

Narcissism, feminine masochism, and paranoia

In 'On Narcissism' (1914c), Freud tells us that the institution of the moral conscience, that invisible judge, was, in the first instance, essentially the embodiment of parental criticism, and later of criticism from society. And that this moral conscience, because of unconscious guilt, comes back to the subject from outside as an unfavourable action. Consequently, I believe that in a female subject held in a victim position, there is an essential original lack, a primordial castration, which generates a deep narcissistic wound and a frustration of satisfaction in the realm of the ego ideal. Thus, the subject seeks to fill this fundamental defect through others, but the invested other reminds her of this deprivation, this narcissistic 'hole', and, above all, the impossibility of achieving the desired ideal of completeness. The dissatisfaction that results from not achieving this ideal can turn into consciousness of guilt and secondary moral masochism. This is how Freud (1915c),[17] through the defensive mechanism of turning back on one's self, develops the process of reflexive sadism in the sense of autosadism or regressive narcissistic sadism. But, after the event, a hated outsider is required as object who, in view of the change of purpose, must play the role of the sadistic subject in the unconscious intersubjective relationship.

This foreign, sadistic other self may be the reincarnation of the enamoured father figure, linked to the subject's primordial narcissistic wound in their frantic quest for filiation. Consequently, the idealised paternal stranger is both desired and hated as a painful expression of lack. In this sense, the following allegation, which manifests both 'autosadism'[18] and the expression of a negative identity of fatality and original trauma – 'I'm a bastard' – is transmuted into a convincing proclamation of external hostility and annihilation: 'He hates me and wants to destroy me'.

On the other hand, from the perspective of the phantasmatic fathering scene – etymologically, 'bastard' (*bâtard*) probably means '*fathered* on the *bât* (pack-saddle) or in the barn' – Guy Rosolato (1969), in his article 'Paranoïa et scène primitive' [Paranoia and the primitive scene], emphasises theories that place masochism at the heart of paranoid delusion. Thus, the homosexual love of the paranoiac undergoes regression and sublimation to masochism. But, in the victim position, where masochism is 'active' in so far as the person is unconsciously 'acting' in seeking victimogenic situations, the regression to the *fustigation scene* seems a determining element. Freud had already underlined this hypothesis in the scene of the beaten child (1919e), a masochistic phantasmatic scene in which the pleasure of being beaten by the father is unmistakable: 'I should not be surprised if it were one day possible to prove that the same phantasy is the basis of the delusional litigiousness of paranoia' (Freud, 1919e, p. 195).

The second phase of this 'properly feminine' phantasy (whatever the subject's anatomical sex), shows that being beaten by the father undoubtedly leads to a masochistic satisfaction where the subject enjoys the hatred of the other. I, therefore, consider that there is a pathogenic regression to the feminine position ('becoming woman again') in this phantasmatic scene, in the unconscious manifestation of masochistic behaviours through which the feminine subject derives phallic jouissance in passivation, punishment, and humiliation.

In Lecture XXXIII of *New Introductory Lectures on Psychoanalysis*, Freud argues that: 'The repression of women's aggressiveness' increases and 'favours the development of powerful masochistic impulses, which succeed, as we know, in binding erotically the destructive trends which have been diverted inwards'. And he continues: 'Masochism... is truly feminine'.[19] This feminine masochism, which affects both women (in a primary way) and men, is characterised by passivation ('undergoing coitus') and castration ('being castrated'), where the subject, now in a position of subjection to the Other, seeks her jouissance in suffering. The female subject usually seeks out and finds the hated-lover who tyrannises her, and this lover gives her what the father was unable to give her.[20]

Love *in* persecution, love *of* persecution

In psychoanalytical literature, it is generally asserted that the paranoiac struggles against the strengthening of their homosexual inclinations, which basically refers to a narcissistic object choice. The other is simply the subject themselves, reflected. What is more, we usually hypothesise that the persecutor, who is more often than not of the same sex as the persecuted, is really the loved one, or the one who was once loved. From this point of view, it can be argued that the persecuted (loving–desiring) erastes, seeks in his unconscious love of the (loved–desired) persecutor eromenos, the position of lack within himself and, thus, his idealised, megalomaniac scopic self through the other who has become the object of his 'enamoration'.

In addition, Freud's 'A Case of Paranoia Running Counter to the Psycho-Analytic Theory of the Disease'[21] is an invaluable aid to understanding the unconscious mechanisms at work in the situation of the persecuted victim.

In this text, Freud presents the case of a young woman who feels harassed by a man. The man had led her into a romantic relationship with him. She claimed that the man had taken advantage of her accommodating attitude to have photographs taken of their tender lovemaking by unseen spectators; it was then in his power to shame her by showing these images, and to compel her to stop trying to resist him. This young woman, overwhelmed by the power of the maternal complex, lived with her elderly mother, for whom she was the sole support. Like my patient, she had no brothers or sisters, and her father had died a few years earlier.

Analysis of the case shows that the loved–hated man is put in the place of the father. It should also be noted that, for Mrs E, the putative 'father' – in a more or less incestuous relationship with his wife, since she is at the same time his aunt – was described as a person clearly younger than his wife. This can easily accentuate

102 Can you be innocent if you love someone guilty?

the bivalence of the 'husband–father' representation as a telescoped image of the persecutor.

On the other hand, if an excessively strong homosexual bond is commonly presented as the condition for the development of a persecutory delusion, Freud, in this 1915 text, draws the conclusion from his analysis that the original persecutor, the agency from whose influence the woman wants to escape, is not, even in this case, the man, but the woman in the persona of the mother. Indeed, the mother disapproves of, and condemns, her daughter's love affair from the outset. And in our observation, Mrs E was 'forced to marry to save the family's honour', she says, but above all, as I understand it, to free herself by defensive counter-investment from the unconscious incestuous homosexual liaison with her mother. In the same way, the mother also disavows her daughter's love for her son-in-law, but also her daughter's love for her father, by masking the latter's identity. Through her close identification with her mother, the *double,* Mrs E is confronted with the disillusionment of the 'father–husband', who has become the object of hatred. Thus, through homosexual regression, the relationship with the same sex is opposed to the patient's efforts to obtain a member of the other sex as a love object. Hence, the repressed (daughter–mother) hatred is displaced on to the husband, who represents the substitute paternal agency. Consequently, in this relationship of homosexual, mother–daughter hatred, the two protagonists, in a bond of great promiscuity, if not in an execrable and devastating fusional relationship, 'love each other to death like Electra and Clytemnestra'.[22] As Michelle Montrelay (1977) writes, the two women 'confront each other, caress each other, kill each other, are reborn, begin again, powerless to separate themselves',[23] as they phallically fend off the other [*se parent*], especially when the father figure, the mediating and separating third party, is absent.

The singularity of this complex psychosexual mother–daughter relationship has been clearly defined by François Perrier (1980):[24] 'There is no woman,' he writes, 'for whom love, the hope of love, the right to love, the assumption of love, does not refer to the mother, and to the "incestuous" mother–daughter–mother relationship'. Yet this fusional, loving, incestuous bond between the daughter and the devouring maternal object, or its fear, gives rise to hatred.[25] In the same sense, we can assume that a mother's incestuous maternal complex for her daughter, extremely powerful and not overcome, is at the root of my patient's *victim neurosis.* As a result, the daughter's masochism, integrated early into her psychic economy, is a perfect reproduction by psychic heredity of the mother's masochism and her seduction.

Indeed, it is important here to specify, as Freud points out, that 'the manifestation of the neurotic reaction will always be determined, however, not by her present-day relation to her actual mother but by her infantile relations to her earliest image of her mother [*Urzeitlich*]'.[26]

Thus, in the analysis of the case I am presenting, the mother therefore becomes the hostile, malevolent observer and persecutor, and the persecution was originally directed against her, 'but now, on this paranoic basis, the advance from a female to a male object was accomplished' (*ibid.*).

Consequently, the loved–hated man (the enamoured husband) has not become the tyrant directly, but through the intermediary of the mother, and by virtue of her relationship to the mother. Moreover, the beloved always remains the idealised father (imaginary father), and instead of the mother, there is the patient herself. For all that, the patient strives to free herself from her homosexual allegiance to her mother.[27] In a regressive shift, instead of taking the mother as love object, she has totally identified with her. She herself, by reversal, has become the mother who was the victim of her alcoholic husband who died in a psychiatric hospital, who was neglected by her second partner, also an alcoholic, who died in a state of destitution, and finally abandoned by her daughter's father.

And so Mrs E, feeling that she had been singled out by the cruelty of fate and resigned to it, declares – through a strong masochistic identification with her mother – her own state as a victim of fate in the *fatum* of the reproduction of the same: 'If my mother was a victim, I could only be a victim myself, from the moment I was born. ...' As a result, the daughter, the filial victim, feels reduced to repeating the maternal feminine masochism, with the aim of perpetuating, or perhaps regaining, a lost unity with the mother.

Hatred of paternal castration

The real lack of a paternal image is experienced by Mrs E as a supreme narcissistic humiliation (being a 'bastard'), which justifies her position as a victim of fate and the essential dereliction caused by her father's absence. In a moment of melancholic depression and paternal abandonment,[28] she asserts: 'Of course, if I'd had a father, he wouldn't have allowed my husband to treat me the way he did, and that has left a deep mark on me for the rest of my life. ...' As we can see, moral suffering and torture are clearly identified and associated with this major paternal deprivation. Mourning is impossible, the complaint inconsolable. Beyond the loss of the father, it is his absence, his gaping hole, that is cruel. This fundamental *lack-of-the-father* reinforces the phantasy of affiliation and parthenogenetic fathering (immaculate filiation and uniqueness of origins), establishing the castrating mother in her unique phallic omnipotence. The latter, through the unspoken fact that she cultivates (secret of filiation), creates a hole in the place of the real father who, in the oedipal conflictual organisation, usually plays the necessary role of the separating and mediating third party. His abandonment, or even non-existence in the child's imaginary world, can give rise to a feeling of essential deficiency and incompleteness, which can lead the 'castrated' female subject to adopt a compulsive and mortifying unconscious masochistic position. Indeed, the negation of the father, beyond the negative effect it produces in psychic life, causes the subject, confronted with the violence of her internal destructive impulses, to repeat the same traumatic primordial victimisation.

In place of the father's name, which caused narcissistic suffering, is the name of the hated husband. Indeed, it is the Name that is the problem in the female masochistic position, because beyond the man who bequeaths his name (husband), it is the Father who is actively sought in masochistic passivation.

Consequently, beyond the father's onomastic secrecy, the dimension of the father figure is pre-eminent in the dynamics of psycho-affective development, even though Freud was initially only interested in the mother's libidinal investment. It was Carl Jung (1909) who was the first psychoanalyst to accord a decisive role to paternity and its vicissitudes, albeit from an essentially phylogenetic perspective. Freud dealt with this dimension of the problem in *Totem and Taboo* (1912–1913). But from an ontogenetic point of view, it is undoubtedly in Schreber's analysis that the father, as the object of homosexual fixation, is made decisive.

In her painful and desperate search for her father, Mrs E. – like Oedipus, the original scapegoat victim, questioning the Oracle of Delphis about his natural parents – develops her drive to know (*Wissendrang*) and her impulse to see[29] in the secret investigation of the unknown and enigmatic. In this way, she attempts to reconcile the earthly and the celestial, the visible and the invisible, birth and destiny, while maintaining that she was 'born under an unfavourable star'. The expression of this painful destiny is accompanied by the search for the legendary father in the mystery of the heavens and astral influences. Mrs E says she is 'a great believer in God and in the influence of the stars', that her 'life is guided by the stars', and that they provide her with 'moral support'. As Gérard Pommier (1985) observes,[30] there is a clear proximity between the religious mystical impulse and feminine jouissance that results from the inaccessibility of the 'Father'. The absence of the father is compensated for by the presence of God, a signifier that is nonetheless paternal, inaccessible, and desired, through which the woman can reach her extreme jouissance.

In fact, the vision of 'seers' and other consulted soothsayers is a veritable mediated hallucination of the lack or primitive scene. As a kind of magical, mythical response, this form of spiritualism reinforces the subject's own internal[31] visions, that is, their intimate unconscious desires. This repetitive compulsion to question the stars also testifies to the individual's fixation with an infantile archaic status, and her alienation from, and dependence on, the phallic parental figure. In this way, acknowledgement from the stars resembles an authorisation from the supreme authority of the ascendants. In this sense, astrology is yet another substitute for the father. Like the father, the astrologer is also supposed to possess knowledge and power. The soothsayer becomes divine, but, like any grandiose, omnipotent figure with a downside, they can be hated and perceived as diabolical.

Hatred of the diabolic masculine as a substitute for the father

'I've got the devil on my tail, …' The diabolical invades Mrs E's talk of persecution, she believes in its influence, its evil action, and, as a result, has asked 'the village abbot to come and bless the house and recite the prayer to St. Michael... to strike down the devil'.

In her investigation of the evil cause, Mrs E 'found' that the satanic figure at the root of all her misfortunes was none other than her husband, as predicted by a 'clairvoyant' during one of her many consultations. Here again, in my comparison between the 'husband–persecutor' and the 'devil', I cannot fail to make another association with the figure of the 'enamoured-father'. This conjecture resonates with Freud's article entitled 'A Seventeenth-Century Demonological Neurosis' (1923d). In this text, the author recounts the story of painter Christoph Haitzmann who, in a pact written in black ink and blood, is said to have given in to the devil, who had tempted him nine times, and committed himself to belonging to him 'body and soul'. The painter, a willing sacrificial victim, is ready to submit himself entirely to the devil, Master of Hell. He feels 'possessed' (*eigen*)[32] by the devil, who replaces the lost father.[33] Note that the relationship with the father was particularly ambivalent, made up of tender obedience but also of repulsion and distrust. For the subject, the father was the original image of both God and the Devil. Indeed, as Freud reminds us, if 'the good and just God is a substitute for the father, we should not be surprised that the hostile attitude, which hates, fears and complains about him, is also expressed by the creation of Satan'.[34] Consequently, the idealised beloved Father, God, is accompanied to some degree by a negative pole of hatred, the Devil.

It is also worth noting that when the mythical Mephistophelian character appears to Haitzmann, it presents with female sexual characteristics, notably large, pendulous breasts. Such an 'unusual' vision seems to Freud to contradict the hypothesis that the Devil is a substitute for the father. Yet, behind this figure of the demonic androgyne,[35] who is nonetheless idealised in the sense of the 'perfect man', the two-in-one 'total being', the painter expresses his hatred of the father (paternal castration), and his repugnance towards the representation of the intensely close sexual bond of the combined parents. Above all, he rebels against his masochistic feminine position by projecting 'the subject's own femininity on to the father-substitute' (*ibid.*).

From this point of view, we can also point to Victor Tausk's (1919)[36] model of the psychotic and mystical 'influencing machine', where the 'feminine' subject experiences an intense 'hainamoration' towards the alienating and persecuting phallicisation of the psychic apparatus. Similarly, in this situation of ambiguity and ambivalence marked by the domination of the Other, which distinguishes itself from the self but does not detach itself from it, there is a projection of the own body, considered in its entirety as a desired and threatening genital organ. With the influencing machine, the body escapes from the security of its internal world. It is attacked by its own objects, which the subject turns against itself by becoming, in among them, the persecutor and the persecuted person.

Returning to our observation, Mrs E, by projection, 'feminises' her hated-husband. She manifests her 'need for belittlement' (*Erniedrigung*), by repeatedly giving a contrasting image of the identity of the man designated as the object of all her torment. The ambivalent description of the enamoured man oscillates between showing a dangerous 'excess virility' of mortifying destruction and a 'femininity' (castrated lover) through supposed homosexuality.

Therefore, beyond this condensation of the 'feminine–masculine' pair of opposites found in the same persecutor character, the victim feels like a victim because she projects the fault committed in phantasy or in reality (cf. The 'sin' of both Mrs E and her mother in their illegitimate carnal relations) on the persecutor – the diabolical, cruel seducer. In effect, the victim presents herself as the docile, innocent, and not unconscious prey who has (passively) undergone the seduction of the executioner. Even if, in a subjective, archaic interaction of painful repetition of the ancient identity, 'victims and executioners remember their younger years in the same way' (Freud, 1897). They are in an interrelated, sadomasochistic, and symmetrical relationship, as each identifies with the other in the phantasy. In fact, in a reversal of roles, the enamoured executioner, the accused sadist, almost always shows himself to be a victim of the victim. This leads us in the direction of Freud's famous assertion: 'A sadist is always at the same time a masochist, although the active or passive aspect of the perversion may be the more strongly developed in him and may represent his predominant sexual activity'.[37]

After Lacan,[38] the ambitendency and intersubjectivity of the opposing positions of complacency and completeness, as well as the reversal in the phantasy of the aggressor–aggressed couple, were particularly studied by Lagache (1960), who sees the domination–submission relationship as a *conflict of demands*: 'The position of demander,' he writes, 'is, virtually, a position of persecuted–persecutor, because the mediation of the demand necessarily introduces sadomasochistic relations of the domination–submission type, which implies all interference from power'.

From another point of view, within a psychogenetic perspective, it is worth noting that the neurotic regression of sadomasochism is rooted in the anal–sadistic stage of libidinal development. In this respect, it is important to note that money, and its symbolic equivalence of faeces, is more often than not at the centre of demand conflicts in the sadomasochistic dialectic relationship between victim and executioner. The painter Christoph Haitzmann made a written commitment to the devil because, following the death of his father, he was plagued by material distress, and was anxiously wondering how to ensure his subsistence. But, as we know, money given by the devil to his victims is always excremental (Freud, 1897).[39]

The sensation of internal organs being destroyed is a sign of an undeniable masochistic movement of the 'feminine' type. In this sense, Helene Deutsch – who wrote 'The taste for unhappiness is incomparably stronger in women than in men' – also defined the masochistic nature of the girl's desires. She explains that little girls often imagine

Dismemberment of the 'insides' through the penetration of a gigantic body and through the expulsion of a child. [...] They refer to the internal organs of the body, that is to say, the stomach and intestines, and the paths of penetration and expulsion are represented by the mouth and the anus. The cruelty of these fantasies corresponds to the strength of the aggressions directed inward.'[40]

Cruelty and delight or masochistic enjoyment of the feminine

The complaints voiced by Mrs E, tinged with eroticism, appear to be not without a certain unconscious masochistic satisfaction: 'He [the enamoured executioner] always uses me,' she says, '... his relentless, Machiavellian pressure ... I am the prey and he devours me with delight. ...' In the victim position, where unconscious feminine destructive masochism predominates, satisfaction is shown to be allied, or closely associated, with pain and unhappiness. In fact, this unpleasant situation gives rise to mixed sensations of anxiety and jouissance, linked to themes of identity and archaic, nostalgic, libidinal life. Consequently, in a sort of identificatory chiasmus, the masochistic victim enjoys their desired and designated executioner 'in the mirror', just as the exhibitionist shares the jouissance of the person who is watching them strip off.

Consequently, in the state of masochistic victimhood, the displeasure presented to the ego by repressed instinctual impulses does not refute the pleasure principle provided by the other source. However, in this situation dominated by the paradox of affects, the superego finds an ideal unconscious partner in the character of the persecutor. Both torment the ego, which seeks its jouissance in suffering.

In fact, moral masochism involves a resexualisation of morality, a regression of morality to the Oedipus complex, and the unconscious demand for fustigation from the parental power. This moral masochism, which has its source in the death instinct, has the significance of an erotic component, because even self-destruction of the individual cannot be achieved without libidinal satisfaction. The pleasure of displeasure, forced and coerced, does not seem to be absent in the enjoyable repetition of dolorism and subjection: 'He finds reasons to compel me until I do it... I'm ashamed of my behaviour... I'm like the reed that bends ...' says Mrs E.

Here, however, the obvious regression goes beyond the mere desire for enslavement and passivity (letting oneself be carried along). It aims for a paradoxically pleasurable state of self-extinction, in the sense of a return to the inorganic, and a search for nirvana as a refusal and refuge from oneself (playing dead to endure life, or having to die in order to live), as Mrs E also expresses it: 'I'm in physical and psychological agony', or again: 'I feel like I'm in a coma, acting mechanically... I let myself go with the flow of events that I am subjected to without reacting. Nothing interests me any more. The future... too distant... aware of my weaknesses, I don't react. ...'

Consequently, through the compulsive feminine masochism of the victim position, the drive regresses and attempts to re-establish a former state (a mute expression of primary death masochism). Similarly, 'victimhood compulsion', like destiny compulsion (*Schicksalszwang*), is, therefore, characterised by the systematic recurrence of unpleasant and mortifying experiences that unfold according to an unvarying scenario, and appear as an external 'demonic' fatality of which the subject, perceived as evil and persecutory, and with no access to an unconscious desire coming back to them from outside, feels like the irresponsible and sacrificial victim.

Notes

1 The question I use as a title for this chapter is taken from Savinient Cyrano de Bergerac's tragedy, *La mort d'Agrippine* [The death of Agrippina] (c. 1466, Act V, Scene V) (1654). *Œuvres complètes*, Paris, Belin, 1977.
2 Following on from Lacan, I deliberately use this concept with this spelling [*énamoration* in French]. The word '*énamoration*' was used by this author on the basis of the Old French transitive verb '*énamourer*' and the adjective '*énamouré(e)*', which refer to an excessive or 'ridiculous' love attachment.
3 Cf. Jacques Brel's beautiful lyrics in 'Ne me quitte pas': 'Laisse moi devenir, L'ombre de ton ombre, L'ombre de ta main, L'ombre de ton chien …'!
4 It has to be said that this highly ideological thinking is steeped in bourgeois conception!
5 This is a primordial 'hatred', uncoupled from primary identification, which could be described as 'pre-objectal'. Cf. Winnicott (1947)[1975].
6 Lacan (1972–1973), p. 89.
7 Freud S. (1900a).
8 It is in this text that Freud turns to Alcibiades' speech in *The Banquet*. In a eulogy of Socrates, instead of a eulogy of love, Alcibiades expresses his powerlessness and ambivalence towards his *erastes*: 'I have been bitten by something more poisonous than a viper, and at the most sensitive point that can be … Heart, soul, call it what you will!' (218a) or again: 'How many times haven't I wished to see him to hell and back! But if I did, I know I'd be ten times sadder; go and sort out my feelings for him!' (215c). Through the massive military 'occupation' of the self by the beloved object, the 'subject' runs the risk of no longer being, of being annihilated by the other, and hatred can then be an attempt to re-subjectivise oneself: 'I hate the love he causes me, because I risk losing myself in it'.
9 Freud (1912b).
10 Freud (1915a), p. 167.
11 Freud (1895). Draft H, p. 208.
12 Freud (1911c).
13 Cf. my approach to the theory of seduction in its close relationship with the masochistic inclination and the position of compulsional, traumatic, and destined victim (Maïdi, 1996).
14 Jacqueline Lanouzière (1991) notes that the notion of secret, etymologically, indicates separation, division, setting apart... 'All derived figurative meanings,' she writes, 'such as mysterious, hidden, have retained the primitive notion of separation'. From this perspective, we can subscribe to the idea that, by keeping the daughter in the dark about her father's identity, the mother separates her from him, but in a certain way also from men.
15 The original French expression used was '*ma mère avait cet homme dans la peau*', and through her use of it the patient expresses her hatred of the jouissance of the sexually combined maternal other. This popular expression, which means loving someone passionately for carnal reasons, clearly evokes the primitive scene. But it also brings to mind the idea of the relational symbiosis of mother and child, fused in a single skin, and the masochism that stems from it. The latter, as Didier Anzieu writes:

Is constituted by the representation that the same skin belongs to the child and its mother, the figurative skin of their symbiotic union, and that the process of defusion and the child's access to autonomy entails a rupture and tearing of this common skin. (1974).

16 Cf. Maïdi (1993). On the correspondence between the feeling of persecution and the experience of abandonment and lack of identity. In this problematic situation of affective ('not enough') and filial deprivation, the subject, through the mechanism of reversal into the opposite, feels dominated by the object of lack and frustration (being 'too over-watched'). The absent is, in fact, there, invisible, like a kind of permanent vigil that escapes sight!

Can you be innocent if you love someone guilty?   109

17 Freud (1915c).
18 Cf. Rosenberg (1991).
19 Freud (1933a), p. 116.
20 Deutsch (1946–47)[1944]. Chapters VI & VII.
21 Freud (1915f).
22 Montrelay, M. (1977), p. 154.
23 *Ibid.*, 153–154. The passionate, tangled bond between daughter and mother is well portrayed by this author, who writes: '...: excess of words, excess of meaning, excess of food, of suffering, of kindness: so much violence in which mother and daughter sink, calling out, wanting to get out of the inextricable, suffocating forest where both are trapped'.
24 Perrier (1980), p. 95.
25 Cf. Stein, C. (1987).
26 Freud (1915f).
27 Note the *lapsus calami* which expresses the repressed homosexual tendency in this dynamic of persecution. Mrs E, who has a friendly relationship with a woman called 'Marie', writes in reference to her husband, in a kind of feminisation of the masculine or vice versa, and in a condensation of the two homophones ('Marie – *mari*' [husband]) which, in terms of orthographic meaning, becomes '*Mon marie ...*' (cf. also below, the Mephistophelian androgyny of the persecutor). From another point of view, Mary's first name is also linked, in the Christian tradition, to the Blessed Virgin and the hypothesis of the fantasy of a parthenogenetic conception, as well as a mythical exemption from Mrs E's mother's 'original sin' through the mystery surrounding the co-generator's name.
28 The early experience of paternal neglect is felt as a veritable 'dereliction'. Like Antigone in her passionate, pathetic complaint to her father: 'My father, why have you forsaken me?' Lacan sees Antigone as a sacrificial victim for her father. Driven by passion, she is condemned to the torment of being 'locked up alive in a tomb'. Cf. Lacan (1959–1960) June 1960, p. 270. Let's remember that the feeling of dereliction is the same one experienced by Christ in the Garden of Olives: 'My God, My God, why have you forsaken me?' '*Eli, Eli, lema sabakthani*?' (*Matthew*, XXVII, 46 and *Mark*, XV, 34). Dereliction is an irremediable despair that drives the feeling of abandonment. The person excluded from divine grace is left to his or her own devices.
29 The scopophilic dimension is an eminently important part of the sadomasochistic problematic. In the sadomasochistic couple, 'seeing and showing' suffering are essential. From this perspective, the opposing duality of active–passive, seeing–being seen, is inseparable. This theme of the gaze is, therefore, prevalent in the intersubjective persecutory relationship (cf. the notion of the 'evil eye' from another point of view). The other's gaze is perceived by the victim as inquisitive, accusatory or castrating. As Mrs E says of her persecutor: 'If his eyes were a weapon, I'd have died long ago.' The partial scopic drive, in its paradoxical form, is the ideal manifestation of the coalescence of the contrasting affects of love and hate, as expressed, for example, by the well-known metaphor of 'devouring with the eyes' an object or something that simultaneously means desiring it *and* destroying it through incorporation–identification.
30 Pommier (1985).
31 In Schreber's case, clairvoyance also plays a decisive role in his persecution disorders. In his study of the mechanism of paranoia, Freud clearly associates the phenomenon of clairvoyance with the mechanism of projection. Thus, when Schreber, as a 'seer', became convinced that a great catastrophe, the end of the world, was imminent, Freud explains that this 'is the projection of this internal catastrophe; his subjective world has come to an end since his withdrawal of his love from it' (Freud, 1911c, p. 70).
32 In letters 56 and 57 to Fliess (Freud 1897, p. 227), Freud, who gradually discovered the manifestations of the sadistic–anal phase and abandoned his ideas on the role of seduction in the aetiology of neuroses, recalls that the medieval theory of possession,

supported by the ecclesiastical courts, was identical to the theory of the *foreign body* and the dissociation of the unconscious. But the obscure question arises: 'But why did the devil who took possession of the poor things invariably abuse them sexually and in a loathsome manner?' (*ibid.*, p. 224).

33 The question of the dead father and his representation with its contrasting meanings is addressed by Freud in his almost ultimate text *Moses and Monotheism* (1939a), in which he writes: 'It is the ambivalence which in general dominates the relationship to the father. [The Latin] "*sacer*" means not only "sacred", "consecrated", but also something that we can only translate as "infamous", "detestable" (e.g. "*auri sacra fames*" "Execrable hunger for gold", *Aeneid*, VI, 816), (Freud 1897, p. 121).

34 Freud (1923d).

35 The androgyne is a phallus (*andros*) in the shape of a woman. What's more, beyond this feminisation by projection, the Devil appears with breasts because, let's not forget, he's obliged to become the painter's 'foster father'. This 'transexualisation' of the devil remains, nevertheless, relative, for let's not forget that during one of his apparitions, the phallicised demon presents 'in addition to the breasts, a large penis ending in a snake' (Freud, 1923d, p. 89).

36 Tausk (1919).

37 Freud (1905d), p. 159.

38 Lacan (1948), pp. 10–30. As early as 1938, in his article 'Les complexes familiaux', Lacan noted that the confrontation of two partners reveals itself to observation not as a conflict between two individuals, but in each subject, as a conflict between two opposing and complementary attitudes, and this bipolar participation is constitutive of the situation itself. Describing a scene of discord between children, he writes: 'Of the child who enjoys the evidence of the domination he exercises and of the one who delights in submitting to it; let us ask ourselves which is the more enslaved?' (Lacan, 1938).

39 Locked in their logic of castration, victims often suffer from 'giving too much', 'feeling drained', 'having been taken away', etc. Numerous authors have highlighted the correlation between the paranoid problem and a fixation on the erotic–anal stage (cf. Schreber's memoirs and my study on the 'Paranoid Feminine', *infra* Chapter 9). See also Rosolato (1976a), where the author, studying Antonin Artaud's paranoid and passionate movement in a kind of triptych linking pain, expulsion and persecution, writes: 'This reiterated experience of pain is the masochistic detour of the testing of the body itself, through all expulsions, down to the most intimate, those of the internal organs, themselves taken for evil persecuting objects' (p. 140).

40 Deutsch (1944)[1946–1947], p. 231.

Chapter 7

Feminine destiny

'And from this destiny he has no escape'. This assertion by Aeschylus[1] confirms, if any were needed, the lazy argument so often used in the face of the subjugating power at work in unfortunate events. Mysterious is this power of fate (*Schicksalsmächte*), to which, for millennia, men have felt 'bound' and can do nothing but submit. Destiny (*Heimarménè*), '*mektoub*' ('it is written'), whatever the name given to this oracular, supernatural, and deified force, we find everywhere the same sense of inescapable Necessity, *Anankè*. A violent, external constraint that haunts and directs the subject until it overpowers them and ruins their freedom. Like a shadow, fate follows them, even pursues them wherever they go. Indeed, the harmful persecuting *fatum* is frequently personified. The feminised subject, placed in a paranoid position, feels they are the object of this sort of phallic, mythical, and impalpable 'executioner' who never lets go. Unable to apprehend the aetiology of their suffering, the subject, forced to endure passivity and tortured by their misfortune, turns to belief in a blurred, veiled, and impenetrable power that sets the inevitable, more often than not unpleasant, course of life's events.

Within this perspective of a strange, invincible, omnipotent, and immutable power that weighs heavily on a person's life, in this chapter I want to show the importance and violence of destiny for a woman who has 'been subjected to' the need for a double medical transplant that was supposed to 'rescue' her from a chronic and irreversible illness.

So, before presenting the clinical facts, essentially dominated by the seriousness and complexity of the 'experience' of organ transplantation and its negative evolution in the 'case' studied below, it should be noted that, whatever the time and place, people, whether men or women, sick or healthy, have always appealed to the value of the phallic omnipotence of fate. By way of example, three names were used indiscriminately in Greco-Latin antiquity to express the idea of this evil external force: *moîra* (*fatum*) the power that dispenses fate, *anankè* (*necessitas*) the conquering and terrifying character of necessity, and *pronoia* (*providentia*), prescience or providence.

As we can see, destiny, which is above all the idea of ineluctable resignation to a superior omnipotence, is not 'what must be' but 'what will be', irremediably. Fatality ('it was bound to happen') or destiny (*Verhängnis*) are the dramatic expression

DOI: 10.4324/9781003414247-8

112 Feminine destiny

of facts 'written' in advance, and therefore unstoppable, as portrayed by the Greek tragic poets.

However, clinical experience has taught us that, while the subject maintains that they are totally neutralised by *fatum*, they do not appear to be entirely neutral in the production of 'fated' misadventures. Their singularly stern and austere superego forbids them any jouissance from favourable events. Indeed, the subject, who is both active and passive in their story, determines, and is determined by, fate. In a way, it could be said that they partly predestine their personal destiny, in the sense that there is simply no such thing as chance in the unconscious. Unbeknown to the subject, they themselves prepare their destiny by repeating harmful events. Similarly, according to the theory refuting the lazy argument of the Stoics, it is possible to argue that the subject acts, albeit constrained by external and/or internal forces (cf. the painful expression: 'It was stronger than me'), but according to their own story, the only 'freedom' to which destiny can still leave room.

That said, as Jean Paul Valabrega rightly points out, it is no easy task to study the problem of this higher power. According to the author:

> The issues surrounding destiny – the respective roles and functions assigned to the innate and the incident, the hereditary and the acquired, the exogenous and the endogenous, the seed and the terrain, trauma and predisposition, essence and accident – continue to pose the most difficult problems.[2]

It is worth noting that the forces of fate have essentially been analysed on a metaphysical and theological–philosophical, if not exclusively phenomenological, level. That is why fate (*Schicksal*), when all is said and done, is not a metapsychological concept. However, it was used by Freud, particularly in a fundamental text from 1920, to describe people of whom 'the impression they give is of being pursued by a malignant fate or possessed by some "daemonic" power',[3] differentiating, however, between the compulsion of destiny (*Schicksalszwang*) and the neurosis of destiny (neurosis of character, of failure...). These fatal events, which occur inevitably, are a periodic recurrence of identical sequences of unfortunate circumstances, to which the subject finds themselves subjected through no fault of their own. Alienation from *Zwang* is radical here. This constraint obliges the subject to repeat what is painful, and in the face of which they encounter their incapacity, their deficient self-control.

Confronted with their weakness, the subject feels and claims to be the powerless object of 'external fatality'. Yet, without knowing it, they are, in fact, trapped by their own inadmissible, unacknowledged, and unconscious desire, which comes back to them like a boomerang from outside. As a result, wherever they go, they constantly have the impression of being overtaken and assailed by this particularly daimonic and demonic terrorising power.

Freud's concept of repetition also helps us to understand failure behaviours, those repetitive scenarios in which people sometimes believe themselves to be under attack and cruelly abused. This gives them the feeling of being the permanent victim of a perverse destiny that reigns supreme, for let us not forget that destiny 'chooses' and pursues its subjects, like a persistent predator hunting its prey.

Based on his analysis of Ibsen's play *Rosmersholm* (1886), Freud[4] asserted that failure is often a 'price to pay' for the subject, an obligation imposed by an unconscious guilt that frustrates the subject's jouissance. Thus, it appears that frequent catastrophic behaviours are both a way of enduring the weight of guilt, and proof that this guilt is not satisfied by them, since it continually demands further failures, further bad luck. As a result, the characteristic function of repetition is to pay for the Other, to atone for a subjective fault that will lighten the load, but without liquidating it. In this forced and necessary repetition of the traumatic, in which the fate of the body is singularly highlighted, the work of the sadistic, mortifying and destructive drive exerts the greatest violence against oneself.

Body of destiny and destiny of the body

Like Oedipus, man is the product of *Tukhè*, Fortune, Chance. Man's destiny, therefore, seems clearly linked to his own history, even to his prehistory. In this respect, the phylogenetic influence is, it seems to me, eminently important in the advent of unpleasant facts of existence. From this perspective, we should speak of a veritable predestination that remains essential throughout life. The subject is, in effect, almost programmed to 'be'. Thus, for example, the mother as spokesperson: 'far preceding the birth of the subject, a discourse pre-exists them'.[5] From this point of view, we know that in the phantasmatic imagination of the parents, the child 'is' long before it is even born.

Similarly, there is an inextricable, undeniable relationship uniting the body and destiny. With this in mind, and taking up Freud's assertion (1923) that 'Anatomy is destiny', I think it would be useful to make a more general statement: 'The body is destiny'.

As Jean Paul Valabrega notes: 'Body and destiny combined once more, brought into contact in an encounter whose suddenness, more than any pre-established or regained harmony, resembles a collision'.[6] The author adds: 'Destiny, or the sense of the Subject, is a fabric whose weft is corporeal and whose warp is mythical'.[7]

In this respect, it is possible to argue that an original trauma, in the sense of an ordeal *from the moment of* birth rather than *due to* birth, lies at the heart of human destiny. Present in every subject, this traumatic experience of primordial 'being' will largely determine the direction and vital path of the subject. In this way, the originally instituted, pre-established destiny affects and traumatises the subject from the very first confrontation with their environment.

'*I missed a step*': bad luck or doomed birth?

Recommended for 'psychological follow-up' by the specialists who had performed a double kidney and pancreas transplant, Mrs G came to see me after first 'complaining' to a departmental victim support service. This woman, in her forties, who I met

114 Feminine destiny

only twice, arrived the first time assisted by her daughter, aged nineteen, and … a crutch. Her foot was in a cast, and she was keen to explain that 'I missed a step' [*J'ai loupé une marche*], and to express her great distress: 'I need help... I don't want to be let down... I feel like I'm not going to make it... Everyone's against me. I have no-one to support me.' This woman, who'd had her kidney and pancreas transplant about a year and a half before, had been suffering with constant 'lower abdominal pain that cripples my life', adding: 'I wake up with stomach ache and I go to bed with stomach ache.' According to Mrs G, these abdominal pains began about five months after the double transplant. As a result, she wonders whether there has been a medical error, whether she has been the victim of a breach of trust, and is, in a way, claiming reparation for the (failed) reparation: 'I had the transplant to be better, not worse …', she protests.

As a result of this poorly tolerated double kidney and pancreas transplant, the patient was treated with antidepressants, without any real success, and is currently taking one anxiolytic tablet a day 'to forget everything', says Mrs G.

It should be noted that despite hyper-anxiety at the idea of the transplant, and considerable fear of an operative catastrophe, the patient had nonetheless agreed to be put on the list and subsequently received the transplant. The surgeons and carers were unanimous about the excellent outcome of the operation. According to the letters and medical documents in my possession, everything went perfectly. Kidney function has become more or less normal, euglycemic without insulin, whereas Mrs G had been treated with insulin since the age of twelve. She had in fact been diabetic for twenty-seven years, putting up with the multiple care requirements associated with this irreversible somatic disease.

Negative narcissistic exception

Mrs G tries to present herself as the negative double of her only sister, aged thirty-five. She compares her unlucky and unhappy family and professional life to that of her sister, who is, instead, said to be fulfilled and 'successful'. This sister has had two children, after 'a great marriage', she points out. She also runs an apparently prosperous business. Whereas Mrs G, who 'didn't have all that', she says with regret, felt unloved from the start by her mother, described as 'mean, demanding, and very authoritarian', and unprotected by her father, portrayed as 'passive and weak'. She also claims to have been separated from them, against her will, and brought up mainly by her grandparents.

When it comes to the two sisters, Mrs G is adamant that *ill fate* has befallen her. She describes herself as the scapegoat, hostage to the family legacy, the bearer of the curse. By becoming, in a way, the parental symptom-bearer, the sick person in the family, she wonders 'Why is this happening to me, why has it fallen on me?' With this heartfelt exclamation, her status as the target of destiny comes to the fore, her guilt culminates: 'I wonder what I've done to deserve this. I feel bad and so alone. I don't know why *everything* is against me …'

These painful expressions reflect a feeling of being the object prey of fate. But this unpleasant experience nonetheless appears to be ancient. It is now reinforced, as it were, by the organic disease that has become irrefutable 'material' proof, a truth that reveals an impossible well-being. This is why, despite the success of the transplant, the complaints and lamentations persist, evoking in this way a *neurotic functioning of character*.

Systematically confined to a negative role in relation to others, the patient also speaks of her wounded narcissism and low self-esteem: 'I feel useless. I find it hard to assert myself.' On the other hand, referring to her only daughter's latest failure at the baccalauréat exam, she laments: 'I can't bear the brunt of everything.' At this point, it is interesting to note that Mrs G, in a process of resignation and fatalism, threatened to 'drop all [medical] tests' after the operation.

Fate is implacable, for, as I pointed out above, the subject is helpless and totally powerless in the face of this obscure force that impotence designates as responsible for unfortunate hardship. This omnipotent, pernicious, and disdainful power seems to be toying with the subject, not even deigning to 'play the game'. As Mrs G laments: 'If you make an effort and don't get rewarded, it doesn't *work* [ça ne marche pas]',[8] an expression that combines ingenuity and the 'as though' of an aggressive defensive reaction, but that allegation may well also be a sign of renunciation, submission, or even an attack on the self in the sense of a feminine gesture of sacrificial fatality. In this case, '*Ne plus marcher*' (no longer working/walking) could be the translation of a 'destinal' will introjected with a refusal 'to live'.

Fate and the mother

In 'The Economic Problem of Masochism', Freud returns to the divine Logos– Ananke duality, writing that:

> ... all who transfer the guidance of the world to Providence, to God, or to God and Nature, arouse a suspicion that they will look upon these ultimate and remotest powers as a parental couple, in a mythological sense, and believe themselves linked to them by libidinal ties. In 'The Ego and the Id', I made an attempt to derive mankind's realistic fear of death, too, from the same parental view of fate.[9]

Thus, fate can be seen as a mythologised representation of parental agency, or more precisely, a 'later projection of the father'.[10] The role of the latter, whether real, onomastic or symbolic, is undeniable in the existence of every human individual.[11] However, while destiny designates the supreme figure of the father, the mother still seems to be its essence. In a way, she is able, if not to generate it, at least to largely instil it into the course of a subject's life. In this way, the mother, who is predominantly perceived to be harmful and hostile, or insufficiently loving and, therefore, anarcissising, provokes a life destined to be peppered with failures, problems, and inextricable catastrophes for the subject subjected to passivity, who is now dominated and overwhelmed by their mortifying autoaggressive impulses.

'Every time I did something, my mother would tell me it was wrong. I wondered what I'd done. She'd often say to me, "You don't know how to do anything. You don't work. You're ill". I took it all the time. Instead of loving me, she really smothered me. With my mother, it's perpetual disappointment.' Beyond this shared disillusionment that sets the mother against her daughter, we can observe in the subject the expression of a painful feeling of having been unwanted and seriously frustrated in the primitive relationship that bound her to the maternal imago. Consequently, the daughter, who considers herself the victim of a mortifying maternal destiny, believes that her evil mother, inauthentic in her affects, anti-narcissistic, devitalising, and disqualifying, betrays her intense unconscious desire for the death of her child.

In several of his analyses, Freud associates the destinal trajectory of the individual with their mother's behaviour towards them. Thus, for example, he writes: 'I have found that those persons who consider themselves preferred or favoured by their mothers manifest in life that confidence in themselves, and that unshakeable optimism, which often seem heroic, and not infrequently compel actual success'.[12]

In 'A Childhood Recollection from *Dichtung und Wahrheit*'[13] alluding to the contribution from 1911, above, Freud writes: 'If a man has been his mother's undisputed darling he retains throughout life the triumphant feeling, the confidence in success, which not seldom brings actual success along with it.' As a result, we could simply say that it is the mother's 'satisfying' love towards her child that animates and drives the child's love of life.

With this in mind, Freud (1966)[14] also states: 'To fall in love with a maternal substitute is to pledge oneself to destiny'. Many authors emphasise the fundamental importance of the mother's 'life-giving' narcissism in her child's psycho-affective and social development. On the contrary, as Joyce MacDougall (1998) points out,[15] the 'toxic', excessive mother, experienced as mortifying by her daughter, can only inflict a negative, morbid destiny on the latter by failing to offer her the useful opportunities that enable her to undertake a relatively satisfying overall life.

The fate of transplantation: Solution and/or problem

While medical transplantation has become an almost commonplace surgical procedure, the somatopsychic process of incorporation–introjection is no simple matter for the person who lives with an external organ, that of a stranger.

First of all, before the transplant, the patient experiences alternating moments of anxiety and hope. Being near death or dependent on a machine[16] are opposed to the possibility of removing the pain, eradicating the suffering. The patient expects the surgeon not to make mistakes, and above all to repair the disorder, the insufficiency.

After the patient has given their 'informed consent', the transplant is carried out. The surprise is often pleasant, and the course of life generally happy. According to Laurent Degos (1994):

> Nine out of ten transplant patients are satisfied with their lives; eight out of ten transplant patients lead a normal daily life, including a return to sexual activity; more than one out of two return to work; and dozens of women have carried pregnancies to term – and had normal children – even after a heart transplant.[17]

The precious incorporated organ creates a link with life. Transplant patients sometimes speak of re-birth, resurrection, and the renewal of existence. The transition is 'lived' as the imminence of death and the return to life. A return to life in which the subject nonetheless finds themselves 'marked' (in the sense of 'transplanted') by change and differentiation compared to their former pre-transplant state.

So, while many subjects derive benefit and satisfaction from the experience, others emerge from it particularly disturbed. Faced with a genuine problem of accommodating the transplant, these people display major difficulties in tolerating the experience of intromission of something into the body. My patient expresses her terrible disillusionment, her exceptional negative status and fateful destiny this way: 'The other transplant patients I meet live well, but that's not how it is for me at all.' Here, the transplanted organ-object is not rejected as such. It is part of a transference dynamic. Current affects of any kind are simply the duplication of the most primitive, ancient affective activity, dominated by negativity and destructiveness.

Thus, acceptance or resistance, or even rejection of the surgical operation, are, strictly speaking, linked to the subject's archaic destiny and history. It is this history, in fact, that underpins the singularity of the transplant experience and the underlying phantasies inherent in this new situation. In this perspective of a global definition of destiny as the history of the subject, the typical state of the transplant patient, characterised by transformation or change, cannot take place without the necessary psychological rearrangements, without psychological effects. Some people take a long time to come to terms with this second condition, or fail in the process of appropriating the life-saving external transplant. Others may never be able to come to terms with it, to live serenely with this new organ they have not really 'chosen'. The incorporation was forced because it was essential, if not vital, and had to be rationally consented to.

In addition to wounded narcissism, the identity of the transplanted subject is shaken, even disturbed. Transplant recipients no longer feel themselves. Their destiny forces them to be an 'other'.[18] A foreign body is present deep inside them. They experience the sensation of having someone else within them, and wonder about their being, their existence. The exogenous incorporated organ inevitably combines with bodily sensations and self-representation. From this anxious questioning of identity stems the recipient's fundamental desire to know details about the donor. This could, in part, facilitate the operation of introjection and projection mechanisms. Obviously, the substance absorbed by the recipient's body is not neutral; it is loaded with values and phantasies, it is part of the other and raises the question of identity boundaries, of the separation between self and other, between death and life in oneself and in the other.

Similarly, the introduction of the foreign-body kidney into the recipient's own body, the cohabitation of the kidney of the deficient-bad self with that of the efficient-good Other, raises the disturbing question of weakness and strangeness.

In addition to the biocompatibility of tissues, there is also a 'psychocompatibility' between the transplanted organ and the patient. There may be a match, an 'adoption', or an unconscious rejection of the transplanted organ. It is, therefore,

118 Feminine destiny

quite likely that medical rejection (*Abstoßung*) is associated with psychic rejection (*Verwerfung*).

In the same way, the biological rejection of the kidney may be related to the feeling of being the object of past and/or present exclusion, either through 'inverted' identification[19] with the now-incorporated organ, or through a hostile feeling towards oneself. The projection of a 'bad whole' has taken place inside the body itself. In this position, where the attack seems to come from within, the subject, while seeking and demanding help and reparation, believes deep down that they do not deserve the attention they are receiving, thus repeating a former situation of an environment experienced as indifferent or rejecting, a psycho-affective environment with little mothering, that is dominated by phantasies of infanticide and destruction.

Thus, the affects linked to the state of the transplant patient are eminently mixed with early memories and memory traces revived by analogies with primitive situations experienced before, such as the confrontation with death, passivity, donation, regression, and initial incorporating experiences. Note that the original model for introducing an exogenous element into a body is that of the mother's breast and her milk into the child's mouth. In this regard, Melanie Klein noted: 'The "good" breast – external and internal – becomes the prototype of all loving and gratifying objects, and the "bad" breast the prototype of all internal or external persecuting objects'.[20] So if the kidney organ is 'refused', it is partly because it is 'endured', and partly because it has been transmuted by telescoping with an unconscious representation into the 'bad' persecuting breast of the primitive dyadic relationship.

We should remember that aggression and rejection have a transference dimension. They refer back to earlier periods when gifts or donations were desired but not received, whereas here, fate dictates that the donation must necessarily be received, without being asked for. Welcoming the external healing organ is 'forced' because it is essential. Here, need supersedes desire.

Furthermore, an intense guilt that is unspoken by the patient, can, it seems, torment them in silence, when the organ to be transplanted is taken from a 'dead' person, a corpse. In this ambiguous situation, death gives life without knowing it, and life gives death without wanting it. The survivor is impeded by a terrible guilt that is difficult to overcome, and can be expressed as follows: 'Thanks to their death, I live'. A statement that can conceivably be made by deduction through crossed destinies: 'So that I may live, they die'. It is, therefore, legitimate to ask whether it is possible to live in relative peace with the ghost of a corpse inside us? The subject is, in effect, now and forever both *enté* – grafted – and *hanté* – haunted – by a foreign body.

Ambiguity of gift, debt and guilt

The patient–recipient experiences the transplant as a fantastic gift that provides them with a vital force and renewed energy. However, the received and incorporated transplanted organ has been likened to a kind of 'poisoned gift'.[21] In fact, from that moment onwards, the transplant patient–subject must assume another position, that of simply transplant recipient. Beyond their new status and identity, they must assume this gift from others, this part of someone else within them.

As Marcel Mauss points out,[22] the gift demands the response of the counter-gift in human societies. The social bond is clearly based on the symmetry of exchanges, on transactions. Therefore, the imperative response to the gift received may be made, sometimes unbeknown to the subject (the donee), in the form of a reciprocal service addressed indirectly to the donor in the form of expiation. Consequently, the recipient's acceptance of the gift is dangerous in that it symbolically places them in debt to the giver. The perceptible paradox of the gift is that it binds the recipient: 'The recipient puts himself in a position of dependence vis-à-vis the donor' (p. 76) The patient must face up to a feeling of debt forever unpaid to the giver. Mauss writes that the unreturned gift, 'makes the person who has accepted it inferior, particularly when it has been accepted with no thought of returning it' (*ibid.*, p. 83).

The guilt of not being able to satisfy the morality of the gift is pervasive. It anchors the subject–recipient in an intolerable and infinite impasse. All the more so as the transplant recipient sometimes experiences the sensation of a disconcerting 'overflow' inside the body, a state of excessive violence. For example, when the patient's own diseased organs are joined by transplanted organs: 'I'm now living with three kidneys and two pancreases!' complains Mrs G.

There is no doubt that the gift tyrannises, induces guilt, and profoundly disrupts the recipient's identity for some time.

It is worth noting that Freud links the feeling of guilt that operates in the psychic life to the *a priori* 'bizarre' fact that some people 'choose' suffering for a better psychosomatic fate. This internal phenomenon, described as a negative therapeutic reaction, is precisely what manifests the dreaded 'work' of debt (*Schuld*), akin to the unconscious feeling of guilt inherent in certain masochistic victim-type organisations[23] that seek expiatory torment and self-punishment.

Negative therapeutic reaction

There is a tendency these days in the medical sciences and psychopharmacological care to leave room for the mysterious, the inexplicable, and the unexpected, with, in particular, repeated use in scientific works of the concept of *serendipity* or *serendipitous*; in other words, that there's an element of chance in medicine. Nevertheless, despite the discovery of this unexpected aspect of medical care, it has to be admitted that some people really do resist being cured. It is as though their destiny condemns them to prefer to suffer than to recover. The patient somehow seems completely locked into earlier, archaic stages covered by primary erogenous masochism and frustration. In *The Ego and the Id*, Freud describes this paradoxical effect encountered in certain people to the course of treatment:

> Every partial solution that ought to result, and in other people does result, in an improvement or a temporary suspension of symptoms produces in them for the time being an exacerbation of their illness; they get worse during the treatment instead of getting better.[24]

120 Feminine destiny

Lacan expresses the impact of the negative therapeutic reaction in this way:

> ... we encounter the specific character of the negative therapeutic reaction in the form of this irresistible inclination towards suicide that becomes recognizable in the last resistances we encounter in these subjects who are more or less characterized by the fact of having been unwanted children. As what must bring them closer to their history as a subject becomes articulated, they increasingly refuse to play the game. They literally want to quit it. They do not accept being what they are. They want nothing of this signifying chain into which their mother has only regretfully admitted them.[25]

This suggests there is an interactive dynamic between intrasubjectivity and intersubjectivity.

As a result, the narcissistic deficit originally suffered develops a singularly ferocious and cruel superego figure. It seeks, and, more often than not, finds, a ruthless and 'perverse' external alliance. In this negative inclination – the work of 'reflexive masochism' – satisfaction is tied up with suffering. Like the drug addict, the subject, author of their own pain, seeks their substance, their dose of dolorism, 'a certain amount of suffering.'[26] In *The Ego and the Id*, Freud (1923b) adds that: '... this sense of guilt is dumb; it does not tell him he is guilty; he does not feel guilty, he feels ill', he insists. The unconscious feeling of guilt, most often borrowed and not integrated by the subject, can also be reversed, with the victim 'choosing' to be guilty by identification.

The most bitter superego agencies are fully at work in this resistance to treatment or inverted reaction. In the same way, the death instinct – which attacks silently from within – is raging here, a situation in which regressive primitive autosadism is hyperinvested.

Sublimation: A bastion against destiny?

As we know, it is particularly difficult to isolate the somatic from the psychic. This is why, given this indisputable interdependence, in certain psychosomatic disorganisations or delirium, the organic disorder may well be favoured or accentuated by the subject's masochistic inclinations. This is the case when, placed in such a position, they unwittingly find themselves the victim of their own sadistic destructive impulses, which are reflected and directed at the ego. Here, suffering is intimately intertwined with an underlying jouissance, a jouissance of the Other within the ego that enables the subject to exist. In this way, aggression, detached from the outside world and directed back at the ego, transforms the latter into the most ambivalent love object.

So, with this type of narcissistically wounded patient, whose real somatic disorder is, it should be remembered, associated with a neurotic disorder, the technical and relational work aims, beyond the necessary repair of the annihilated maternal imago which has been subjected to the violent assaults of the patient's devastating

Feminine destiny 121

phantasies, at a fundamental rectification in the subject's instinctual destiny. It is a question of specifically and ideally helping sublimation[27] in the sense of diverting the aggressive and destructive instincts that are here inverted or introjected in the direction of autosadism or narcissistic death masochism, and to encourage in these subjects, as Rosine Debray points out: 'economic modifications enabling them to circumscribe the place assigned to their illness in their general economy, and therefore make them more resistant to secondary complications'.[28]

Indeed, while 'it cannot provide a complete defence from suffering; it creates for them no armour impenetrable to the arrows of fortune',[29] sublimation can serve as a bastion against the repetition of cruel and trying events, and even, to a certain extent, prevent pain from taking root in the body or moving preferentially towards it (bodily recourse).

Certainly, sublimation can temporarily deflect and prevent self-destructive energy, and fate then has little hold on the individual, as Freud states in *Civilization and its Discontents*. Nevertheless, this complex and certainly ambitious task is fraught with pitfalls when dealing with patients whose psychic economy is singularly guided by the iterative need for passivation and domination through repeated unfortunate behaviours. Subjects who unconsciously refuse to get better and resist change, thereby justifying their place as a sacrificial feminine object. In this respect, let us just note that the, sometimes intense, anguish that accompanies this work of overcoming would attest to the deep and fierce antagonism of the amphibological ego, always divided between the pleasure of an early death and the turmoil generated by the idea of its own annihilation. Nothing could be more exquisite than the reduction of excitation to zero, than death conceived as the extreme sedation of tensions.

However, failing to bring about their real and radical demise, the person 'worked' by the negative remains painfully trapped in an equivocal position governed by the 'in-between', a situation of psychic agony and dereliction, where life, which is complacently intertwined with death, remains as though suspended. Therefore, without the necessary mental elaboration that would give them the opportunity to escape the tyranny of fate that was in part self-initiated, the person, sclerotic in mortifying feminine masochism, can only endure and survive in order to live, suffer in order to be, and be in order to suffer. As Mrs G eloquently puts it: 'Death doesn't frighten me. I don't live. I survive... yet I like life.'

Notes

1 Aeschylus (1902).
2 Valabrega (1980), p. 97.
3 Freud (1920g), p. 21.
4 Freud (1916d).
5 See Aulagnier (2001)[1975].
6 Valabrega (1980), p. 73.
7 *Ibid.*, p. 75.
8 Cf. the patient's 'plastered foot' following the missing of a 'step' (*marche*). In the original French the 'faux pas' here is a genuine expression of a perfectly 'successful' 'missed' act.

9 Freud (1924c).
10 Freud (1928b).
11 Cf. Chapter 6, 'Can you be innocent if you love someone guilty?'
12 Freud (1900a). Note added in 1911.
13 Freud (1917b).
14 Freud and Bullit (1966), p. 151.
15 Cf. MacDougall (1998).
16 The cumbersome nature of the artificial kidney used for kidney failure means that the machine has to be separated from the body, and purification sessions have to be carried out three or four times a week.
17 Degos (1994), p. 87.
18 Perhaps it's interesting to note the analogy between the signifiers *enté* ('grafted') and *hanté* ('haunted') ... by a foreign body?
19 The 'good' external organ becomes somehow 'bad' or 'dying' by condensation with the painfully severe and negative self-perception.
20 Klein (1952).
21 Note, moreover, the ambiguity of the word '*gift*', which, in ancient Germanic languages meant both 'gift' and 'poison'.
22 Maus (2002)[1924]. *The Gift: The Forms and Reason for Exchange in Archaic Societies* (M. Douglas, Trans.). Taylor & Francis.
23 I'd like to make a distinction here between the masochistic position and that of victim. Although these two notions can be associated, they must not be confused, because beyond suffering, what prevails in the victim state is the *complaint* and the demand for *reparation*, which corresponds to the 'price of pain' (*pretium doloris*).
24 Freud (1923b), p. 49. It should be noted, however, that in 'Remembering, repeating and working-through', Freud (1914) already refers to this state of 'aggravation in treatment' or *reversed* reaction, with the probable presence in the patient of a benefit from the illness.
25 Lacan (1957–1958a), p. 228/section 246.
26 Cf. Freud (1924c).
27 It is worth noting that in Freud's early writings, sublimation, as a *purification* process, is linked to a kind of 'psychic dialysis'.
28 Debray (1983), p. 36.
29 Freud (1930a).

Chapter 8

Feminine hypochondria

Recognised and described by ancient medicine (the 'disease of the hypochonders'[1] according to Hippocrates, the 'hypochondriac disease' according to Galen), hypochondria is one of the oldest words in medical and psychoanalytic vocabulary.[2]

Hypochondria has almost always been defined as the constant fear or belief of being affected by a serious illness. It is a syndrome built on the subject's intense anxieties about their health, despite negative results from tests. In the hypochondriac complaint, the illness is invisible, unknown, inaccessible, mysterious, and hidden, and the subject's suspicion of the disease, sometimes accompanied by pain, reveals or predicts mortal danger. Nowhere is the hypochondriac's world better described than in the literary example of Argan, in Molière's The Imaginary Invalid (1673), which provides a remarkable clinical illustration that led to the now-abandoned term Arganism being proposed to designate hypochondria.

Of the many 'definitions' of hypochondria, we can take the one given by Dubois d'Amiens in 1833:

> A very distinct monomania, characterised by a special and exclusive dominant preoccupation, that is, either by an excessive and continual fear of bizarre and imaginary illnesses, or by the intimate persuasion that illnesses, real in truth, but always ill-defined, can end only in a disastrous manner.[3]

Narcissistically hyper-attentive to the inside of their body, the hypochondriac is attentive to the slightest signal that may emerge from their anatomical organs. Everything is scrutinised and deciphered in a negative, worrying, and threatening way. In his famous *Manuel de psychiatrie*, Henri Ey[4] summarily places hypochondriasis within melancholia. He associates it with asthenia, depression and neurotic anxiety.

Hypochondria and melancholy

Claudius Galen had already understood hypochondria as being closely related to melancholy. Similarly, 'sufferings of the soul', particularly fear and sadness, had earlier been described by Hippocrates (460–377 BC) and linked by him to atrabile, or black bile. Following Hippocrates, ancient medicine considered that a disorder

DOI: 10.4324/9781003414247-9

124   Feminine hypochondria

of one of the four humours (yellow bile, phlegm, blood, black bile, corresponding to the four elements, four seasons, and four temperaments), and in this case an excess of atrabile, could favour an attack on thinking. Thus, from Hippocrates to Philippe Pinel (1745–1826), hypochondria was associated, even amalgamated, with melancholy. Moreover, Jules Cotard described the syndrome that bears his name hypochondriacal delusion as a complication of melancholia (1880), before it was called 'delusion of negations' two years later.[5]

Regarding the sensations of hypochondria, the language and the specific relationship to representations, Freud notes in *Studies on Hysteria* (1895d): 'when a neurasthenic (a hypochondriac or a person affected with anxiety neurosis) describes his pains, he gives an impression of being engaged on a difficult intellectual task to which his strength is quite unequal'. He later adds: 'He is clearly of the opinion that language is too poor to find words for his sensations and that those sensations are something unique and previously unknown, of which it would be quite impossible to give an exhaustive description' (p. 136). According to Freud, anxiety neurosis and hypochondria are linked to an excess of libido due to sexual continence (libidinal stasis). In hypochondria, the anxiety arising from this excess of unfulfilled libido becomes fixed and focuses on bodily sensations.

It is useful to distinguish hypochondria from hysterical suffering and from melancholic pain. Hypochondriacal obsession is generally accompanied by an eroticisation of the body. There is a libidinal interest in the symptoms. As in hysteria, hypochondria involves a certain jouissance. However, while the link between body and psyche is not broken in hysteria, this does appear to be the case in hypochondria. The body–psyche connection is missing. The subject feels dispossessed of their body, a stranger in their own home. The body is always, more or less, a stranger and never one's own. In 'The Unconscious' 1915e, Freud described hypochondria as a 'language of organs', contrasting it more broadly with hysteria's 'language of the body', but also indirectly with the incarnation of melancholy.

From a clinical point of view, it is necessary to differentiate between hysteria, hypochondria, and somatisation, in other words, the three major clinical entities that directly raise the question of the relationship between the psyche and the body. Hypochondria must be compared and specified in relation to hysteria. In hysteria, the subject *puts on a show,* a spectacle. The hypochondriac, on the other hand, *gives voice* to what is going on inside them, what is hidden behind the scenes. The hypochondriac's complaint is, above all, a difficult discourse. You could say that the hysteric shows, while the hypochondriac demonstrates. The former is on the side of seeing, while the latter is on the side of having and knowing, echoing scientific medical discourse.

As for the process of somatisation, it is distinct from the hysterical conversion process in that it directly affects the somatic body. The body is genuinely affected. It is not a question of 'fake illness'. With this in mind, Freud wrote:

A difference between hypochondria and organic disease now becomes evident: in the latter, the distressing sensations are based upon demonstrable changes; in the former, this is not so. But it would be entirely in keeping with our general conception of the processes of neurosis if we decided to say that hypochondria must be right: organic changes must be supposed to be present in it, too. But what could these changes be?' [6]

For Freud, both hypochondria and organic illness are characterised by a libidinal shift back on to the body. He thus compares somatic illness and hypochondria. Whereas the somatic patient

> withdraws his libidinal cathexes back upon his own ego, and sends them out again when he recovers [...] the hypochondriac withdraws both interest and libido... from the objects of the external world and concentrates both of them upon the organ that is engaging his attention.
>
> *ibid.*

Hypochondria, actual neurosis

Freud considers hypochondria to be one of the three actual neuroses, along with neurasthenia and anxiety neurosis. These actual neuroses are pathologies of the libido.[7] He contrasts the ego-libido, the domain of hypochondriacal anxiety, with the object-libido, the domain of neurotic anxiety. Thus, according to Freud, hypochondriacal complaints are pathological manifestations of the 'ego-libido', as described by the hypochondriac's feeling of omnipotence, which can systematise the demanding behaviours and confrontation with the medical profession.

In this regressive, aggressive position, the subject attacks in particular a close family member, a relative or, externally, a doctor. Conflict, in the form of a misunderstanding or non-understanding (of the complaint), is external. Internal conflict is lacking.

It should be noted that each of these actual neuroses is linked to a psychic disorder, as if it were its source: anxiety neurosis with hysteria, neurasthenia with obsessive neurosis, and hypochondria with paraphrenia.

Even more clearly, Freud suggests that hypochondria is to paraphrenia and paranoia what anxiety neurosis and neurasthenia are to hysteria and obsessional neurosis.[8] Freud even went so far as to claim that hypochondria was 'the somatic equivalent of paranoia',[9] a *paranoia somatica*. This would be a kind of introjection, even incorporation, of the attacking object that strikes from within.

Freud came to speculate that all the organs of the body, over and above their normal functions, play an erogenous role that is sometimes so immoderate as to disrupt normal functioning. In other words, erogeneity is a general property of all organs.

In this respect, Ferenczi believed that the hypochondriac structure is imposed by anal eroticism.

He wrote:[10]

> The true hypochondriac is an anal erotist who manically projects onto an external cause (illness) his anal–erotic coprophilic interest which has been displaced to

other bodily organs. The entire hypochondriacal delusional system serves as insurance against the insight of anal–erotic wishes. The colossal abhorrence of anal erotism makes it so that this kind of libido is sublimated at all costs, and where that does not succeed – it must be *projected* as far as possible by the ego ... There are further intimate connections between anal erotism, homosexuality, hypochondria and *paranoia* ... a man interprets his homosexual anal erotism (operations on the rectum) first hypochondriacally and feels all kinds of lethal illness in himself; only later is it *detached* by persecution mania. Hypochondria is, after all, also a persecution mania: only one is being persecuted not by another person but by the *'illness.'* ... Hypochondria's therapeutic intransigence and similarity to paranoia can be explained by this mechanism; so projection is not easily reversed.[11]

Ferenczi also noted: 'It usually comes down to anxiety about illness or formation of hypochondria when one of the sublimations (particularly the money complex) is severely injured or destroyed'.[12]

Paul Schilder talks of a form of depersonalisation in the hypochondriac. In his understanding, the body is fragmented, as though 'split', to use Melanie Klein's expression.

Rosenfeld[13] proposes a distinction between hypochondria as a chronic psychosis, temporary psychotic or neurotic hypochondriac states, and hypochondriacal anxieties.

For his part, Pierre Fédida affirms that hypochondria has a central role between paranoia and melancholia. This author understands it as a defence against threats of decomposition and cadaverisation, a struggle against annihilation and for psychic survival. From a conjectural perspective, Fédida maintains that the incriminated organ may play 'the role of representative of an absent ancestor whose tutelary protection is accorded only at the price of this enigmatic ongoing recollection of pain'.[14]

Transnosography: hypochondria/psychosis

Polymorphic and ubiquitous, hypochondria has no independent place in psychopathology. Clinical practice indicates that preliminary hypochondriacal tendencies are consistent in psychosis. The paradigmatic case of Schreber is a case in point. Hypochondria is on a path that can lead to psychosis.

Freud, in a famous phrase, asserts its importance in psychoses: 'I shall not consider any theory of paranoia trustworthy unless it also covers the *hypochondriacal* symptoms by which that disorder is almost invariably accompanied'.[15] The hypochondriac feels persecuted by their own body. As stated earlier, hypochondria as an organisation is very close to paranoia.

It is important to distinguish between hypochondria and hypochondriacal complaint. For not all hypochondriacal complaints are clearly 'delusional'. As for the destabilisation of reality, this is also part of certain hysterical presentations, in which patients become engulfed in catastrophic thoughts and affect-laden discourse, putting them out of touch with reality. It is quite possible to argue for the existence of mixed forms of hypochondria, or on the links that can be forged between hysteria and hypochondria, in relation to the question of the feminine.

Freud remained extremely concerned about the metapsychological status of this notion, as he wrote[16] in 1912 to Ferenczi:

> I have always felt the darkness in the question of hypochondria[17] to be a great disgrace to our efforts but have come up with nothing but suppositions. The problem seemed to me to be: characterization by means of a particular organ source or a particular process. And, with a view toward obsessional neurosis, I opted for the latter, while you choose the former. With regard to the process, I thought of hypochondria as the third actual neurosis and the somatic basis for paraphrenia, as anxiety neurosis is for hysteria. So I drew the erogenous contributions of the organs, which are annexed to the ego rather than to the libido, but with negative sign, but nothing consistent has come out of this, and I don't want to force anything that doesn't seem ready.

In psychoanalytic literature,[18] hypotheses and clinical cases are more prevalent than convictions about the etiology of this condition. As early as 1912, Ferenczi sees hypochondria as inconstant, capable of change, and a transient condition linked to different positioning of the libido and different modes of defence.

For Freud,[19] it is important to relate hypochondria to psychosis, in conjunction or correspondence with what actual neuroses represent for transference neuroses.

Libidinal drive stasis, put forward in two texts from 1912[20] and 1913[21], includes a possible application for the ego-libido. The movement of disobjectalisation, the withdrawal from real or phantasmatic objects, signals a failure of psychic elaboration.

Feminine masochism, narcissism, and hypochondria

An analogy can be drawn between the hypochondriacal sensation and the unconscious feeling of guilt and consequent need for punishment. Let us recall Freud here:

> The practical significance of this discovery is not less than its theoretical one, for the need for punishment is the worst enemy of our therapeutic efforts. It is satisfied by the suffering which is linked to the neurosis, and for that reason holds fast to being ill.[22]

With the support of narcissism, seen as the return of object-libido to the ego under the strong action of external factors, Freud confronts neurotic anxiety – linked to the subject's partner and the object-libido – and hypochondriacal anxiety, linked to the own body and the ego-libido. Freud begins his observation about narcissism with the consideration that, in psychosis, delusions of grandeur – megalomania – and turning away from the outside world are united.[23]

Thus, libido detached from the external world has been provided to the ego. Freud adds: 'The hypochondriac withdraws both interest and libido – the latter specially markedly – from the objects of the external world and concentrates both of them upon the organ that is engaging his attention'.[24] The archetypal pain-sensitive organ is the aroused genital organ, the epitome of which is penile turgidity. This arousal is reflected in the body itself, with erogeneity becoming the character of all the organs. Here, jouissance prevails, and the death instinct reigns, beyond the pleasure principle. Some patients renounce recovery, seeking to satisfy an unconscious need for punishment: 'People in whom this unconscious sense of guilt is excessively strong betray themselves in analytic treatment by the negative therapeutic reaction which is so disagreeable from the prognostic point of view'.[25]

Primary homosexual relationship and hypochondria

Hypochondria, an 'enigmatic' pathology, seems to be a typically 'feminine' problem, or a profound expression of the feminine. The majority of women with hypochondria have a complicated relationship with their mothers, and, thus, with their own femininity. It is very often a question of bad, unrewarding, frequently ill and/or tyrannical mothers (or mother figures) to whom the patients have remained 'attached'. This relational difficulty seems to be the result of too much promiscuity in the unsatisfactory mother–daughter bond, or of a despotic, controlling relationship from an excessive and abusive mother (narcissistic seduction).

Is there a 'susceptibility to hypochondria'? To this question, we can say that the anxiety that predominates in parental relationships is an essential criterion. Deep, archaic, 'schizo-paranoid' anxieties have marked the hypochondriac's primordial relations with the maternal object. These hypochondriacal anxieties renew early, archaic anxieties, but also present-day anxieties engendered by the instinctual flow.

In hypochondria, the question is to know which traumas, which 'kernel of truth', could be at its origin, far removed from the *après-coup* of individual history (Schreber's childhood). It is important to stress the seriousness of early narcissistic wounds, early childhood anxieties and emotional deficiencies in the past of a hypochondriac. In particular, Anna Freud noted the resurgence of hypochondriacal anxieties in subjects separated from their parents. Hypochondria is said to be linked to loss and the experience of abandonment.

Justine:[26] 'I can't stand being me any more'

Justine is a sixteen-year-old teenager. She regularly takes part in beauty contests. Referred by her family doctor, she comes to the clinic for 'unbearable anxiety'. She complains of abdominal pain. She says she suffers greatly from this situation, painfully feeling 'a knot and cramps in the stomach'. She pathologically dreads her 'stomach making a noise'. She is alert to the slightest rumbling, for she experiences a feeling of shame when she 'imagines something and what others might think' of her.[27] It takes considerable effort, in her opinion, to comply with the requirements of propriety and decency. She watches for any signs or calls that might indicate betrayal or a flaw in her body. The need for mastery is considerable. She is an intelligent teenager, an excellent student, but she is also afraid of 'being stupid, of being rubbish'. Her speech is dominated by complaint, as she says: 'I can't stand being me any more.[28] I can't stand what I am any more... I always feel like I'm being *watched*.'[29]

The divorced mother is described as fragile. She was depressed when pregnant with Justine. The father is a doctor. Even today, the daughter has 'a lot of anger towards him', adding: 'I don't think he loved me enough.'

This brief observation illustrates the complex and ambivalent perceptions of a body that can be both a container that encloses, and a body that expresses the suffering of many different ailments. The internal body seems to be the Pandora's box of all the anxieties born of childhood and adolescence, and a window-body, a narcissistic façade through the gaze of the other, but at the same time fearful that this gaze may see inside herself,[30] her intimacy, her thoughts, her anxieties, hence the paranoid aspect common to adolescence.

On the subject of hypochondria, Augustin Jeanneau[31] (2002) wrote: 'Thought that can do nothing persists in questioning a body that knows nothing'. For this author, the mental register is inadequate to its somatic object. The body is insufficient or inappropriate. The body is specified by this double characteristic: it is both the dwelling place of the psyche and, indeed, something of a jailer, as well as an object of the world delivered up to the gaze of the other. In this case, there is also the dread of others listening to the body.

The fear of 'making noise' in spite of oneself is experienced by the adolescent as though it undermined the silence of the body, so important to the sense of well-being.[32] Michel Fain[33] (1990) refers to the rupture of the 'silence of the body' in hypochondria as a 'rift in reassuring perceptions'. This silence corresponds to familiar background noise...

There is almost an antinomy between *Having* (all that is in oneself, and also what is lost, such as one's childhood), and *Being* (seen, beautiful, loved), in the phenomenological sense of this notion: in other words, in its relationship to the 'flesh', as Merleau-Ponty points out, through which the thought and felt body reveals the sensitive becoming of Being.

But isn't this the inescapable fate of every being, incarnate, both body-self and imaginary-self? Justine has introjected her mother's suffering, but she also wants to radiate outwards. Similarly, her mother's confidences are an overflow; not yet a woman herself, the daughter is invaded by this woman–mother, who creates a kind of 'collusion'[34] with her own feminine future: what 'woman' will she be one day?

Sophie or hatred of the mother

Sophie, a beautiful, intelligent woman of forty-five, is seeking help for 'harmful thoughts'. She says she feels frightened whenever pain arises in her body. She 'sometimes has stomach ache'. Above all, she's afraid of being affected or

130 Feminine hypochondria

'touched' (*touchée*) by a disease that, she says, 'would be transmitted' to her body. Her husband is a specialist doctor with a high reputation, as is Sophie's brother, whom she consults remotely for advice and guidance, following medical examinations, for example.

This woman had 'already sometimes seen shrinks for problems with anorexia'. She says: 'I used to eat nothing during the day and do a lot of sport.'

This problem disappeared with the birth of her son, who, she points out, has the same first name as Sophie's father.

Today, the problem is rather her eldest daughter, aged twenty-three, who is overweight. 'She's always hungry,' bemoans the mother.

Straight away, as though to emphasise the negative fate of her existence, Sophie claims to have 'attempted suicide at the age of five, by trying to jump out of the car'. She was told about this event, which a few years later she denies recounting, by one of her two brothers who were 'much more valued by the mother'. Sophie is the only daughter in a sibling group of three children.

Highly sensitive to the question of knowing, she says she is 'afraid of not measuring up', because her mother 'always made her feel inferior'. This patient, who seems preoccupied, says she 'sees the worst in everything'. She is very attentive to the judgemental gaze of others. Above all, she says she 'can't stand' being looked at or touched by her mother, who is described as 'frosty'. One hardly needs reminding of the importance of the two, closely associated, partial drives in the first mother–child encounters: the first relationships by means of touch and gaze are fundamental. The baby makes contact with their mother first through touch, then through gaze.

On this subject, Sophie recounts a difficult scene. When she was in hospital, her mother came to see her 'hidden behind some sunglasses'. Sophie says she couldn't 'see' her, and 'since that day,' she says, 'I can't stand my mother looking at me'.

The daughter has many grievances with her mother. It seems the latter discouraged her daughter from pursuing dance. The daughter felt wounded. She believes her mother denied her the right to be 'feminine', to 'discover and show off her body'. She thinks her mother took issue with her *being* what she *is* or would like to be. 'My mother used to force me to eat. I have the feeling she didn't want me to be feminine.' Sophie considers these few essential elements to definitely be at the root of her 'late puberty, which occurred around the age of fourteen'.

The patient says that while her mother denied her the right to be a little girl, she, on the other hand, was very sensitive to her own image as a woman. Sophie says she suffers from a lack of 'complicity' with her mother, described as 'frightening' and 'disgusting'. She continues her criticism, saying she has a 'toxic mother who sees evil everywhere (illness, death, etc.)'. According to the daughter, her mother is nonetheless 'not afraid of illness, even though she's always complaining about her joints. Living for her is terrible, because she thinks she'll live a long time... She has no taste for life. ...' Sophie stresses the difficult relationship she has with her mother, who is described as scornful and persecuting on the telephone. She says she feels hatred towards her mother, but she is not at all at peace. The mother is said to have 'had a breakdown', and blamed her daughter for her condition.

Sophie also claims to have suffered greatly from her father's lack of protective presence. He died ten years earlier at the age of sixty. He would 'always go to confession in church'. His daughter was 'astonished by this attitude'. She thinks he was 'looking for God's mercy... unlike us sinners'. 'Me too,' says Sophie. 'Every evening I'd make myself suffer in front of the window with my arms outstretched.' She adds: 'My father was in awe of the Saints... I'm sensitive to the way God looks at us... even though I don't believe in it... My father was a very self-righteous man. He was always afraid of having done something... I'm sensitive to giving, to generosity, to knowing how to give, the gift of God. ...' Deeply affected and hurt by her father's death, Sophie tries to de-idealise him: 'I thought I admired my father. As the years go by, I admire him less. As time goes by, I am noticing all his faults. He did me a lot of harm. I blame him for having been under my mother's authority … directed by his wife. He avoided conflict. He never opposed her... He didn't defend me much... My mother has supreme authority... going up against her isn't easy.'

I met with Sophie about ten times. She was doing much better, particularly because she was working professionally on some art projects. She was passionate about making these personal creations which were 'recognised' by her family and the public at large. Two years after our sessions had finished, the patient informed me that her mother had committed suicide by 'intentional drug overdose'.

Notes

1 For thousands of years, hypochondria has been considered a 'disease of the hypochonders': the area below the ribs.
2 Cf. Freud (1897)[1986]. Letter of 24/11/1887 to his friend Fliess.
3 Dubois d'Amiens (1833).
4 Ey (1960)[2010].
5 Quoted by Cotard in his 1882[1994] text, 'Le délire des négations', pp. 311–328. Lacan used this syndrome to formalise the notion of the in-between-death and the concept of jouissance. Jouissance, a libidinal excitation that returns to the body itself, accounts for the clinical fact to postulate the death drive. Cf. Lacan (1954–1955)[1988].
6 Freud (1914c), pp. 82–83.
7 Freud, S. Drafts B (1893) and K (1896), and Further remarks on the neuro-psychoses of defence (1896b). In *The Standard Edition* Vol. 1.
8 Freud (1914c).
9 Freud (1907b).
10 Freud & Ferenczi (1908–1914), p. 358.
11 *Id.*, p. 358.
12 *Id.*, p. 359.
13 Rosenfeld (1958).
14 Fédida (1995).
15 Freud, S. (1911c), p. 56, note 3.
16 Freud & Ferenczi (1908–1914), p. 360.
17 Freud uses abbreviations: 'hyp.' for hypochondria, 'hy.' for hysteria, 'neg.' for negative.
18 Aisenstein, Fine & Pragier (1995). See in particular the articles by A. Fine and G. Pragier for their synthetic review of the literature.
19 Freud (1914c).

132 Feminine hypochondria

20 Freud (1912c). The title of this article is misleading. Freud uses the term neurosis here, as he often does, in the old sense of functional affection without organic lesion. Here, Freud is talking about the onset of any mental pathology.
21 Freud (1913i).
22 Freud (1933a). Lecture 32, 'Anxiety and the instinctual life', pp. 81–111.
23 Freud (1914c).
24 *Id.*, p. 83.
25 Freud (1933a). Lecture 32, 'Anxiety and the instinctual life', pp. 81–111.
26 This first clinical situation was presented in greater detail in my book *Clinique du narcissisme* (Maïdi, 2012).
27 Already Pierre Janet, in his description of 'shame obsession', distinguishes 'self-shame obsession' from physical shame concerning dissatisfaction with one's body or bodily functions, which he would call 'function phobias' concerning eating and anal functions, for example.
28 This is 'the fatigue of not being oneself', to paraphrase the title of Alain Ehrenberg's 1998 book, *La fatigue d'être soi*. In this instance, the young subject feels alienated and deprived of his or her freedom to be.
29 Here, the notions of the gaze and the superego agency that firmly guards desire are clearly associated.
30 Adolescents have this dreaded fear of being transparent (trans-parent?), with no control over their image or body.
31 Jeanneau (2002).
32 Cf. The 'skin-self': the body is an envelope between inside and outside, here perhaps too permeable.
33 Fain (1990)[2010].
34 In our care services, we often see these granddaughters (still young) who are too confident about their mother and her adult problems, and who need to be put back in their place as children. I developed this issue of generational confusion and narcissistic seduction in my book (Maïdi, 2008).

Chapter 9

Feminine paranoia

It is almost inconceivable to study the question of the feminine without giving a fundamental place to the psychoanalytic understanding of paranoia. We cannot ignore the particularly close links between this notion and organisations of a hysterical and hypochondriac type,[1] or with the enigmatic economic problem of masochism.

What is more, contrary to popular belief, it would seem that cases of feminine paranoia[2] are more frequent than those of masculine paranoia.

To illustrate the problem of feminine paranoia, I have nevertheless chosen to analyse Daniel Paul Schreber's *Memoirs of My Nervous Illness*[3] in a dialectic with one of my own patients.

As a reminder, Schreber seeks to be turned into a woman. He wants to be a woman, a coital mother, pregnant,[4] giving birth, but also passive, offered, penetrated, humiliated, all in uninterrupted jouissance (Freud, 1911). 'It really must be rather pleasant to be a woman succumbing to intercourse',[5] he asserts. The question of the feminine dominates Schreber's psychic space. Moreover, the absence of female characters in his delusions proved their omnipresence, as Ronald Fairbairn (1945)[6] has rightly pointed out.

Passivation and feminisation of Schreber

Throughout the pages of Schreber's autobiography, he never ceases to lament, to cry out for 'help', to undergo 'eviration' (transformation into a woman), 'to be delivered'. He complains, 'so that my soul was handed to him, but my body – transformed into a female body... was then left to that human being for sexual misuse and simply "forsaken,", in other words left to rot' (*MNI*, p. 63).

The former president of the Saxon Appeal Court laments being offered up to 'human games',[7] being the plaything, becoming an object, suffering 'soul murder', being 'made to look like (*Darstellen*) a transient person of feminine pusillanimity', being in a position of passivation and feminisation.

Schreber describes the vicissitudes he went through. He tries to give a witness account of what he calls the 'signs of feminisation' on his body. Thus, he writes:

DOI: 10.4324/9781003414247-10

134 Feminine paranoia

> Twice at different times... I had a female genital organ, although a poorly developed one ... [*MNI*, p. 18]
>
> In consequence of the miracles directed against me, I had a thing between my legs which hardly resembled at all a normally formed male organ. [*MNI*, note, p. 65]
>
> My breast gives the impression of a pretty well-developed female bosom; this phenomenon can be *seen* by anybody who wants to observe me *with his own eyes* ... anyone who sees me standing in front of a mirror with the upper part of my body naked would get the undoubted *impression of a female trunk* [*MNI*, p. 248].

Schreber experiences, sometimes with a certain voluptuousness, a sense of divine rays breaking into his body and penetrating, but also 'most probably ... Professor Flechsig's ... *whole* soul' (*MNI*, p. 86).

> The nerves concerned have, through the power of attraction of my nerves, been absorbed into my body, in it they have taken on the character of female nerves of voluptuousness and apart from this have given my body a more or less feminine stamp; they have in particular given my skin a softness peculiar to the female sex.
>
> (*MNI*, p. 90)

The narcissistic feminine and paranoia

In his recounting of the Schreber case, Freud (1911c) presents narcissism as a characteristic of the object choice:

> Recent investigations[8] have directed our attention to a stage in the development of the libido which it passes through on the way from auto-erotism to object-love.[9] This stage has been given the name of *narcissism*. What happens is this. There comes a time in the development of the individual at which he unifies his sexual instincts (which have hitherto been engaged in auto-erotic activities) in order to obtain a love-object; and he begins by taking himself, or his own body, as his love-object, and only subsequently proceeds from this to the choice of some person other than himself as his object.[10]

According to Freud, the narcissistic stage is 'inevitable' in the course of development, but some people become fixed there permanently.

The work of the following generations of psychoanalysts confirmed the role of narcissism in the psychogenesis of homosexuality. In 'President Schreber' (1911c), Freud again links homosexuality and narcissism. We can recall the considerable influence of belittlement and vexation in what Freud calls the 'social rebuffs' in the development of paranoia, which are to be examined as narcissistic wounds. In this context, Freud depicts the path of the libido from autoeroticism to object-love.

It is also possible to wonder whether, for certain subjects, becoming a homosexual does not arise from early narcissistic trauma,[11] the existence of which is announced by a fixation on the specular image.

Largely inspired by the study of Schreber,[12] Freud writes in 'On Narcissism' (1914c):

> We say that a human being has two original sexual objects – himself and the woman who nurses him – and in doing so we are postulating a primary narcissism in everyone, which may in some cases manifest itself in a dominating fashion as his object-choice.[13]

We find this narcissism in the object-choice through the phenomenon of idealisation of the ego in the sexual object, as presented, for example, in Leonardo's homosexuality. Indeed, Leonardo depicted condensed portraits of himself and his mother prodigiously: ephebes with a feminine smile; women inspired by the grace of a young man's face. These are his 'two original sexual objects'.[14]

In *Group Psychology and the Analysis of the Ego* (1921c), the theme of the double examined in 'The "Uncanny"' (*Das Unheimliche*) enabled Freud (1919h) to examine the fate of narcissism, the primary identification relationship with the mother, homosexuality, the repetition compulsion, and the struggle against annihilation anxiety. Freud considers that the appearance of the double, which has 'grown out of the terrain of unlimited love of self, that of primary narcissism', takes place in a climate of disquieting strangeness, even of imminent threat of fragmentation, which reflects a return of the repressed. The *Unheimliche*[15] situates the double between annihilation anxiety and castration anxiety, between primary narcissism and the later stages of ego development.

Is the paranoiac a 'true' victim?

Richard von Krafft-Ebing described how the primary paranoia that affects the young subject can be identified by its well-systematised delusions. This is in contrast to the so-called late paranoias, also known as paranoides. According to Emil Kraepelin, in systematised delusions with a paranoid structure (*Treatise*, 1883–1905), there is a 'complete preservation of clarity and order in thought, will and action'. Similarly, in so-called 'persecutory' delusions (Lasègue, 1816–1883), which are 'characterised by a systematic and coherent development of a persecutory drama', we note in the content of the discourse an 'irreducible and lucid argumentation', as well as a 'fundamental affective and aggressive tone. …'

On the other hand, in passionate delusional productions, the *litigious* delusion is generally characterised by the prevailing need and unshakeable will to make a demand triumph that the environment generally refuses to satisfy. In this situation, the subject finds themselves in a permanent sensation of deprivation and frustration. They also have the inflexible conviction that they alone hold the truth (almost mathematical certainty), that they are, in short, completely sincere, unlike people (usually acquaintances) who are presented as frustraters in the sense of rejecting and abandoning. In this respect, it is worth recalling that in his paranoid torment, Schreber suffered from being 'forsaken' (*liegen gelassen*).[16] He suffered from being a reclusive victim, from being 'isolated', cruelly left to himself or to his ruthless, uncompromising Other.

It is useful to note, as Ernst Kretschmer[17] did with his concept of *sensitive paranoia*, that the pathological process of paranoia is not only, in certain cases, linked to that of the personality of the paranoiac, but also to the patient's social interactions and relationships as a whole. Indeed, paranoia can be 'reactive', and the paranoiac a 'genuine' persecuted person who is placed in a 'genuine' passive and humiliating situation. To quote Kretschmer: 'We call "reactive" a psychic state in which the lived experience, possibly the situation linked to the environment that gives rise to this state, has not been created solely by the personality itself'.[18] The paranoiac, placed in a feminine victim position, also has their 'authentic' enemies.[19] Gradually excluded and literally 'persecuted' by those around them, who adopt a policing and 'conspiratorial' attitude to this exclusion, they become increasingly 'undesirable', isolated from the group, quarantined and placed in 'secrecy'. As a result, the subject is sometimes a 'real' victim of a paranogenic and fundamentally repelling environment. So, at the outset, the organisation of a persecutory feeling may be the expression of a simple mode of defence against an authentic privation–frustration from a hostile, tormenting, despotic environment that is seriously disconcerting through its senseless violence.[20]

From this perspective, the merit of systems theory was in its inclusion of environmental factors in the genesis of psychotic illness, and counterbalancing the equally simplistic concepts of psychotic constitution or predisposition. It should be remembered that this approach[21] excludes any differential diagnosis, situating the object of reflection not in the individual, but in their interrelationship with the world. Thus, in the system of interactions that is the family, the patient is no longer primarily an individual, but a point of relationship. And the illness appears as the result of a series of pathogenic interactions between the existence of the patient and their environment. Similarly, the parthenogenesis of psychosis originates in a system of constraints in which the future sufferer evolves from childhood. It is this relational system that Gregory Bateson called 'double bind'[22] in 1956.

When the communicative function is impaired, the subject suffers as a result of their early and continuous confrontation with 'ambiguous' or 'paradoxical' messages emitted by the environment. Thus, the 'designated patient' or 'predestined stooge', as Paul-Claude Racamier called them, must 'suffer and survive in paradoxes'.[23] In this way, the patient, the designated victim or 'scapegoat', appears to be the symptom of the parental couple's pathology.

Harold Searles[24] was one of the first psychoanalysts to recognise the value of the Palo Alto School's conception of paradoxes as sources of insurmountable pathogenic internal and intense conflict. This author offers a kind of definition of the very often unconscious 'technique' that involves driving the other person mad. He says: 'The establishment of any interpersonal interaction that tends to foster affective conflict in the other – that tends to make different areas of their personality act against each other – tends to drive him mad'. The various existential modalities identified by the systemic school have also been identified by other, more individual approaches, such as the psychoanalytic school, through clinical observation of the relationship of the psychotic with their mother. As I shall discuss in this chapter, this relationship is dominated by the violence of the arbitrary, frustration, intrusion and persecution.

Micheline Enriquez (1984) neatly sums up the genuine violence suffered by the 'paranoid' person by highlighting the feminine victim position of the latter confronted with the violence of the arbitrary. According to this author, the paranoiac

attempts to resolve at least two major contradictions linked to their encounter with the arbitrary:

a   the arbitrariness of having been subjected by others to the denial of the validity of a perception or experience whose truth and reality they were sure of. (...)
b   the arbitrariness of having undergone this physical and psychic constraint in the name of an ideal, of a supreme value which justifies it, whereas it is only the expression of a hatred, a rejection, an unconscious desire to persecute...

Enriquez adds: 'At the root of all paranoia is the experience of harm, of attack:

–   on meaning, thought, and the right to think;
–   on senses, sensory information and psychic emotions.'[25]

From a clinical point of view, psychoanalysis has undoubtedly made a major contribution to the study of paranoid organisation and the understanding of the mental functioning of this condition, highlighting in particular the importance of the problem of *seduction* and the *feminine* in the determining factors of *paranoia*.

Seduction, femininity, and paranoia

As early as 1895, Freud made a connection between paranoia and childhood memories or sexual scenes. In 1896, he drew distinctions between defensive psychoneuroses, hysteria, obsessional neurosis, and paranoia. In 1897, he connected paranoia with myths about the origin of the child (cf. letter 57 to Fliess, 1897). Then, in 1908, Freud discusses 'Hysterical Phantasies and their Relation to Bisexuality', pointing out that *paranoid phantasies are of the same nature as hysterical phantasies*, but become directly conscious and 'rest on the sadomasochistic components of the sexual instinct'.[26]

Freud repeatedly associated paranoia, directly or indirectly, with infantile sexual memories, sometimes of the most archaic kind. More explicitly, he does so in his 1915 text entitled: 'A Case of Paranoia Running Counter to the Psycho-Analytical Theory of the Disease.'[27] So, although the phantasy of the primal scene is not specific to paranoid manifestations, there is a particularly close link between paranoia and the original phantasy. Indeed, the organisation of impressions (noises,

138 Feminine paranoia

whispers, voices, etc.) in relation to memories buried in the unconscious is frequent in paranoia. This speculative and conjectural elaboration concerning the primal scene–paranoia relationship was essentially carried out by Freud in his study of the 'Wolf Man' (1918b), who presented a form of (hypochondriacal) paranoia. It is worth noting that, in the phantasmatic scene of primordial seduction, the patient takes the place of the mother, in other words, the place of the 'woman' in the subject's imagination. In this way, they can remain 'attached' to this phantasmatic scene, which then becomes dominant in the unconscious psychic content. In these people weakened by the original object relationship and an insecure environment, phantasy spills a long way over into reality.

In the post-Freudian period, Melanie Klein examined the question of the phantasy of parental coitus through child sexual theories in *The Psychoanalysis of Children* (1932b),[28] theorising on the oral incorporation of the paternal penis by the mother. Parental coitus is, thus, internalised in the paranoiac (or the paranoid episode). Remember that in this primordial scene, parents are experienced as bad objects who are subjected to sadistic attacks. Similarly, according to speculative hypotheses, the subject, feeling alienated from the parental union, seeks to dissociate themselves from this alliance that is being formed without them. Through their insistent presence, they attempt to separate the couple from the parents. As a result, the primal scene highlights the paranoiac's difficulties in structuring identification, and a search for 'fusion' in the maternal feminine mode. Beyond the quest for identification with the maternal example, the paranoid subject exercises a kind of psychic union with the mother. The subject's phantasy of oral regression can be seen as an unconscious desire for coitus with the mother[29] and, in this way, an aggression against the paternal penis. It should also be noted that feminine masochism, in what might be called *victim paranoia*, is very often linked to oral phantasies: being greedy, absorbed, intoxicated, poisoned, soiled, sliced, flayed, castrated, penetrated, etc.[30]

In this perspective of the feminine dimension, of the hollow, of receptivity, of orality (incorporation) in paranoia, we note a problem linked to gendered identity structure and identification (introjection). Ida Macalpine and Richard Hunter[31] have developed the idea that beyond unconscious homosexuality, what prevails in the subject are phantasies of male pregnancy and bisexuality. In a way, this condition represents an uncertainty about the reality of differentiated sex or, conversely, the production in reality of the sexual phantasy of the androgynous myth (man and woman at the same time). In this case, the subject is acting out a phantasy of asexual procreation or a 'primitive' conception that has not been successfully and efficiently repressed.

On the other hand, Freud's work succeeded in showing, particularly in his analysis of President Schreber's *Memoirs*, the essential psychic mechanisms at play in paranoid psychosis, emphasising the undeniable importance of the 'paternal complex'. Remember that for Schreber, God is the 'sublimated symbol' of the father *par excellence*.

Consequently, it is suggested that there is a point of fragility in paranoia 'somewhere between the stages of autoeroticism, narcissism and homosexuality'.

According to Freud (1914c), in paranoid psychosis, there is a narcissistic and autoerotic investment of the ego[32] and the secondary function of the delusion is to objectalise the libido, in other words to attempt a transition from narcissistic (ego-) libido to object-libido. Although the delusion supports the sometimes very 'raw' phantastical life (internal reality), it is paradoxically an attempt to maintain the link with the environment (external reality).

Karl Abraham (1908) nevertheless contrasts these two types of investment (narcissistic and objectal) in dementia praecox, and assumes that persecution has an erotic origin, with the persecutor initially being none other than the sexual object itself. Paranoia would, thus, have a clearly autoerotic and homophilic value. It implies a mediated narcissistic relationship. In effect, it is oneself that is reached through the other, designated as the harasser and persecutor. The other is oneself. In this way, the feelings the person attributes to the other are their own affects. The mechanism of projection seems to be predominant here, as though a part of the subject's masculine self has become detached from the now significant feminine part, which returns to them from outside in the form of persecution.

Feminine masochism and paranoia

It should be remembered that Freud and Ferenczi consider paranoia to be inseparable from the reversal of love into hate. Freud[33] writes that he who is now cursed and feared as the persecutor, was once adored and deified. 'The main purpose of the persecution asserted by the patient's delusion is to justify the change in his emotional attitude'. This is particularly evident when the subject indicates one or more familiar objects as persecutors, if not a member of their own immediate family. This is how, for example, the parents themselves, who are collusive and the first targets of affects, are presented as the executioners, responsible for the harassment and hate–rejection to which the subject is victim, particularly when the latter is an only child or more or less explicitly wishes to be (cf. the Schreber case). Here, it is essential to note that the feeling of narcissistic deficiency (original lack) is at the heart of the child's complaints. This recalled and consubstantial feeling is omnipresent in the mind of the adult. Schreber's pain at being 'forsaken' is particularly expressive in this respect.

Referring to the second phase of the 'A Child is Being Beaten' (1919e) phantasy, an unconscious masochistic phase, Freud asserts that subjects with this phantasy 'develop a special sensitiveness and irritability towards anyone whom they can include in the class of fathers', and attempt to realise their fustigation phantasy in which the subject is the object of punishment. Freud then adds: 'I should not be surprised if it were one day possible to prove that the same phantasy is the basis of the delusional litigiousness of paranoia'.[34]

In my clinical practice, I also find this fustigation phantasy in pathological situations of harassment marked by two key factors: sexuality and identity, with the sadistic harasser representing the father. At the same time as the victim–child experiences pleasure at being beaten in the phantasy, they also feel a real sense of filial

140 Feminine paranoia

existence and identity. In other words, the phantasmatic fustigation scene can be read in the opposite way: 'If he beats me, it is because he really is my father.' As a result, this scene reinforces the feeling of filial belonging. It helps address anxious concerns about identity in the sense of the nagging question: 'Who am I?' As a result, the fixation on the scene evokes an uncertainty or lack, sometimes more or less maintained by the mother, regarding the identity of the father (Name-of-the-Father).

As Freud suggested, there is an undeniable link between the phantasy of being beaten, female masochism, and paranoia. Taking up and developing these same ideas, Robert Bak[35] also supported this theory, insisting on the fundamental presence of masochism in paranoia. According to Bak, paranoia represents 'delusional masochism,' and 'homosexuality is sublimated, not original'. Masochism lies at the root of paranoia. Laplanche defended this idea with *Life and Death in Psychoanalysis* and his article 'La position originaire du masochisme dans le champ de la pulsion sexuelle'.[36] For him, 'pathological masochism, Schreiberian masochism,[37] would be a particular, and naturally aberrant, case of this original position of masochism'.[38]

Projection and paranoid persecution

For Freud, delusions of persecution are always the result of projection, which takes the homophilic statement 'I, a man, love a man' and produces first its negation: 'I don't love him, I hate him', then the inversion of persons: 'He doesn't love me, he hates me'. Through this projection, what should be felt internally as love is perceived, from the outside, as hate, and the subject can thus avoid the danger that the irruption of homosexual desires in his consciousness would put him in. (Defensive) projection thus enables the subject to avoid confrontation with their own homosexual phantasies.

It should be noted that in his text on Schreber, Freud admits and recognises the weakness of the projection mechanism in accounting for the problem of paranoia, subtly developing the notion of repression, which is singularly well analysed in 'On Narcissism'. Thus, while admitting the impotence of the projection mechanism at work in paranoia, Freud invites us to look to narcissism and repression in the advent and development of persecutory delusions. In this sense, Freud affirms: 'We may say, then, that the process of repression proper consists in a detachment of the libido from people – and things – that were previously loved'. The object-libido is converted into narcissistic libido, which contributes to the formation of the megalomaniac delusion in the sense of a regression-fixation to the ideal, omnipotent ego.

Moreover, the delusion has a defensive virtue in the verbal production of persecution. It is even salutary against the onslaught of self-destructive impulses. The delusion also appears as a means for the paranoiac to ensure the cohesion of their ego, while at the same time recreating reality. But the delusion authorises and externalises the subject's regression. As Freud showed, it is a question of regression for the paranoid subject, to the stage of fundamental narcissism. For Klein, all psychosis reveals a state of fixation or regression to an infantile primary stage. Persecution develops precociously, because in the relationship with the primary (partial) object represented by the breast, a cleavage appears very early on, through this maternal organ, which can appear at times as ideal and good, and at other times as persecuting and bad, during the stage that Klein specifically calls paranoid. It is, thus, possible to imagine that the paranoid reaction may be based on the revival of the subject's early contradictory affects towards the first object figure, partially represented by the breast.

Lacan's foreclosure of the Name-of-the-Father

Like Freud, Lacan highlights the decisive role of the paternal complex in paranoid organisation, notably in his seminar on psychoses (1955–1956), by emphasising the notion of *foreclosure*. He says:

> What is at issue when I speak of Verwerfung? At issue is the rejection of a primordial signifier into the outer shadows, a signifier that will henceforth be missing at this level. Here you have the fundamental mechanism that I point as being at the basis of paranoia. It's a matter of a primordial process of exclusion of an original within, which is not a bodily within but that of an initial body of signifiers.[39]

Lacan maintains that what is deficient in the paranoiac is the paternal metaphor, in other words the signifier of the Father (the Name-of-the-Father) and, hence, the 'phallus' signifier. This is foreclosure because instead of the Name-of-the-Father, there is a chasm that creates a hole in the subject corresponding to the place of the phallic signifier, producing in them a dark and disquieting distress when confronted with this phallic signifier.

If the metaphor of the Name-of-the-Father doesn't occur, or at least if its process fails in such a way that the Name-of-the-Father signifier doesn't replace the signifier of the primordial object of the mother's desire, it follows that the entire psychic organisation will be disrupted. Lacan defines this as the 'foreclosure of the Name-of-the-Father'. He highlights the idea that the foreclosure of the Name-of-the-Father is linked to the mother's disqualification of the true father's authority. 'For psychosis to be triggered', writes Lacan, 'the Name-of-the-Father – *verworfen*, foreclosed, that is, never having come to the place of the Other – must be summoned to that place in symbolic opposition to the subject'.[40]

It is in this perspective that Schreber's psychosis begins, at the very moment when he is called upon to occupy a symbolic function of authority himself; in other words, to symbolically take the place of the father, an assumption of paternity to which he can only react with acute hallucinatory manifestations.[41] The construction of his delusion will provide a solution, replacing the failing paternal metaphor with a 'delusional metaphor', designed to give meaning to what for him is totally devoid of it, to create his own reality through the emergence of phantasy in the external world.

As for unconscious homosexuality, in Schreber's case we should speak not only of transexuation, that is, a process of devirilisation marked by castration, but also

142 Feminine paranoia

of genuine *androgynisation*, in the sense that, I recall, he writes: 'I have to imagine myself as man and woman in one person having intercourse with myself, or somehow have to achieve with myself ...' (MNI, p. 250). This delusional process of androgynisation is not subordinated to the desire for another man, but to his mother's relationship with the paternal metaphor and, thus, with the phallus. The child is, in effect, obliged to be this maternal phallus. As Lacan states in his Écrits: 'unable to be the phallus that the mother is missing, there remained the solution of being the woman that men are missing'[42] or the woman of God (the Father).

Primitive homosexual hatred and paranoia

In 'Quelqu'un a tué quelque chose' [Someone has killed something], Piera Aulagnier (1986)[43] points out that the psychotic, schizophrenic or paranoiac, has lived with a parental couple cemented by hatred. 'The person who is no longer an *infans*,' she writes, '"will hear" hatred and the desire for murder circulating in the couple. But what about before that moment? What about the effects on the origins of the violence tearing apart the surrounding psychic milieu?'[44] In this sense, the 'parental scene' dominated by hatred between the protagonists is different from the 'primal scene' marked by the parents' loving interactions.

Note that while the relationship to the mother is central when it comes to schizophrenia, in paranoia it is the relationship to the 'combined' and 'tangled' couple that is fundamental. Thus, Schreber's primal scene may have been marked by the amalgamation and association of the two parental imagos, maternal and paternal, breast and penis.

Similarly, I would speculate that, despite Schreber's mother's 'subjection' to her husband, there was a 'silent' relationship of hatred in the parental couple. This was revealed indirectly in the aggressive, intrusive upbringing by Schreber's tyrannical, invasive, and frustrating father, and his mother's no less aggressive 'silence'. For, beyond the mother's incompetence in 'educating' her son implied by the father, the son's deprivation also concerns the mother more widely. It is *the* primary relationship of pleasure that is controlled and sometimes prohibited by the separating father. As well as frustrating the son, the father also deprives the mother (his wife) of the primary seductive relationship. By invading the maternal realm in this way, the frustrater father, who was said to have some appalling character traits, penetrated and shattered the particular intimacy between the mother and the child in her arms. He disturbed this reciprocity and the immanent co-excitation of the generalised seduction scene developed by Laplanche. Schreber senior's prohibition, seeking to remove all sexuality from self-preservation, was addressed 'as much *to the mother* as to the child'. In fact, these censures banished maternal excitation at the same time. In this sense, Jacqueline Lanouzière writes:

> Drawing on the ideas formulated by Dr. Schreber concerning the conjugal libidinal life, reduced to its simplest expression in order to make desire last, a prolonged form of the art of renunciation inculcated in children, we can indeed

assume that Daniel-Paul's mother, like Catarina, may have experienced particular difficulty in repressing her erotic drives that the baby, in the absence of the father, could satisfy, finding himself placed somewhat like Leonardo in the position of a complete sexual object.[45]

The mother's hatred of her husband is consequently expressed in some way through the son's illness and other pathologies in the siblings, such as the suicide of Schreber's sister. In this way, the son's paranoia is, by identification, one of the mother's evident expressions of her 'contained' antipathy towards the father. We could say that the son identifies with the woman whose original prototype is quite simply the figure of the mother. Likewise, Schreber sees himself as the passive, submissive feminine through the person of his own wife. Her miscarriages engender in him a mixture of hatred and melancholy compassion.

Moreover, for Piera Aulagnier,

> the psychotic is the person who cannot think of the *function* independently of the characters who were for him the first representatives and become it forever. He cannot think of himself as *a* son, but only as *the* son of the latter, instead of recognising the chain of generations in which the parental function succeeds the filial function, and in which he himself would thus be in a position to exercise it in turn and pass it on to his children.[46]

This point of view is all the more pertinent when it concerns an only child (cf. the following clinical observation), whose separation from the parental couple proves to be a highly problematic operation.

It would seem that the relationship of persecution, although initially real, subsequently helps the psychic survival, or even survival itself, of a person who claims to be a 'victim' of this situation. This person thus appears curiously loyal to their initial suffering. This is how Aulagnier puts it: 'In order to preserve their life, the "I" is obliged to invest this other, another, "I" or anonymous agency, who is supposed to want their death, to hold the power and become the cause of it'.[47] Thus, to exist, the damaged subject needs to unconsciously 'create' and designate their persecutor. In order to be, they need to suffer and occupy the position of victim. From the original genuine victim, the person unwittingly becomes a 'consenting' secondary victim. Masochistic pleasure serves as a bulwark against mortifying impulses and destruction. And persecution becomes an unconscious strategy in the fight against suicide.

Seduction, frustration, and harassment in feminine paranoia

Psychopathological psychic harassment, whether interpersonal and sexual, or intrasubjective and 'moral' in origin, cannot be dissociated from its origins in the theory of seduction that was explored in great depth by Laplanche.[48] The inoculation

144 Feminine paranoia

of a primary trauma, in other words the intromission or implantation of *le sexual* in the child–adult object relationship, reappears in reality. What was experienced early on comes back in the present reality. It returns. Following Lacan and a number of other authors, Laplanche presented a way of examining the genesis of psychoses by working on two notions linked to the untranslatability of enigmatic signifiers: intromission (failure *to* translate), which makes up pathological states, and implantation (failure *of* translation), which acts in normative neurotic states.[49]

On the other hand, in people with a persecutory and victim-orientated organisation, we regularly find in their history feelings of lack and deprivation, which are quite simply *a priori* and original complaints. In this respect, in her text 'Schreber et le sein' [Schreber and the breast],[50] Lanouzière stressed the 'sexual', particularly oral, frustrations endured by Schreber in early childhood. The mother, invaded by Schreber's father, deliberately 'frustrated' her son in fundamental exchanges and 'early seduction'. In effect, she virtually 'deprived' him of any sensation associated with oral pleasure, with the aim of instilling in him the art of renunciation for his 'well-being'. But such pain and torment inflicted on the child, Lanouzière writes,

> ... in addition to the rage and despair that such a will can arouse, the breast cannot be fantasised as an object whose withdrawal is linked to the existence of a sexual rival for whom it is intended and who demands it, and thus linked to the elaboration of a first oral primitive scene, but as an attribute of absolute and arbitrary power' (p. 36).

The mother does not deprive her child for the sake of another, within the perspective of Oedipal regulation, but for the sake of an imposed moral and educational foundation. Thus, the child, unable to elaborate and overcome the loss, is invaded by the obsessive persecution of the idea of renunciation. In this way, he becomes a 'victim' of the primordial lack to which he is subjected by the combined parental couple, which is nevertheless governed by the father in the case of the son's paranoia.

Daniel[51]

Twenty-three-year-old Daniel, whose gender identity is at first difficult to recognise,[52] is a young man with the frail physique of a smooth-cheeked teenager.

The stereotyped, prim speech, monotonous in tone and delivered without discontinuation, is dominated by feelings of terrible injustice, immoral and 'criminal' abandonment, of being a 'sacrificial victim', and even 'scapegoat for all the world's misfortunes'.

From this young man's story, we learn that he is the only child in the family. Daniel's satisfactory studies led him to prepare for the entrance exam to the prestigious *Grandes Écoles*. But 'psychological problems', he explains, prevented him from pursuing his studies as he had wished. So, at the age of twenty-one, he left his parents to join a large company as a 'trainee auditor'. A year later, he is, he says,

'... against (his) will, officially placed on long-term sick leave by his superiors'. He also complains a great deal about his parents, who he believes abandoned him.[53]

Still, despite his 'fierce opposition', the care staff at the clinic where Daniel was receiving treatment, 'taking into account the opinion of (his) parents, forced, obliged and compelled him against (his) will to undertake colossal expenses... to move into housing' and consequently separate him from the parental couple. In addition to becoming a victim of a 'terrible financial catastrophe', he felt that his condition (in contrast to his defence formulated above) dominated by regression, incapacity, and disability, meant an almost permanent presence and attention from his loved ones was indispensable. Daniel repeatedly expresses the major fear of being, like Schreber, 'forsaken', sacrificed, abandoned, abused'. Castration anxiety (emasculation) and oral frustration are also evident in Daniel's comments, in which he refers to his parents as being guilty of having 'cut him off'.

> Persisting in his complaint and expressing his need for support and help, he writes: My behaviour clearly showed that I was totally incapable of leading an autonomous life in a home independent of my parents. My behaviour was extremely infantile, puerile, and I presented significant intellectual and emotional delay. It was essential for me to continue to be supported for a long time by living with my parents.

So, while Schreber reproaches God for his selfishness, our patient complains of his parents' insensitivity, and more particularly of the indifference of the father described by the son as an individualist. In this regard, consider what Schreber writes in his *Memoirs* about God's selfishness: 'These egoistic actions have been practised against me for years with the utmost cruelty and disregard as only a beast deals with its prey'. (*MNI* p. 308). Here, and more generally, the figure of God cannot be separated from that of the Father. Similarly, the selfish, even sadistic, aims denounced today by the son are, of course, linked to the ancient, cruel frustrations experienced by the subject in early childhood. These same frustrations are obviously, as I stressed earlier, of a sexual nature. It is a trauma associated with the primordial sexual deprivation in the bond between child and mother, the primary homosexual relationship.[54]

Maintaining his accusations against and denouncement of his 'torturers', Daniel, in a logic of inferences (the discourse is most often supported by mathematical equations) concludes and deduces that the hospital and its staff whose 'mission is to care and heal, deliberately provoked suicidal tendencies in (him),' due to his isolation and confinement 'in a cell,'[55] but also due to his parents' failure to monitor his compliance with his medication. On this subject, he threatens: 'If I took all the drugs at once, which are accumulating at home in enormous quantities, I'm quite sure I'd succeed in committing suicide, because I'd have swallowed the lethal dose several times over'. Here, the medication evokes the ancient Greek *pharmakon*, in that it possesses the dual properties of both remedy and poison. But, in paranoia, where regression–fixation to the oral stage is significant, medicine is often received

146   Feminine paranoia

as a harmful, foreign element, confused with the threatening persecutor. By refusing to accept what may be hidden (*caché*) in the drug (*cachet?*), Daniel is expressing his distrust and regressive suffering, potentially linked to the displeasure (bad breast) and oral frustration he experienced at an early age.

Feminine masochistic impulses, in their extreme expression of jouissance, are concretely translated into an attempt at anorexia that could be described, on a conscious level, as rational and economic, or even strategic, since the subject's aim is to drastically reduce the 'expenditure on food... to go on hunger strike'. Daniel thus threatens to sacrifice himself rather than make great sacrifices, by choosing undernourishment as a solution.[56] However, this was somewhat unsuccessful since, after several days of forced starvation, he was subjected, he claims, to 'horrible physical suffering and atrocious torture' which led him to put an end to this forced and coercive fast.

The hymn to death and its drive are omnipresent in Daniel's life. For him, happiness is to be found in death. In 'It's happiness to die' – the title is in English – he writes: 'There is nothing more wonderful than death'. The annihilation of life is particularly eroticised. He adds: 'I am condemned to eat... like an animal,'[57] and 'condemned to live a life without life, a life without death'. Here again, the ambivalent feeling of both cruelty and omnipotence (the experience of immortality) is particularly prevalent. The megalomania is at its height, as the 'martyr' of all persecutions; he presents himself as the 'victim of hatred, of the hostility of everyone who is predisposed to attack (him) and commit the worst atrocities against (him). ...'

But, as a victim of others, he is also a victim of himself, through a kind of inter- and intra-systemic cleavage, of the introjected and/or incorporated 'Other' within himself (cleavage of the ego). The complex and complementary relationship between a masochistic ego and a sadistic superego is evident here: '... My splitting in two that is with me incessantly, tortures me as excruciatingly as if my body were sliced in two with a gigantic blade that wanted to divide me into two parts, to split my body. ...'

Ultimate masochism and victim sacrifice find expression in a handwritten request to the public prosecutor in which he 'demands' his death by euthanasia or self-murder, forced, he says, to put an end to all the 'atrocious and horrible torture and suffering' to which he would fall prey. An immolated sacrificial victim, he also voluntarily wants to put himself to death 'so that society no longer suffers all the damaging acts that people impose (on him) to accomplish by telepathy. ...'

Despite the significant amount collected from the subject, who essentially tells of his state as a victim and his negative feelings, I met with Daniel on only two occasions, knowing that he would continue to benefit from therapeutic follow-up within the context of the sector's medical–psychological service. It was during the second session that he gave me a copy of two documents addressed to the magistrate. These were two manuscripts about a hundred pages long. In a very loose style of writing, marked by a profusion of superlatives that attempt to emphasise his role as victim, the patient, like Schreber,[58] amply describes his 'personal vicissitudes' and his internal and external harassment.

The transcribed complaint is frantic and poignant. In the first manuscript, Daniel cries out in writing, recording his grievances with his parents, who, according to the patient, are in league with the nursing staff for abandonment ('leaving [him] forsaken'), and seeks help, mainly from his parents, in order to benefit from their assistance and find solutions to his financial problems.

In the second document, the subject pleads for an end to his suffering by simply ending his life. In particular, he expresses his 'request for euthanasia to put a definitive end to the atrocious torture, and horrible physical suffering, Dantean torments'.

Having given this succinct presentation of a few elements of Daniel's life and some of his singular grievances, I shall specifically highlight the dominant themes in connection with the 'feminine' position in an organisation of a 'paranoid' type, and make as many links as possible with Schreber's productions in his *Memoirs* and Freud's analysis of them in the 'The Schreber Case'.

Both Schreber, a martyr in his own way, and my patient, complain in writing about their place as victim: one by writing his memoirs, the other by recounting his setbacks. They also both bemoan the permanent disturbances (*Störungen*), psychic harassments and other tortures of the mind (*MNI*, p. 291) that, Screber says, 'are beyond human comprehension'. Passivated and feminised, confined to the position of victim, he, like my patient, demands 'a reward... for the pains and privations I have suffered' (*MNI*, p. 290). Both report the 'violence' of their family environment, as relayed by medical staff.

When the worst is yet to come in persecution

The paranoiac dreads the future. They fear what or who awaits them. They fear the worst and traps. They distrust what or who cannot be seen. It is in this way that Daniel, in a deluge of superlatives, declares:

'This is the sinister, tragic, horrible, appalling, awful, atrocious, Dantesque, monstrous future that awaits me. This is how my existence will evolve'. Similarly, he writes: 'My future therefore turns out to be entirely catastrophic, and I am truly threatened by the most terrible misfortunes imaginable'.

This apprehension about tomorrow is also prevalent in Schreber's speech: 'I'll become a corpse, who'll be on the pavement and not in an amphitheatre' or 'What's going to happen to this cursed story?' The future is so dreaded that it is also represented under the guise of a terrifying, persecuting living being: 'My future is an enemy waiting for me at the corner of the street, hiding round the corner', says Daniel. This intense anxiety about tomorrow seems to be linked to a troubled ego and its identity. The ego seems to be stricken by dislocation, even dissolution: 'What am I going to become? Who am I?' says Schreber. The subject feels that he is disjointed and fragmented. Everything within and around him is broken. Nothing holds together. The alteration of identity and the uncertainty of the ego engender a more general uncertainty in the face of reality. This would explain, by inverse reaction, the paranoiac's need for certainty in their relationships with others. In effect, they

148 Feminine paranoia

constantly need to provide proof, logic, and evidence attesting to their innocence and their status as a victim.

Transformation, division, and splitting of the self

In victim paranoia, the subject's ego is also disunited. It transforms itself and takes on other, sometimes antagonistic identities. It can, thus, become a double and contradictory character, both victim and persecutor. A martyr to their own unconscious, the oscillating, variable ego is multiplied:

> I'm constantly changing person and I never stay myself. I transform incessantly into a multitude of different people. So I'm nobody and everybody at the same time, which is absolutely atrocious and appalling. I split myself into an invisible person who accompanies me incessantly, torturing me just as horribly. …'

We find these same feelings of loss of identity, or of a strange and sinister experience of multiple threatening personalities that abolish or suffocate the original subject, according to Schreber's statements. He writes: 'I had possessed several individualities under one and the same skull... A man with several heads', or, in the sense of Cotard's syndrome, when he evokes his split and disunited body: 'I am a leprous corpse, dragging behind me another leprous corpse'. It is a genuine sensation of depersonalisation and a frightening loss of identity that violently affects the paranoid subject. He is prey to an authentic dispossession of the body. Indeed, it is precisely the body that is affected or 'escapes' the subject. Thus, the loss concerns the ego in its entirety; that is to say, in its full and absolute psychosomatic entity.

Logical loss and the logic of loss

Invaded by ideas of lack and castration, the paranoid subject seems doomed to lose. This loss is based on rigorous and implacable argumentation. It is, according to the person, 'logical'. As Lacan pointed out more generally, psychosis is a veritable 'attempt at rigour'. An almost logical–mathematical attempt. Indeed, in paranoia, there is a hyper-investment in mathematical science as Law.[59] The subject thus seeks to skilfully place 'arguments' and other discursive 'demonstrations' to formally attest to their feminine position as victim, the proof of lack. The mathematical discourse of the paranoiac attempts to support the subject's uncomfortable and harmful position through the axioms included. Paranoia is an attempt at logic that provides irrefutable material proof.

'My future is the tragic result of the inequation: expenses > income, which implies the equation: expenses – income = decrease and exhaustion of savings. This equation becomes expenditure – income = debt, bailiffs, overdraft, eviction from home, then homelessness'. Through this infallible and alarmist reasoning, Daniel expresses his suffering from giving more than he receives. 'Inequation donation > receipt = debt', he asserts. In this argumentation, where the logic of loss and complaint is resolutely put forward, the subject clearly feels 'cheated', 'robbed', 'emptied', 'abused'. The victim of a conspiracy, he feels obliged and condemned to lose.

We find similar relentless reasoning in Schreber who clearly demonstrates the injustice and persecution of which he is the victim: 'As for me, I have a truly overwhelming body of arguments in favour of its veracity. …' Schreber attempts to bring to light the evidence and reveal the charges against the people who persecute and harass him: unimpeachable, cruel evidence that, in his words, 'go beyond human comprehension'.

Like the melancholic, the paranoid subject also complains of relentless loss. In this respect, Daniel says he gives too much in spite of himself, giving too much because he is influenced by the environment that forces and threatens him. Drawing on a diagnosis of his mental disorders, he denounces the conspiracy that was hatched against him.

> The fact of spending enormous sums of money, as I did, or to be more precise, as I was forced to do, is a mental pathology. Indeed, the manic attacks of manic-depressive psychosis, an extremely serious mental illness, prompt the patient to spend vast amounts, beyond his means.

He adds, probably inspired by nosographic definitions borrowed from classic psychiatric and psychopathological textbooks[60]:

> During manic episodes, the patient is extremely enthusiastic, motivated, redoubles his energy and has visions of grandeur. He undertakes a multitude of grand projects, and in particular, spends enormous sums of money. And the patient is completely unaware of the pathological aspect of his behaviour. In the space of a few days, the patient ruins himself completely during a manic episode, and when he runs out of money and is in debt, he enters a depressive phase antagonistic to the manic behaviour... In this way, the nursing staff at the centre forced me, coerced me and made me, against my will, have manic episodes, incurring colossal, enormous and gigantic expenses, whereas their role, their mission is to cure, treat, avoid and prevent manic episodes in patients suffering from manic-depressive psychosis. This is extremely serious and totally unacceptable. It must be severely punished and sanctioned at both a criminal and disciplinary level.

Schreber, for his part, insists in his writings on the constraints imposed upon him. He wrote, for example, that he was forced to *think non-stop* (imperative of the continuity of thought). In the same logic of having 'thought too much' [*trop pensé*] and enslavement to the other, my patient complains of being abused and forced to spend (*dé-penser*) without counting, being obliged to *pay*. Spending is experienced by the subject as a harrowing loss that can lead to decline. Both Daniel and Schreber relate their torment, which is notably linked to the continuous 'too much of too much', the 'excess of excess'. Regarding this excess, one suffers from thinking too

150 Feminine paranoia

much, or thinking relentlessly, while the other complains of spending too much, or spending relentlessly. Indeed, one thinks (*pense*) ... the other spends (*dé-pense*). Schreber's compulsion to speculate is replaced in my patient by the compulsion to calculate. There is a kind of infinite, free, and uncontrollable haemorrhaging of self that evokes the melancholic feminine inclination of the paranoid subject.

Stolen thoughts and lost identity

Xenopathic phenomena are evident in paranoia. These include the 'dispossession of the self' (Lévy-Valensi), the 'dissidence of the self' (de Clérambault) and the experience of the self as 'a foreign body' (Ey). The subject regularly expresses this phenomenon of self-subtraction in the sense of a loss of identity, where being and having merge: 'I am (have) [*est (ai)*] no longer myself'. The subject experiences a feeling of veritable confiscation of the self, a stranglehold on the whole person. So, in addition to the body, it is reason that is attacked. For Schreber, this type of psychic intrusion leads to the liquidation[61] of his subjectivity, his individuality. Consequently, the 'soul murder' (*Seelenmord*) or 'soul abduction' (*Seelenraub)* from which Schreber suffers not only involves 'the surrender of a soul to another person' or 'appropriating his mental powers' (*MNI*, p. 38), but, beyond theft or loss, it is a genuine destruction in the sense of ripping away the most cherished part of oneself: one's intimacy and thoughts. Schreber's many complaints of castration or emasculation (*Entmannung*) are particularly eloquent in this respect. It is a question of extirpating the male identity and transforming into a woman. Torture of the body is accompanied by 'mental torture', says Schreber (*MNI*, p. 128, note 63).

Daniel affirms this same unbearable, frightening and torturing experience. He writes: 'In addition to atrocious physical suffering, horrible, atrocious, dreadful and appalling moral torture is incessantly added'.

This particularly painful sensation of mental torture is permanent. It is all the more cruel because the supposed culprits are, at first sight, imperceptible. Nowhere is the subject at peace.

> I hereby lodge a complaint against a number of people who are morally torturing me telepathically. These people morally torture me by imposing thoughts on me that are foreign and painful. There are also other people who steal my thoughts, and I want them punished with at least ten years in prison and a fine of at least one hundred thousand francs.

They're stealing my thoughts, so I no longer have any thoughts. So there's absolutely nothing I think that goes unnoticed. All my ideas are then known by the people who steal my thoughts. And on top of that, these people use my thoughts to hurt me. These people who steal my ideas divulge my thoughts and ideas to others, so that everyone knows and understands what I am thinking.

With regard to the painful feeling of psychic transparency, Schreber also suffers from the guessing of his thoughts by others: 'The rays I am dealing with, insatiably eager as they are to know constantly what I am thinking'. He suffers from moral plundering, from an appropriation of his ideas and other interests by others: '... the surrender of a soul to another person perhaps for prolonging early life, for appropriating his mental powers, for attaining a kind of personal immunity or some other advantage ...' (*MNI*, p. 38).

The body hears

Although the paranoid subject cannot see his harassers, he nevertheless cannot stop hearing them. In fact, it is the body in its entirety that hears them. The body is specifically infiltrated and traversed by the voices. Whereas visual hallucinations retain an exteriority, auditory aggression is a genuine intrusion into the body. As a result, auditory hallucinations are experienced in an intensely intrusive, penetrating and persecutory mode. In this respect, Daniel writes:

> I very often hear voices... In fact, it's not with my ears that I hear these voices speaking to me. I usually hear all these voices speaking to me with my kneecap at knee level, with my feet, with my pancreas, with my intestine or with my lungs. So I'm really not deaf. In fact, I'm the opposite of deaf, since I can hear voices even though no one is talking to me, and there's absolute silence around me.[62] Even if I put 'who is that?' balls in my ears, the noise of the voices speaking to me is not diminished, since I hear these voices with organs other than my ears. What's more, all these voices are constantly saying abusive things to me, and really nasty things.

Insults are a fundamental feature of the clinical phenomenology of paranoia. In his delusional and hallucinatory production, Daniel adds: 'Numbered voices speak to such-and-such an organ at such-and-such a time. For example, voice Number...' These auditory phenomena also predominate throughout Schreber's delusional narrative. He evokes harassing, dangerous voices that break in and overlay his body: 'Internal voices that have been talking to me non-stop ever since'; 'The voices that penetrate me, loaded with poison from a corpse, preserve the poison's harmful power for as long as possible.'

Hearing appears here to be linked to origins. We know that the paranoiac progressively replays their painful past marked by persecution from the early years of their life. Indeed, in every hallucination there is 'the return of a forgotten event from the earliest years, of something the child saw or heard at a time when he could barely speak'.[63]

Similarly, through the incessant harassment of the voices, the subject expresses their displeasure at hearing their own thoughts. It is worth recalling that for Freud (1896),[64] the voices a paranoiac can hear 'could not be memories that were being produced in a hallucinatory way, like the images and sensations, but were rather thoughts that were being "said aloud" [*Laut gewordene*]'. The voices may also have their origin in the repression of thoughts that have the significance of reproaches

152 Feminine paranoia

provoked by an event similar to the childhood trauma. They are symptoms of the return of the repressed, but at the same time, adds Freud, these voices are 'consequences of a compromise between the resistance of the ego and the power of the returning repressed – a compromise which in this instance had brought about a distortion that went beyond recognition' (*id.*).

In paranoia, the repressed reproach uses the defensive route of projection. The subject becomes suspicious of others, but especially of their own ideas attributed to others. It is the 'other' who influences their thinking. As a result, the reproaches that recur in delusional ideas have no protection, since they are addressed to the other, the persecutor.

The anxiety of being 'forsaken'

The victim usually emphasises the plot that is being hatched against them. The subject feels abused, passivated, constantly forced to act and be according to external decisions and judgements imposed on them. As a result, they call for help. They ask for protection and assistance. There is the spectre and threat of danger everywhere. It is clear to Daniel that salvation can only come from the parents who have failed in their duty to support their only son. So he complains that he has been harshly excluded and distanced from the family environment, or, more precisely, from the parental couple; that is to say, in some way deprived of the ancient pleasure of the Oedipal relationship: 'To top it all off, there are aggravating circumstances surrounding the fact that the (medical) staff forced me to move into accommodation independent of my parents' home.' With these words, the patient clearly expresses his need for attention and care, but also his belittling of himself, even his infantilism and regression:

> My state of health makes it essential that I always live in the presence of someone who watches over me to make sure I don't fall ill, in this case at my parents' home... incapable... impossible to live alone... unable to live in accommodation independent of my parents' home ...'

It is necessary 'that I always live in the presence of someone ... Otherwise,' adds Daniel, 'I would constantly be committing puerile, infantile acts, worthy of a five-year-old.'

In his *Memoirs*, Schreber denounces the outside forces working against him. They are said to take advantage of his invalidity and his 'femininity' to sacrifice him in some way, to offer him body and soul to his enemies:

> In this a plot was laid against me... the purpose of which was to hand me over to another human being after my nervous illness had been recognized as such, or assumed to be, incurable, in such a way that my soul was handed to him, but my body – transformed into a female body and, misconstruing the above-described fundamental tendency of the Order of the World – was then left to that human being for sexual misuse and simply "forsaken" in other words left to rot' (*MNI*, p. 68).

The terror of being abandoned, left to fend for himself, is constant. Being alone, with no support, becomes a fearsome and unbearable ordeal that evokes the idea of infanticide: 'A child is killed'. The feeling of isolation leads to a feeling of a slow, violent death. In this regard, Schreber writes: 'The dread of "being forsaken" played a major role, so that every night I went to bed in my padded cell I doubted whether the door would open again at all in the morning' (*MNI*, p. 98).

Feminine masochism and persecution

The expression of a 'feminine' position reaches its peak when, in the person's assertions, they feel continuously harassed, when persecution is at its height. The cruellest thing is that the victim 'carries' within themselves the antagonistic other self that torments and persecutes them. Like their shadow, their double accompanies them everywhere: 'There's an invisible person who's always with me, who wants to hurt me.' The persecutor can multiply on the outside. And it is the person's whole environment that takes on the face of hatred.

> Everyone has a grudge against me, everyone criticises me, points the finger at me and is constantly reproaching me, violently, horribly. I'm the scapegoat for all the world's misfortunes and for everything people hate. So I am incessantly subjected to the anger, rage, fury, irritation, wrath, and hostility of all these people... I am the victim of everyone's hatred, hostility, rage, anger, fury, abuse and insults.

In terms of linguistic expression, it is interesting to observe the hyperbolic aspect: strength of the words, accumulation of related signifiers (anger, rage, fury), emphasis, lyricism and so on. There's a kind of inflation of meaning (related to the inflation of the ego?).[65] What is the function of the discourse in this excessive metaphorisation? Is it to compensate for the foreclosure of the signifier of the Name-of-the-Father?

The word repairs the lack. It is 'magic', writes Freud in 1890 in 'Psychical Treatment'. In this sense, it can have a curative value. In psychosis, however, we should remember that words are subject to the primary process. Like acts, they are unbound, reflecting a verbal discharge of internal psychocorporeal excitation. In this form of auto-therapy, the bad is expelled through verbal language. Words are discharged from the mouth in the same way as anal excrement.[66] Like an evil foreign body, language inhabits and possesses the psychotic person, who therefore needs to constantly eject it from themselves.

A martyr inside and out, Daniel writes:

> I am therefore a victim of the worst atrocities and horrors that can exist in the world... I am systematically beaten and kicked. Everyone systematically wants to shoot me down, whereas I always want to go up... I am incessantly pursued and attacked by various and multiple creatures and occult forces. I am invaded by ghosts and spirits that gnaw and suck at my body.

154 Feminine paranoia

In his *Memoirs*, Schreber describes at length the persistent and general malevolence of his environment, which is unleashed against him. For example, he complains of 'insults thrown in [my] face', 'verbal and physical attacks ...' (*MNI*, p. 283) as well as the 'unceasing talk of voices causing mental unrest' (*MNI*, p. 302). Schreber was constantly receiving abuse. The environment was totally hostile to him. He saw himself, he says, as the enemy to be destroyed (*MNI*, p. 153), 'passing him off' as someone 'other' by 'shaping' his mood. His status as a martyr is restated everywhere. As a whipping boy, for example, in his conflicts with the other residents: 'in all instances concerning other *patients* I was always the attacked party' (*MNI*, p. 181).

All these misfortunes, which explain the strange and unpleasant feeling of being the target of external ferocity in collusion with internal violence, lead the subject to demand 'reward ... for the pains and privations I have suffered' (*MNI*, p. 290), the reparation of *pretium doloris*. In this regard, Schreber presents himself as the helpless prey against his offenders. He writes: 'These egoistic actions have been practiced against me for years with the utmost cruelty and disregard as only a beast deals with its prey' (*MNI*, p. 308).

It should be noted that in the paranoid delusion, beyond the psychic torment dominated by harassment, the patient undergoes a hallucinatory physical ordeal. Thus, for example, Daniel reports the extensive bodily torture and sadism to which he is subjected:

> My numerous torturers incessantly amuse themselves by sticking numerous knives and sharp blades, heated red-hot, into my body, which tortures me horribly and excruciatingly... Blacksmiths incessantly strike my feet by giving them violent blows with anvils and very heavy hammers to break and fragment them.

Paranoia somatica

In paranoia, persecution affects and gnaws away at the inside of the subject's body, which is both its object and its source. In effect, the subject is attacked from within by the inside of their body: the aggression is also internal. The pain is profound. Destructive and deadly impulses are specifically at work against the person. Daniel abundantly describes his painful organic experiences, a situation in which everything seems blocked off. Life seems fully threatened:

> My nose and nasal passages are constantly blocked and obstructed. I am tortured with excruciating agonies of choking. My throat is constantly tightened, contracted as if I were incessantly in agony being strangled by someone or undergoing hanging. My thorax is constantly and violently irritated by excruciating torture and by extremely violent and acute pain. In fact, my thorax is constantly and incessantly devastated by a gigantic and enormous fire within. I'm suffering all the atrocious tortures of a person burned alive at the stake... My abdomen is also the site of atrocious torture and absolutely horrible, unimaginable pain. In fact, as far as my abdomen is concerned, everything is going on as if there were

a violent, relentless and merciless war between, on the one hand, the contents, the interior, which wants to get out, to disseminate itself in the outside world, and on the other hand, the peripheral walls which prevent it from doing so... My stomach constantly and incessantly manufactures violent poisons that intoxicate me and torture me atrociously, and these poisons spread throughout my body to make me suffer atrociously... My legs constantly threaten to collapse under the colossally heavy weight of my body. My legs will then collapse, dragging everything, absolutely everything, in their path, which will be a horrible, dreadful apocalypse. My feet are extremely painful... And to top it all off, the entire surface of my skin is constantly crossed by violent and excruciating itches that irritate me colossally in an incessant and infernal way... My horrible sufferings and excruciating tortures are multiplied by the number of entities of cells or molecules there are in my body, that is to say by billions of billions of times... These occult forces and spirits that constantly assault me have fun pummelling, fiddling with my intestines and guts and twisting them into an inextricable and infinite number of knots, each of which hurts terribly.

The imperialism of the discourse ('crowning') is at its peak. There is also an abundance of mathematical metaphor. We constantly see use of addition (of terms), multiplication to infinity (of suffering), division (of the body down to its smallest cells) and so on.

Let us not forget that Schreber, too, devotes a great deal of space in his collection to his physical torments. In particular, he describes the degradation of his bodily integrity and the persistent attacks on his internal organs (*MNI*, p. 142 *ff.*). In his *Memoirs,* he writes:

the whole perfidy of the policy conducted towards me is clear. Whenever the need to defecate is produced by miracle, some other person in my environment is sent to the lavatory – by exciting the nerves of the person concerned – in order to prevent me from emptying myself; this I have observed so frequently (thousands of times) and so regularly that one can exclude any thought of it being coincidence (*MNI*, p. 206).

In paranoia, investment in numbers is significant. It is used as irrefutable support, indisputable proof. Chance has no place in the persecutory speech I characterise as 'paranological' [*paranologique*].

The question of the persecuting body, in particular, features prominently in the work of Piera Aulagnier. For this author, this form of somatic paranoia involves a displacement of the persecutory relationship and hatred towards the parents on to the body. 'The subject introjects persecution and hatred, becoming the battleground for a persecuted–persecutor relationship between their own I and their own body'. The body is perceived as both victim and aggressor. The subject, violated and attacked from within, has this strange and testing sensation, as though their body were inhabited by a demonic and malevolent foreign body.

In 'La filiation persécutive' [Persecuting parenting], Aulagnier[67] writes:

> A relationship in which the I attributes to a representative of the space outside-I, and therefore to a representative of reality, a power and a death wish towards itself, even though the presence of this representative, like the bond that unites them, are necessary for the I to keep itself alive.

Similarly, it can be said that somatic persecution is generated by an initial, early conflict between mother and *infans*. An original antagonism that becomes a struggle between the subject and their body. Thus, the hatred felt towards the mother is transmuted into hatred directed against their own body. The present organic pain seems linked to the memory of the body suffering in the past. As a result, there is a return to primordial bodily affects, to to an event already experienced but not remembered by the subject.

Mephitic Mephistopheles in the paranoid body

Like the sense of hearing, the sense of smell is linked to origins. The odour of the devil that spreads through the subject's body is the smell of the introjected negative other. In Schreber, unpleasant olfactory sensations predominate. Foul odours associated with evil, disease and poison penetrate and attack the body.[68]

> On the other hand I had on my body at various times fairly definite signs of the manifestations of the plague. There were different varieties of plagues: the blue plague, the brown plague, the white plague and the black plague. The white plague was the most disgusting; the brown and the black plague were connected with the evaporations of the body, which in the former spread ... (*MNI*, p. 94).

In the language of the paranoiac, there is a need to classify and enumerate the elements of their suffering. It is presented as a kind of exhaustive catalogue, a dictionary of suffering. This need to display and expose the negative undeniably reveals the form of the melancholic feminine in paranoia. The subject also seeks, in some way, to be a unique object of study. They present as a privileged subject of knowledge. They surrender their body, an object of exception and attention, to the knowledge of humanity.

Similarly, the odour of the devil plays a considerable role in Schreber's delusions. On the subject of von W...'s soul, he writes:

> It threw the putrid matter which caused the abdominal putrefaction into my belly with such ruthlessness, that more than once I believed I would have to rot alive, and the rotten smell escaped from my mouth in a most disgusting manner into my stomach, with the most consummate brutality, the putrid matters that engender intestinal rot, so that more than once I thought I should rot alive, and that the most nauseating cadaverous odour exhaled through my mouth (*MNI*, p. 146).

Feminine paranoia   157

Yet, unpleasant olfactory sensations also generate a reaction of oral jouissance and a satisfying effect. '... the taking up of putrid matter by pure rats is connected with a kind of voluptuous sensation for them', Schreber relates (*MNI*, p. 175).

Anxiety about the loss of knowing/having [*savoir/avoir*]

The paranoiac is clearly a megalomaniac. This is evident from the form of their discourse. The hypertrophied ego seems to absorb the totality of sensations and existences, as well as the totality of signifiers. Narcissism expands infinitely. The paranoiac is the glorified sufferer. Suffering is glory. Their glory is in suffering. It is interesting to draw a parallel with the narcissistic collapse of the melancholic, for while the paranoiac loves to extol suffering, the melancholic, although exhibiting it, tries to shame their pain.

In the paranoid subject, the feeling of megalomania is often explicitly stated, or hidden behind the fear of the collapse of intellectual and other capacities. As our patient puts it: 'I'm so moronic, stupid, and idiotic that I haven't even managed to find a profession.' This fear of sinking into imbecility similarly characterises Schreber's plaintive written account: '... destroy my reason or make me demented' (*MNI*, p.125); '... mental capacities are extinct... the advent of dementia' (*MNI*, p. 170); 'I will resign myself to the fact that I am stupid' (*MNI*, p. 171); 'Because I am somehow stupid' (*MNI*, p. 205), etc. In this way, the fear of the collapse of intellectual potential masks the feeling of self-expansion, which, in turn, veils a sense of emptiness within oneself, giving rise to the strange feeling of dispossession of the ego that is subsequently rationalised in paranoid illness.

The 'disseminated' body

> It's as though my head was constantly going to explode, and those around me are in danger of having the splinters of my skull hurled at them at high speed. Alas, and to my great misfortune, my death by skull explosion never occurs, so that I always remain alive to endure the most atrocious and horrible tortures... I am the victim of an absolutely awful and intolerable situation. Indeed my body has to follow the same process as my thought, in other words it has to break up, fragment, in effect, in the way that my thought is disseminated all over the world in all the places of the world. My body must be disseminated in all the places in the world that exist... I want this penetration of my body into the whole world.

With this excerpt from Daniel's discourse, we are back to division, but not fragmentation. The division here is a subtle way of multiplying, breaking down limits and extending to infinity. The idea is to disseminate [*dis-séminer*], that is, to create division and fertilisation through penetration. The paranoiac, penetrated from everywhere, also wants to penetrate 'everything' (thoughts, intentions, hidden meanings) and, in a paternity complex (cf. Schreber), wants to sow everything [*tout ensemencer*]. It is a delirious demiurge, having failed to integrate the function of

158 Feminine paranoia

the father. Indeed, the question of paternity is omnipresent: it is necessary to fertilise (Daniel) or be fertilised (Schreber) in order to fully Be.

The question, however, is to know why the overflowing imagination takes the
place of a lack of the symbolic. The pathology of 'too much' in paranoia, where
everything is excessive, reveals the cruel and painful ordeal of frustration, or 'not
enough', felt by the subject in the present and/or endured in the past. Fundamentally castrated, in a permanent state of 'lack', the paranoid subject therefore wants
to merge with the entirety of the real.

'You have to die in order to live'

Successful psychosis generally excludes suicide. Therefore, by fighting against
psychic collapse and destruction of the self through the organisation of a paranoid
delusion, and also thanks to the work of symbolisation that enabled him to write
his *Memoirs*, in a way Schreber helped himself against his illness; his psychotic
strategy was effective at least in alleviating his suffering.

Unbinding (*délier*) and/or to be delirious (*délirer*) are two strategies for fighting
against psychic death. Psychosis, an organised and defensive behaviour, is, in a
way, a process of self-healing and a sign of self-preservation. Suicide, on the other
hand, presents as an aberration of the preservation instinct. Only in the midst of
intense megalomaniac delusion, marked by denial and paradox, does suicide represent psychic immortality: 'You have to die in order to live'.

The act of suicide is seen as a salvation. Attempts at autolysis act not only to put
an end to suffering, but, more unconsciously, to respond to a desire for castration
inscribed in the 'Other'. This is clearly expressed by our patient, who seeks to 'be
suicided' rather than commit suicide himself, even though he reveals an impres-
sive list (always a catalogue!) of methods of self-destruction. He wants the other
to 'give' him death:

> I beg you, kill me, give me death, because I want to die urgently, as soon as pos-
> sible. If I were refused euthanasia, I would kill myself, that's logical. I'll commit
> suicide by fire, by (gas) explosion, by drowning, by electrocution, by hanging,
> by decapitation, by committing hara-kiri, by throwing myself under a big lorry,
> by lying down on a railway track, by throwing myself into the void, from the
> top of a cliff or a skyscraper, eaten alive in a zoo by lions or tigers, by throwing
> myself into the furnace for incinerating the waste from bins. The refuse collec-
> tors will unknowingly transport me, along with the rest of the waste and rubbish,
> to the crematorium[69] for the city's refuse and I will perish by being burnt alive
> along with the rest of the rubbish. This method of suicide is all the better for the
> fact that my body is nothing but vulgar waste, and that I'm a piece of rubbish,
> both figuratively and literally... I'll kill myself crushed in a car at the scrapyard,
> buried alive, by swallowing the blades of a razor or cutter, by strangling myself,
> by using a firearm stolen from a policeman. I'll shoot myself several times in the

skull, aiming for my eyes so that the bullets enter my skull through my eyes...
This list of ways by which I'm going to commit suicide is not exhaustive and
proves to be very incomplete... Besides, committing suicide is easier said than
done... However, I'd rather die by euthanasia than by suicide. So, I beg you, kill
me, give me death …

In his *Memoirs*, Schreber also confesses to having been haunted by the idea of
suicide on several occasions: 'Being buried alive was also repeatedly mentioned
as a way of ending my life' (*MNI*, p. 65); 'God's omnipotence has decided that the
Prince of Hell is going to be burned alive' (*MNI*, p. 152).

Regression, castration, and anal eroticism

Auto-erotic narcissistic regression is clearly expressed in Daniel's words: 'I risk
becoming a convict who spends all his time licking his toes with his tongue in his
room, or rather his cell.'

In the paranoid organisation, in addition to the exaltation of narcissism and the
expression of masochism, there is undeniably a regression–fixation to the archaic
stages of libidinal evolution. In this respect, the expression of sexuality and anality
is paramount. Indeed, in this perspective, it is a question of expelling (*ex-pulsion*),
detachment, and 'letting go', which are abundantly developed in the account:[70]
'waste, refuse, rubbish, etc.'. Likewise, in the exhaustive, meticulous, entomolo-
gist's inventory, there is an undeniable anal attitude, an attitude that one might be
tempted to describe as anal-ytic. The problem of anality, amply explicit in the discourse of the paranoid subject, heralds the megalomaniac position and a probably
reactionary aggressiveness, as Daniel announces: 'My faeces will flood …'. Or
Schreber, in his delusional paranoia, bluntly announcing: 'He who has succeeded
in placing himself in a relationship similar to the middle with the divine rays has,
so to speak, the right to sh... over the whole world.'

It is interesting at this point to evoke from a metapsychological point of view the
digestive cycle described by Karl Abraham.[71] The first stage, notes the author, is
marked by the loss of the object, which triggers the first stage of expulsion. What
is bad is rejected. The phantasmatic bodily effort attempts to eliminate the internal
object. The second, liberating, stage of expulsion can evoke procreation and identification with the mother in childbirth.

As early as 1906 (21 November), Freud asserted that 'each bowel movement
is celebrated as a delivery'.[72] In this respect, let us not forget that the child is considered as *lumpf*, according to the particular word little Hans used to designate
excrement.[73] In popular parlance, French mothers often affectionately refer to their
children as *ma crotte* ['my poo'].

Later, regarding 'Wolf Man' (the report of the analysis dates from 1918), Freud
highlights in the problematic of the subject, the impact of the primal scene – return
to the maternal breast – sexual encounter with the father – second birth: excremental

160   Feminine paranoia

child. The phantasy derived from the primal scene is broken down by Freud as follows:

> the wish to be born of his father... the wish to be sexually satisfied by him, the wish to present him with a child... expressed in the language of anal erotism [where] homosexuality has found its furthest and most intimate expression.

The phantasmatic excremental child born from the primitive scene clearly evokes the 'cloacal theory' and that of anal childbirth. It is an 'intestinal feminine'. This 'Theory', elaborated by Freud in his article 'On the Sexual Theories of Children' (1908c), was later developed by Lou Andreas Salomé. She writes:

> It is not for nothing that the genital apparatus remains close to the cloaca [...], they also resemble each other in the primitive technique of manifesting through the periodicity of pushing and impulses. Just as anal pushing is originally uncontrollable, genital pushing presents itself as involuntarily overwhelming the ego.[74]

Anal eroticism and the castration complex (cf. 'the Wolf Man'), therefore, highlight the existence of phantasies of homosexual desire and the inclination towards victimophilia in a masochistic position of the feminine type. Indeed, the question of the feminine is particularly dominant in disorders with a paranoid and persecutory aspect.

> I'm going to become a tramp, a homeless person, a vagabond, a beggar. I'll beg for charity from people who spit in my bowl instead of putting in a coin... I'll sleep outside, under the stars, freezing cold, in the icy wind. I'll sleep lying on a pavement, next to or on top of dog poo, getting drenched in urine by dogs urinating on me. If I have the habit of sleeping with my mouth open and outside, then dogs will urinate into my mouth, after lifting a leg, and while I sleep, I will drink the urine of dogs urinating into my wide-open mouth... Dogs passing by my corpse will delight in taking a piece of meat from my body or a bone from my skeleton to crunch on and sharpen their teeth.

The relationship of persecution also invokes the regressive problematic of orality. Daniel, translating his cannibalistic phantasy, has the feeling of being literally 'devoured' from both within and without. From this point of view, the investment of the oral dimension in Schreber's discourse is striking:

> In quite another of other instances later I received souls or parts of souls in my mouth, of which I particularly remember distinctly the foul taste and smell which such *impure* souls cause in the body of the person through whose mouth they have entered. (*MNI*, pp. 86–87)

Feminine paranoia 161

The question of the dimension of orality, which is particularly present in victim paranoia, seems to point, as I stressed earlier, to early frustrations linked to the breast and maternal care.

Sacrificial giving, masochism, and megalomania

Like Schreber, Daniel is determined to put himself at the service of science and humanity:

> After my death, can all my organs be recovered by medical personnel, and then transplanted to patients who absolutely need a transplant to be cured or survive. I give my body to science... Medical staff will be able to recover all my organs immediately after my death and transplant them into patients in need. This could save many human lives.

As with Schreber, the body becomes a scientific object. In this psychopathological organisation, there is a constant reference to science and knowledge. The paranoid subject knows everything about themselves. They study themselves endlessly. By surrendering themselves to the knowledge of others, they are convinced that they are also contributing to the knowledge of the universe. Their body, their suffering, their perceptions and their explanations are the very image of the universe, and they add up, or try to add up, the reality of existing circumstances in an encyclopaedic enumeration, through the reality of their experience. The 'proof' that they exist is that they are not only the centre of the world, but also, in a way, the centre of the discourse. Without them, would the world exist? Through this discourse, they give name,[75] like the 'Almighty', to the origins of both good and evil. So the paranoiac has knowledge about themselves, and about the world, that others do not know. What would the world be without them? They are Nothing (waste) and Everything. They are the sacrificed but also the saviour (of other lives). The paranoiac evokes the apocalypse. Suffering is the apotheosis. Ultimately, they 'embody' the absolute Evil of the Universe that glorifies them.

Sacrificing oneself, or being sacrificed, to save other human beings (humanity) is an ambition at once megalomaniac and characteristic of a victim. Were martyrs not offered to appease the wrath of the gods in ancient times?

Schreber gives his body the exceptional characteristic that merits the attention of scientists: 'I believe that expert examination of my body and observation of my personal fate during my lifetime would be of value both for science and the knowledge of religious truths' (*MNI*, p. 3). 'My aim is solely to further knowledge of truth in a vital field, that of religion' (*MNI*, p. 7). 'To offer my person as object of scientific observation for the judgement of experts' (*MNI*, p. 307). '... such peculiarities of my nervous system will be discovered by dissection of my body ...' *ibid.*)

Unlike the melancholic and other 'masochistic' depressives, who are suffering subjects, the paranoiac is distinguished by their circumstantial delusion. They

162 Feminine paranoia

analyse (anal-yse) suffering as a scientific object. They are as much the suffering object as the object of suffering. Suffering is confused with knowledge. They are the body of this knowledge. The suffering of self is also associated with the suffering of humanity. There is a megalomaniac fusion of self with humanity. Unable to live alone, the paranoid subject needs to merge with humanity. So, by sacrificing themselves for humanity, they save 'their own life'. As we can see, the paranoiac is 'eaten away' by paradox. In this mental disorder, the subject is completely inside their discourse. In a way, 'flesh has become word'. Likewise, pushing the study of suffering to its inhuman frontier ('It's indescribable, inhuman, beyond human comprehension …'), they try in their way to posit a 'beyond man' as something below man ('I'm just waste, a piece of rubbish …'). They are the nothing as well as the Everything. In this sense, the non tenable nature of this antinomic and particularly painful position is characteristic of the paranoid feminine.

Feminine or 'Sacrifixion'[76]

The paranoid subject announces and denounces: 'A child is killed' or, more precisely, 'The son is killed'. This assertion expresses an equivocation of meaning and implies the intensely experienced phantasmatic of the dead child. Our patient and Schreber both identify strongly and directly with Christ, the scapegoat Victim. Daniel, an only child, writes:

> I am atrociously tortured. More than the man who has been tortured and tormented throughout human history, more than the man who is burned alive on a flaming pyre, or the victim struck a great many times by a million sharp, red-hot metal bars simultaneously... I am subjected to all the atrocious tortures of a person burned alive on a pyre. I am constantly subjected to the excruciating torture of knives and sharp blades that are constantly cutting and skinning my thorax, so that I am a victim sacrificed at the stake and subjected to the most excruciating tortures... If euthanasia were denied me, I would die by crucifixion. Crucifixion being the best way to die. I'll go to a crucifix and climb on it. In this way, I will perish, crucified. My whole existence is a genuine martyrdom and an unbearable ordeal. So I'll crucify myself so that society no longer suffers all the damaging acts that people telepathically force me to accomplish.

Schreber, too, assimilates himself to the figure of Christ:

> Something like the conception of Jesus Christ by an Immaculate Virgin – i.e. one who never had intercourse with a man – happened in my own body, that is, by a virgin who had never lain with a man, occurred in my own body (*MNI*, p. 17, note 1).

At the end of Chapter XXII, the identification with Jesus Christ[77] is more clearly explicit: '… the picture emerges of a martyrdom which all in all I can only compare with the crucifixion of Jesus Christ' (*MNI*, p. 258). The overt confusion with Christ and the 'delusion of redemption' have a fundamental value in (religious) paranoia.

It should be remembered that, in his delusional discourse, Schreber believes he has been invested with a redemptive mission to save the world. The redemptive role is one of the major manifestations of paranoia. It expresses the patient's mystical megalomania, a feeling of unlimited grandeur, as seen, for example, in this excerpt that recounts the battle between the victim (Schreber) and his persecutor, God himself: 'In this apparently unequal combat between a weak, isolated man and God himself, I emerged victorious, despite having undergone much suffering and privation, and this proves that the order of the universe is on my side'.

Paranoiacs suffer from a fixation at the stage of primordial narcissism and the ego ideal. As a consequence, in this mental disorder, the liberated libido is concentrated on the ego, which, thus, finds itself greatly amplified. In this situation dominated by object narcissism, the subject's ego is the one and only sexual object. What wounds Schreber's narcissism is precisely his adoption of the feminine position in relation to his father (God), a position that in itself entails castration. Castration is somehow 'overcome', or relatively tolerated, in so far as God (the Father) himself becomes a (sexual) partner. As a result, (the unique) Schreber loves and is loved by God. In this way, the paranoid subject has a mythical or mythological idea of their life, in both conception and existence.

It is necessary to die to spare others from harm. Daniel assimilates himself to Evil as determined by an external power (violent people, occult forces...):

> There are also people who force me to do acts that make me dangerous for society. So I'm being remotely controlled, remotely operated by people who demand that I do things that are harmful to society, and I absolutely have to die to prevent this terrible plague from continuing.

In his delusion, Schreber also believed that he was called upon to save the world, prompted by a divine stimulus that was transmitted to him through the language of nerves and in a particular tongue (*Grundsprache*). For this, he would have to be changed into a woman. To be transformed into a woman is also, beyond soul murder, a kind of murder of identity: the murder of the soul is, in a sense, the murder of the man. The man in him must be killed in order to be loved by men.

Consequently, it is a sacrificial devotion whose aim is the preservation of the world. But Schreber, in his megalomania, claims an exceptional status: 'A human being,' he writes, 'who in a certain sense can say *that eternity is in his service, can afford to ignore all nonsense in the certain knowledge that ultimately a time must come when nonsense exhausts itself ...*' (*MNI*, p. 288). In the same vein, Dr Weber, in his forensic report of 9 December 1899, says of Schreber: 'He believes he was called to redeem the world and restore lost bliss to humanity'.

As Freud said, paranoid subjects, narcissistic and proud, love their words and their delusions as much as they love themselves. But, contrary to the noble

164 Feminine paranoia

commandment, they no longer love others as they do themselves. There is no longer an other, only the other in them, through them. They are the origin and the end of the other. From this point of view, the religious injunction, which may seem absurd, paradoxical, or unnatural – 'love thy neighbour as thyself' – precisely re-establishes the universal law of symbolic castration that operates in both differentiated sexes: 'the other is your equal, you are only the other's equal'.

Notes

1 Hypochondria is the somatic equivalent of paranoia. The latter, as Freud points out (1911c), 'almost always includes hypochondriacal symptoms'.
2 See the paradigmatic case study of feminine paranoia studied by Lacan in 1931 under the title 'Structures des psychoses paranoiaques'. Lacan followed the case of Marguerite Pantaine, nicknamed Aimée. We would later learn that she was the mother of psychoanalyst Didier Anzieu. She had been committed to Sainte-Anne following an assassination attempt on a famous actress, Huguette Duflos. The patient presented a paranoid delusion with themes of grandeur and supreme missions. See Lacan (1932)[1980].
3 Throughout this chapter I refer to Daniel Paul Schreber's *Memoirs of My Nervous Illness* (2000). The *Memoirs* are henceforth cited as *MNI*.
4 Let's recall this delusion of pregnancy as he himself describes it in his *MNI*, p. 18):

Twice at different times ... I had a female genital organ ... and in my body felt quickening like the first signs of life of a human embryo by a divine miracle God's nerves corresponding to male seed had been thrown into my body in other words fertilization had occurred.

There is a reminder of the divine conception of the Virgin Mary.
5 *Ibid.*, p. 46.
6 Fairbairn, W. R. D. (19545)[1956].
7 *Menschenspielerei.*
8 Sadger (1910); Freud (1910c).
9 Freud (1905d).
10 Freud (1911c), p. 60.
11 On this question, see also my book (Maïdi, 2008).
12 In the chapter of 'Psycho-analytical notes on an autobiographical account of a case of paranoia' devoted to the mechanism of paranoia, Freud (1911c) writes:

On the basis of this clinical evidence we can suppose that paranoiacs have brought along with them a *fixation at the stage of narcissism*, and we can assert that the length of *the step back from sublimated homosexuality to narcissism* is a measure of the amount of *regression* characteristic of paranoia.

Paranoia is an illness that involves the regression of the object libido towards narcissism and, on this regressive path, the resexualisation of sublimated homosexuality in social bonds. Freud's study of the case of President Schreber, which led him in 1911 to set out the mechanism of paranoia, led him a little later to conceptualise the theory of narcissism.
13 Freud (1914c), p. 88.
14 Freud's concept of the double is linked to the emergence of a theory of narcissism. The word, used for the first time in 1910, appears in *Leonardo da Vinci and A Memory of His Childhood*. Leonardo's turn towards homosexuality is described as follows: the boy's first love for his mother succumbs to repression, yet he keeps her by putting himself in her place, identifying with her

and takes his own person as model in whose likeness he chooses the new objects of his love ... He finds the objects of his love along the path of *narcissim*, as we say; for

Narcissus, according to the Greek legend, was a youth who preferred his own reflection to everything else and who was changed into the lovely flower of that name.

15 It is worth recalling the anecdote that led Freud to formulate this concept, based on the familiar yet strange self-image perceived in the reflection of the compartment door. The disquieting is also closely linked, almost consubstantial with the familiar, which is what makes this concept so rich.

16 Lacan's translation '*laissé gésir*' [left lying] has the merit of emphasising the mortiferous aspect and forced passivity to which the victim is subjected: to be without movement, fallen, overturned, lying down, 'abandoned to putrefaction' and so on. In this spirit of dereliction and abandonment, the less forceful, figurative, and colloquial expression 'let down', often found in the feminine clinic, seems to me to be equally appropriate.

17 Kretschmer (1888–1964) was one of the first psychiatrists to take an interest in relational and social psychopathology, 'typical social constellations'.

18 Kretschmer, E. (1918)[1963], p. 3.

19 In this respect, we could say that President Schreber is an exemplary 'case' of the paranoid feminine victim.

20 In this respect, current studies on moral harassment are finally giving justice to the victims of the 'little sadists' who swarm the world of work, the argument of paranoia being used by the aggressor to outbid him!

21 Ethnologist G. Bateson, founding father of the famous 'Palo Alto School' in 1952, was at the origin of this so-called *systemic* theory, which was applied more specifically to schizophrenia by D. Jackson in 1954.

22 'Double bind' has sometimes been translated into French as '*double entrave*' [double hindrance]. Cf. for example Rosolato (1976b).

23 See Racamier (1991) and (1990).

24 Searles (1959).

25 Enriquez (1984), pp. 151–152.

26 Freud (1908a).

27 Freud (1915f). On this metapsychological issue, I would like to draw your attention to the essential text by G. Rosolato (1969), 'Paranoïa et scène primitive', pp. 199–241. See also, by the same author, the question of the father in the production process of paranoia in the chapter 'Du père'.

28 Klein, M. (1932b).

29 See Freud's *Inhibition, Symptoms and Anxiety* (1926d) and the Wolf Man (1914–1918).

30 These fantasies of punishment can be compared to the torture inflicted on Prometheus, the 'saviour of mankind'. In this respect, it is worth noting the surprising juxtapositions between the sacrifice of Christ and the martyrdom of Prometheus.

31 Macalpine & Hunter (1953).

32 The question of narcissism and autoeroticism, in a way homophilia and homosexuality, is central to paranoia. In this condition, the libido is withdrawn from the object. As a result,

The cathexis lost by the image of the object is first replaced by belief. Where the libido has gone is indicated by the *hostility to the object*, found in paranoia. This is an endogenous perception of libido withdrawal. In view of the relation of compensation between object-cathexis and ego-cathexis, it seems likely that the cathexis withdrawn from the object has returned to the ego, i.e., has become autoerotic. The paranoid ego is consequently hypercathected, egoistic, megalomaniac'. (Freud, 1907a).

33 Freud (1911c).

34 Freud (1919e), p. 195.

35 Bak (1946). This work is cited by J. Laplanche in his article 'Séduction, persécution, révélation' (1993), *Psa. Univ.* 1993, 18, 72, pp. 3–34.

36 Laplanche, J. (1968)[1992], pp. 37–58.

166 Feminine paranoia

37 Schreiberian masochism is evident in this request for poisoning:

In the contact kept up with Professor Flechisg's nerves I constantly demanded cyanide or strychnine from him in order to poison myself (a drop of venom-juice, as it was called in the basic language); Professor Flechsig – as a soul in nerve-contact with me – did not refuse this demand, but always half promised it … (*MNI*, p. 65).

38 Laplanche (1993), p. 18.
39 Lacan (1955–1956), p. 150.
40 Cf. Lacan, J. (1957–1958b), p. 206.
41 Among other etiological elements, there seems to be a particularly close relationship between Schreber's professional promotion to the very high office of President of the High Court (*Senatspräsident*) of Leipzig, and the triggering of his paranoid crisis. In this context, it's worth noting Freud's work on people who 'fail' in the face of social and professional advancement (see the dreams of punishment in the *Traumdeutung*, or the well-known text entitled 'Those who fail in the face of success').
42 Lacan (1957–1958), p. 197.
43 Aulagnier (1986), p. 359 *sq.*
44 *Id.* p. 370.
45 Lanouzière (1990), p. 43.
46 Aulagnier (1975).
47 Aulagnier (1986).
48 Other elaborations on the theme of traumatic and generalised seduction include Jean Laplanche's 'Séduction, persécution, révélation' (1993). Cf. also by the same author *Vie et mort en psychanalyse* (1970), and *Nouveaux fondements pour la psychanalyse* (1990).
49 Laplanche (1968).
50 Lanouzière (1990).
51 The first name of the case presented here was chosen essentially for its unisex character, which was originally real. Coincidentally, it relates to the repetition of the first name Daniel in the Schreber family.
52 In fact, he's a young man with a feminoid physique.
53 In this respect, it is worth noting that the subject's paranoid masochism allows him to perceive the interlocutor as an 'adversary', a fusion of the two parental images. However, in this situation of parental union marked by a coalition against the son, the father occupies a predominant position.
54 According to Kestemberg's concept of primary homosexuality, which defines primordial relational exchanges with the primary object invested as both different (otherness) and similar (homology), this is 'the first stage in the early conquest of the object'.
55 Schreber also describes his confinement, referring to it as 'my time in the cells' (*MNI*, p. 184).
56 Schreber also expresses this quest for the end through hunger:

I therefore decided to end my life by starving to death and refusing all food; the inner voices always reiterated that it was my duty to die of hunger and in this way to sacrifice myself for God, and that therefore any partaking of meals which my body demanded was a weakness unworthy of me.

Hence the feeling of a '*feeding system*' when the guards 'force' him to swallow food 'with the utmost brutality' (p. 64). 'Starving oneself' is a regressive pathological behavior that refers to the relationship of child-feeding by a frustrating mother who gives the child no opportunity to 'enjoy' from and through her mouth in the primordial 'sexual and carnal' connection.

57 In the paranoid, eating (Daniel) or defecating (Schreber) is considered a purely primary activity: 'something every animal is capable of doing. …' (*MNI*, p. 206). However,

Feminine paranoia   167

the aversion of these two factors, orality and anality, precisely show their unconscious attraction and the investment of the afferent bodily zones.

58 Schreber, a 'model' of clinical pathological victimology, of a victimised feminine. Similarly, certain members of Schreber's family display victimised characteristics. Schreber's father (Daniel Gottfried) described himself as a 'victim' at the end of his life (1830). In a short autobiographical document, he describes himself as a hypochondriac, suffering from a number of ailments and disorders. His father died of a perforated ulcer at the age of fifty-three. Three years earlier, he had accidentally received an iron ladder on the head. He had darkened and suffered from a severe obsessive neurosis with homicidal impulses. Schreber's brother (Daniel Gustav) committed suicide by gunshot at the age of thirty-eight. He was suffering from 'progressive psychosis'. Daniel Paul Schreber's second sister, Sidonie, died unmarried, mentally ill.

59 Cf. below the singular and subtle forms of mathematical discourse that Daniel uses to demonstrate his position as a victim.

60 Such as Schreber quoting Kraepelin and his famous *Treatise on Psychiatry* (1st ed. 1883, 6th ed. 1889).

61 The term 'liquidation' is welcome, because in paranoid illness, in addition to the threatening persecution that hangs over the subject (the other wants him dead), the person has the feeling that 'everything is leaking out of his head and body'.

62 One of the fundamental problems of paranoia is linked to paradox and double obstruction, which this example illustrates perfectly: the subject claims not to be deaf, since he hears voices that don't exist.

63 Freud (1937d).

64 Freud (1896), pp. 119–139.

65 The richness of written language is evident in Schreber's numerous euphemisms used in the 'fundamental language' (*Grundsprache*) to make himself understood by God, e.g., punishment for reward, poison for food, juice for poison, godless for holy, etc. (*MNI*, pp. 26–27).

66 Cf. for example the particularly close association between words and the digestive cycle in Louis Wolfson's *Le schizo et les langues* [Schizophrenia and Languages], Paris, Gallimard, 1970.

67 Aulagnier (1986), p. 320.

68 '… in quite a number of other instances later I received souls or parts of souls in my mouth, of which I particularly remember distinctly the foul taste and smell which such *impure* souls cause in the body of the person through whose mouth they have entered' *(MNI*, pp. 86–87).

69 Schreber devotes a short chapter in his *Memoirs* to 'Concerning cremation' (see *MNI*, p. 296, VII Concerning Cremation).

70 See Klein (1932b).

71 Abraham (1915–1925).

72 Freud, in 1907b, p. 61.

73 Freud (1909b).

74 Andreas-Salomé L. (1915). 'Anal' and 'Sexual', in *L'amour du narcissisme*, Paris, Gallimard, 1980. Author's translation.

75 Cf. the creative function of the verb: 'And God created the earth and called it "earth"', etc. (Genesis).

76 I use this neologism to evoke the condensation of the signifiers *Sacrifice* and *Crucifixion*, or identification with the figure of Jesus Christ.

77 Another famous victim, 'Wolf Man', also identifies with Christ, revealing his repressed homosexuality and his feminine, passive, masochistic attitude towards his father.

Chapter 10

Feminine masochism

In his famous work *Psychopathia Sexualis*,[1] Richard von Krafft-Ebbing considers masochism[2] as

> a peculiar perversion[3] of the psychical sexual life in which the individual affected, in sexual feeling and thought, is controlled by the idea of being completely and unconditionally subject to the will of a person ... This idea is coloured by a lustful feeling.[4]

Krafft-Ebing also examines what he called at the time 'masochism in women'. He writes: 'In woman, an inclination to subordination to man ... is to a certain extent a normal manifestation'.[5]

He adds: 'Thus it is easy to regard masochism in general as a pathological growth of specific feminine mental elements—as an abnormal intensification of certain features of the psycho-sexual character of woman'.[6]

Erotic feminine masochism in its excrescence could be found in what Krafft-Ebing called *sexual servitude* (*subjection*), and the erogenous inclination for passive abuse and humiliation.[7] Krafft-Ebing states:

> In woman voluntary subjection to the opposite sex is a physiological phenomenon. Owing to her passive role in procreation and long-existent social conditions, ideas of subjection are, in woman, normally connected with the idea of sexual relations. They form, so to speak, the harmonics which determine the tone-quality of feminine feeling.[8]

For Krafft-Ebing, 'feminine erotic masochism' is determined by the need to experience and represent situations of submission or humiliation. As Krafft-Ebing points out, in woman, the idea of sexual intercourse is generally linked to the notion of submission.

In this sense, the idea of submission in women can be eroticised. Women are not 'naturally masochistic'. Their natural anatomical difference does not incline them to masochism. For Krafft-Ebing, feminine 'masochism' is essentially *erotic* in nature. This masochism, which is specific to the female sex, can be found in men who choose submission to guide and regulate their sexual feelings.

DOI: 10.4324/9781003414247-11

Rousseau's feminine masochism

In the first part of his *Confessions*,[9] Jean-Jacques Rousseau[10] depicts traits of his 'effeminate character' and some of his masochistic behaviours. He examines his 'bizarre taste', definitively fixed at the age of eleven as a result of being spanked by Miss Lambercier, a taste he deems 'ridiculous and shameful': 'To fall at the feet of an imperious mistress, obey her mandates, or implore pardon, were for the most exquisite enjoyments …'[11]. This extract clearly shows the need for submission, humiliation, and punishment in front of women.

Rousseau recounts in his *Confessions* (Book 1, Part 1) how imposing Mademoiselle Lambercier had been, then aged thirty, when he was boarding at the age of eight, and an apprentice with this woman's brother. Her irritation when he failed to answer one of her questions promptly, and her threats to whip him, made the most profound impression on him. Having once received corporal punishment at the hands of Mademoiselle Lambercier, he experienced, apart from the pain and shame, a sensual, voluptuous sensation that gave him a violent urge to receive yet more punishment.

Rousseau writes:

> As Miss Lambercier felt a mother's affection, she sometimes exerted a mother's authority, even to inflicting on us when we deserved it, the punishment of infants. She had often threatened it, and this treat of a treatment entirely new, appeared to me extremely dreadful; but I found the reality much less terrible than the idea, and what is still more unaccountable, this punishment increased my affection for the person who had inflicted it. All this affection, aided by my natural mildness, was scarcely sufficient to prevent my seeking, by fresh offences, a return of the same chastisement; for a degree of sensuality had mingled with the smart and shame, which left more desire than fear of a repetition. I was well convinced the same discipline from her brother would have produced a quite contrary effect; but from a man of his disposition this was not probable, and if I abstained from meriting correction it was merely from a fear of offending Miss Lambercier, for benevolence, aided by the passions, has ever maintained an empire over me which has given law to my heart.

This even, though, which was desirable, I had not endeavored to accelerate, arrived without my fault; I should say, without my seeking; and I profited by it with a safe conscience; but this second, was also the last time, for Miss Lambercier, who doubtless had some reason to imagine this chastisement did not produce the desired effect, declared it was too fatiguing, and that she renounced it for the future. Till now we had slept in her chamber, and during the winter, even in her bed; but two days after another room was prepared for us, and from that moment I had the honor (which I could very well have dispensed with) of being treated by her as a great boy.

Who would believe this childish discipline, received at eight years old, from the hands of a woman of thirty, should influence my propensities, my desires, my passions, for the rest of my life, and that in quite a contrary sense from what might naturally have been expected?[12]

Studying the Rousseau case, Alfred Binet wondered:

> What can we say... about this strange, paradoxical phenomenon to which we have given the happy but enigmatic name of "the pleasure of pain"?... What enjoyment can we find in the physical pain of feeling bruised by blows and in the moral pain of feeling overwhelmed by the anger or disdain of a woman?[13]

Binet, who analysed the 'Rousseau case' in depth, rightly draws attention to the masochistic significance of this case, saying:

> What Rousseau loves in women is not only the furrowed brow, the raised hand, the stern gaze, the imperious attitude, it is also the emotional state of which these facts are the outward translation; he loves the proud, disdainful woman, crushing him at her feet with the weight of her royal anger.

It could be said that, in his own submission, Rousseau loves and seeks out the woman who proves insubordinate. However, in the scene of corporal punishment (the spanking), there was probably a co-seduction, a libidinal co-excitation of the two protagonists. That is why Miss Lambercier stopped this corporal punishment, so as not to arouse the child's voluptuous masochistic perversion. She no longer wanted to play at it...

Freud links the erotic feminine aspect of masochism with male 'perverts' and female sexuality. He states: 'Thus masochism, as people say, is truly feminine. But if, as happens so often, you meet with masochism in men, what is left to you but to say that these men exhibit very plain feminine traits?'[14]

Masochism and dreamlike punishment

The existence of phenomena containing self-punishment was first set out by Freud (1900a) in the *Traumdeutung* (*Interpretation of Dreams*) on *dreams of punishment*. He explains that it is a kind of obligation imposed by censorship for the fulfilment of a desire. Similarly, the dream and its content are the ideal means of expressing unconscious masochism. In the *Traumdeutung*, for example, Freud grouped together, under the heading of 'counter-wish dreams' (*Gegenwunschträume*), dreams of unpleasant content which, in connection with sexual components, are born of the metamorphosis of aggressive and sadistic inclinations into their opposite.

Freud calls the authors of these dreams 'ideal' masochists because, he points out, 'they do not seek their pleasure in bodily pain, but in humiliation and sorrow'. For them, these dreams of suffering, contrary to desire, are merely the fulfilment of desire, the remission of rejected and repressed masochistic tendencies. Indeed, the painful feeling of displeasure that reappears in the dream does not exclude the existence of a repressed desire. This is why it is easy to establish a relationship

Feminine masochism 171

between the unpleasant character of these dreams and the fact that the dream is a distortion. The dream is disguised and the fulfilment of desire misrepresented, difficult to recognise because of a repulsion, a will to repress, against the fabric of the dream or against the desire it expresses. In this way, the disfigurement of dream content appears to be the result of censorship. Analysis of painful dreams reveals that the dream is the (deformed) fulfilment of a (repressed) desire.

Freud also refers to what he calls 'punishment dreams', which he distinguishes from dreams that fulfil desires. These *expiatory dreams* occur mainly in people who have risen rapidly to an important social position. In the conflict between the self-importance and insolence of the parvenu, and self-criticism, the dream seeks out and finds an ally in self-criticism. This is the return of an unpleasant experience in the dream activity. The punishment dream 'pulls' on the side of lack and castration. In this way, the excessive fantasy of ambition finds itself blocked in the dream and transformed into degradation and debasement. This 'inverted' or contrary desire can be attributed to a certain psychic masochism. At the time, Freud wrote: 'All joy belongs to the day, when one has succeeded, and the dream, on the contrary, drags with it the ghost of a sad era, finally overcome'. So, these regressive, masochistic punishment dreams recall failures and negative or painful experiences that we try to forget in our daytime experience, or that we have overcome through personal success or social achievement.

A female character who completely collapses after achieving the triumph she had fought so hard to achieve is Shakespeare's Lady Macbeth, in a tragedy of ambition and remorse. Freud analysed Shakespeare's play at length in 'Some Character-Types Met With in Psycho-Analytical Work' (1916d). Lady Macbeth who, during an episode of sleepwalking, appears haunted by the innocent blood she has caused to be shed, takes her own life, while Macbeth, surrounded in his castle by the men of Malcolm, son of the murdered Duncan, King of Scotland, throws himself into the fray and perishes. Remorse, itself a punishment of the internalised paternal representative (moral conscience), can lead to self-murder or the murder of the Other within oneself.

The desire for displeasure

Dreams with painful and unpleasant content are, thus, the satisfaction of an unconscious and repressed masochistic desire, the fulfilment of which would be felt by the dreamer's ego as unpleasant. This marks the opposition between unconscious and conscious, repressed and ego, desire and reality. In contrast to the pleasure it can generate, desire here is the cause of displeasure and anxiety. To illustrate these situations, Freud gives personal examples in the *Traumdeutung*, and also recalls the well-known tale of the three wishes that a fairy promises to grant to two peasants, where we can see that the fulfilment of desire for one can be a source of worry for the other, when there is no agreement between the two.

Paradoxically, however, dreams of displeasure have a liberating effect on negative affects that are repressed and buried deep in the unconscious. In the same way

172   Feminine masochism

as nightmares, which are dreams of anxiety, they translate the pure and simple fulfilment of a desire, just like dreams of appeasement. These unpleasant dreams (*Unlusttraum*) can, thus, be 'punishment dreams' (*Züchtigungtraum*), where the unconscious desire is a punishment (a role later discovered by psychoanalysis to be devolved to the superego,) inflicted on the dreamer for a forbidden, repressed desire. Consequently, 'punishment dreams' (*Straftraum*) are realisations of unconscious desire. As Freud points out in *Beyond the Pleasure Principle* (1920g), these dream productions of punishments simply 'replace the fulfilment of a strictly forbidden desire with the punishment it deserves, and are therefore the fulfilment of desire in reaction to the rejected drive'. This interpretation, which seems logically dubious – the punishment of a forbidden desire would itself be a desire – retains all its relevance from a metapsychological point of view.

Sadomasochism of compulsion neurosis

There are also self-punitive manifestations particularly in the symptomatic expression of *compulsion neurosis* (*Zwangsneurose*). From his earliest studies on the subject of this pathology, Freud describes self-reproaches (*Selbstvorwurf*) and remorse; then, in *Notes Upon a Case of Obsessional Neurosis* (1909d), he traces the masochistic and self-punitive behaviours that make up this compulsion disorder. It is certainly the whole symptomatology and the suffering it contains that makes the obsessive their own persecutor.

In 1896, Freud gave a definition of obsessions according to which they are 'invariably transformed *self-reproaches* which have re-emerged from *repression*, and which always relate to some *sexual act* that was performed with pleasure *in childhood*'.[15] In 1909, he found this explanation open to criticism 'from the point of view of form, even though it is composed of the best elements'. According to Freud, it would be more appropriate to speak of compulsive thinking, and to highlight the fact that compulsion formations can have the meaning of a wide variety of psychic acts: wishes, temptations, impulses, reflections, doubts, orders, and prohibitions. Freud recursively highlighted the aetiopathogenic specificity of obsessional neurosis from the point of view of psychic defensive mechanisms (displacement of the affect on to representations more or less distant from the original conflict, isolation, retroactive cancellation); from the point of view of the instinctual life (ambivalence, fixation on the anal stage and regression), and from the topical point of view (internalised sado-masochistic relationship in the form of tension between the ego and a particularly cruel superego).

In the case of Ernst Lanzer, the 'Rat Man', Freud (1909d) had him recognise his repressed hatred for his father and how a relative renunciation of genitality leads to a regression of the libido to the anal stage, where it becomes a desire for destruction, essentially turned inwards. In the sadistic component of compulsion neurosis, we find, in effect, the turning round on the subject's own self, without there being any passivity towards another person. Here, sadism is auto-erogenous, narcissistic, and self-objectal. The need to torment becomes torment inflicted on oneself (*Selbstquälerei*), self-punishment and not masochism.[16] The subject is their own persecutor. Like the *Heautontimoroumenos*, they are a victim of themselves. In obsessional neurosis, like the corresponding phenomenon in melancholia, satisfaction is achieved when the sadistic and hateful tendencies that target an object are turning round against the subject's own self, who is now confused and mixed up with this now inaccessible object.

It should also be noted that the obsessive person, by means of self-punishment (internal punishment), is able to take revenge on the original love objects, and to torture those they love through their illness. As a result, the obsessive always reaches, or believes they reach, others through the subterfuge of their illness.

Moral masochism, the need for punishment and unconscious guilt

One of the factors behind the emergence of masochism as regression and turning round of sadism upon the subject's own self is the consciousness of guilt (*Schuldbewusstsein*) and its eroticisation. The feeling of guilt, which has a dominant place in Freudian metapsychology, is at first described by Freud mainly in obsessive neurosis, in the form of self-reproach, obsessive ideas, compulsions to perform unbearable and unhappy (essentially aggressive) acts, and the struggle against these thoughts and inclinations. Here, too, the feeling of guilt is partly unconscious, in so far as the origin of the present desires is not known to the subject.

In 1924c, Freud, in his indispensable article 'The Economic Problem of Masochism', deals with *moral masochism*, recognised essentially as a generally unconscious feeling of guilt (*Schuldgefühl*), or, more appropriately, a need for symbolised punishment on the part of parental power. In this situation, writes Freud,

> by their behaviour during treatment and in life the individuals in question give the impression of being morally inhibited to an excessive degree, of being under the domination of an especially sensitive conscience, although they are not conscious of any of this ultra-morality. On closer inspection, we can see the difference there is between an unconscious extension of morality of this kind and moral masochism. In the former, the accent falls on the heightened sadism of the super-ego to which the ego submits; in the latter, it falls on the ego's own masochism which seeks punishment, whether from the super-ego or from the parental powers outside.[17]

Consequently, while sadism of the superego and masochism of the ego cannot be considered simply as symmetrical sides of a same tension, both do involve an inter-systemic relationship between the ego and the superego or powers analogous to it; in both circumstances there is, in fact, a need for satisfaction through punishment and suffering. It is worth pointing out, however, that while sadism of the superego is more often than not highly conscious, the masochistic inclination of the ego usually remains barred from the person's knowledge and must, generally,

174 Feminine masochism

be removed from their behaviour, which is governed and dominated by iterative, deadly jouissance.

In this respect, consciousness and morality arise, according to Freud, following the resolution and desexualisation of the Oedipus complex. Moral masochism, on the other hand, resexualises and Oedipalises morality. There is, therefore, a regression of morality and a 'return' of the Oedipus complex. In this situation marked by regression, the subject may well have preserved all or part of their morality alongside their masochism, but a large part of their moral awareness is dissipated and allows itself to be supplanted by masochism and dolorism.

Active masochism: Negativity in treatment and in life

The moral masochism caused by unconscious guilt and the need for punishment can also, paradoxically, be at the root of transgressive criminal acts.[18] The 'fault' has to be repaired 'after the fact' [*après-coup*] by the reprobation of the sadistic moral conscience, by the symbolic Law or by the punishment of destiny, the great parental power. We could speak of a veritable *active masochism* here, for, in order to provoke punishment by this ultimate parental representative, the masochist must act 'negatively', unknowingly, and against themselves. Ultimately, they must perpetrate everything that can work against their own interests, extinguishing the prospects open to them in the real world and eventually destroying their own person.

In 'Some Character-Types Met With in Psycho-Analytical Work', Freud (1916d) drew attention to the particular type of person who '... fails in the face of success'. These are people who cannot bear satisfaction on a specific point, linked to their unconscious desire. Their problematic contains the following contradiction: whereas external frustration was not pathogenic, it is the possibility given by reality to satisfy the desire that is intolerable and provokes self-frustration. In this way, the subject defends themselves and denies themselves satisfaction, but demands another kind of satisfaction: that of the pain of lack and incompleteness. In this painful condition, the person becomes the object of their own castration. An attitude which, in extreme cases, can lead to existential extinction and death. These are, in effect, people who do not seem to be able to bear their 'happiness'.[19]

For some subjects the onset of the illness therefore occurs with the fulfilment of a desire, for social or professional advancement, for example. Under these conditions, the ego concedes a desire, provided it is always curbed, controlled, and unattainable. The desire is accepted only as a phantasy. As soon as it approaches fulfilment and threatens to become reality, the ego 'dissociates' itself from this aspiration and vigorously prohibits its realisation.

As a result, unconscious feelings of guilt play a prevalent economic role in a large number of neuroses, and present solid obstacles in the way of recovery. This is why some people react to the progress of treatment in the opposite way and seek out the need to be ill. The sense of guilt that is silent for the patient finds satisfaction here in the state of illness, and in suffering as punishment.[20]

Feminine masochism   175

It was in the course of treatment that Freud came to take a keen interest in what he called the *negative therapeutic reaction*. The analyst has the impression, he writes, of 'a force which is defending itself by every possible means against recovery and which is absolutely resolved to hold on to illness and suffering.'[21] In *The Ego and the Id*, Freud provides an in-depth description and analysis of the negative therapeutic reaction. In some subjects, he writes:

> Every partial solution that ought to result, and in other people does result, in an improvement or a temporary suspension of symptoms produces in them for the time being an exacerbation of their illness; they get worse during the treatment instead of getting better.[22] This strange reaction to treatment is paradoxical, to say the least. It is a sign of the work of the negative within and against the self, which is the direct expression of moral and feminine masochism.

In his *New Introductory Lectures on Psycho-Analysis* (1933a), and, more specifically, in the 32nd lecture entitled 'Anxiety and Instinctual Life', Freud points out that the need for punishment, an expression of the unconscious feeling of guilt, is the major reason for resistance in treatment: it is 'the worst enemy of the therapeutic effort'. So, in these cases, neurotic suffering, in perpetual repetition, is replaced and transposed by another suffering caused by an accident, a traumatic failure or a new illness.

Masochism, thus, appears as the result of a turning round of the destructive drive against the ego. It is a reversal of sadism against the self. In the same way as drive stasis, the turning round of destructive forces implies a libidinal regression. In effect, there is a shift from object-libido to narcissistic libido. Similarly, narcissistic retrenchment entails a regression to archaic, primordial masochism. In this way, 'instinctual repression', which is in itself a perfect form of auto-sadism, slows down and prevents a large proportion of destructive instinctual components from being exercised in life. These are recuperated and exploited by the superego. The sadism of the superego and the masochism of the ego thus combine and complement each other to 'work' against the person.

It is worth noting, however, that the cultural repression of the impulse is fortunately not pathological in itself. It is even necessary, if not indispensable, for the respect of otherness and the harmonious maintenance of relational equilibrium and social exchange. Drive stasis does, however, become threatening and dangerous only when it is used excessively by the subject, generating intense feelings of guilt which in turn produce masochism in a circular fashion. In this respect, it can be noted that moral awareness becomes all the more bitter and sensitive the more the person refrains from any outward aggression. As a result, the more the (passivated) subject restrains their aggression, the greater the self-blame, and the more cruel and destructive the (activated) sadism turned against the self. Finally, the dangerous nature of moral masochism stems from the fact that it has its source in the death instinct, that it corresponds to the part of this instinct that has avoided its outward release in the form of destruction. When the mortifying forces of the instinct cannot

176 Feminine masochism

be released outwards, they are exerted against the self, thus forming masochism. Here, moral masochism and feminine erogenous masochism, marked by inversion rather than perversion, are very similar and complement each other.

Masochism certainly provides pleasure, and turned-around sadism has the feminine value of an erotic component. Indeed, even self-destruction of the person cannot be achieved without libidinal satisfaction. In fact, while masochism is generally harmful to the subject, it is not necessarily permeated only by the destructive and deadly 'negative', even if it is pleasurable. On the contrary, it is even culturally valued, primordial. It is a categorical imperative that lies at the heart of the structuring of the self, the constitution of morality and moral consciousness (*Gewissen*). The eroticisation of destructiveness and the 'detour' of a part of the death instinct that serves as protection against primary processes thus play a crucial role in 'compressing' against unbinding. In this way, by performing a task of 'binding agent', the masochism imperative to life clearly shows that it is at the service of the life instinct, and that displeasure too can be the guardian of life.

Feminine masochism as the negative of sadism

In his *Three Essays on the Theory of Sexuality*, Freud (1905d) examines the notions of female sadism and masochism, with their respective active and passive forms. Commonly, the notion of sadism oscillates between the resolution of an attitude that is simply active towards the sexual object, followed by violent conduct, to the perverse one of the unique union of jouissance at the debasement and humiliation of the object and the abuse inflicted upon it. On the other hand, the term masochism encompasses all the passive feminine attitudes chosen in relation to the sexual life and the sexual object, the ultimate of which seems to be the linking of pleasure to the physical and psychic suffering endured by the sexual object. But masochism, as a perversion, seems to be further removed from the sexual objective than its opposite; does it appear in a primary way, or does it originate in sadism through means of a transformation?

For Freud at that time (1905), masochism was nothing more than an extension of sadism, that prohibits itself and falls back on the subject's own self,[23] which thus immediately takes the place of the sexual object. In extreme cases of perversion, clinical analysis highlights the association of a large number of elements (castration complex, feelings of guilt) that constrain and fix the primary passive feminine sexual attitude. Freud also points out that sadism and masochism occupy a special place among perversions, in so far as the opposition between activity and passivity that forms their basis is part of the general characteristics of sexual life. Consequently, the characteristic feature of this perversion is in the fact that its active (masculine) form and passive (feminine) form are generally found paired together in the same person. The study of sadism reveals the presence, alongside prevalent sadistic tendencies, of masochistic pleasure, and vice versa. The masochist is a repressed sadist[24] even if the roles of each are not generally interchangeable.

The pair of opposites particularly perceptible in perversions is regularly found in the psychoanalysis of neuroses, with the fundamental dualism that makes up the notion of conflict specific to the human being (conflict between desire and defence, between different systems or agencies, between drives, Oedipal, etc.). The activity–passivity pairing, which is notably realised in the sadism–masochism opposition, is considered by Freud to be one of the great polarities characterising the subject's sexual life, which is found in couples that follow its succession: phallic–castrated, masculine–feminine.

It should be remembered that the notion of bisexuality, introduced into psychoanalysis by Freud under the influence of Fliess, assumes that every human being is constitutionally thought to have both masculine and feminine sexual dispositions, which are reflected in the conflicts encountered by the subject in assuming their own gendered identity. So, the feminine (*das Weibliche*) of masochism, that is found in both men and women, is not femininity (*die Weiblichkeit*), which would be the set of characteristics specific to women ('being castrated, undergoing coitus and giving birth in pain') as opposed to masculinity or virility. As part of the masochistic triptych (erogenous, moral, feminine), *feminine masochism*, therefore, reflects a fantastical or fanciful elaboration that situates suffering in the psychological domain. This form of feminine masochism is, therefore, not unique to women. Linked to the question of symbolic castration and the problem of narcissism, it should be associated with the *fustigation phantasy*,[25] a feminine masochistic phantasy developed by Freud (1919e) in his key text 'A Child Is Being Beaten', subtitled 'A Contribution to the Study of the Origin of Sexual Perversions'.

Masochism and introjected or auto-objectal narcissistic sadism

In 'Instincts and their Vicissitudes' (1915c) Freud examines the destiny of the instincts, and lists, alongside repression and sublimation, *reversal into its opposite* and *turning round upon the subject's own self*. He immediately points out that these two processes – the first concerning the objective, the second the object – are, in fact, deeply intertwined, as can be seen in the two main examples, that of sadism–masochism and voyeurism–exhibitionism. Indeed, it seems impossible to describe separately any single element of these dualities.

The reversal from sadism to masochism presupposes both a shift from activity to passivity and an inversion of roles between the (active) person who inflicts suffering and the (passive) person subjected to it. This process may stop at an intermediate stage, where there is a turning round upon the subject's own self (change of object), but where the objective has not become passive but simply considered (making oneself suffer). In its complete form, where the transition to passivity is achieved, masochism implies that 'an extraneous person is once more sought as object; this person, in consequence of the alteration which has taken place in the instinctual aim, has to take over the role of the subject'.[26]

In this way, masochism, a partial instinct that is the complement of sadism, can be understood as a turning round of sadism on to the own self. However, sadism, or the destructive drive, turned outwards and projected, can also be introjected once

178 Feminine masochism

again, thus regressing to its original situation. This gives rise to secondary masochism, which is added to the primary masochism.

We can, thus, say that masochism is sadism turned round upon the subject's own self. As emphasised above, it is generally achieved during the 'cultural repression of the instincts'. This leads to a feeling of guilt, and moral conscience becomes all the more tyrannical and pressing as the person denies themselves any aggression towards others. Restricting aggression towards the outside world brings harshness and, thus, aggression to the person's ego-ideal. The greater the control over aggression, the more intense becomes the aggressive tendency of the ideal against the ego. It is like a displacement, a turning round on to the own ego and a restrictive and violent compression of the destructive impulses within the self.

It should also be remembered that the superego born of identification with the paternal model is the dialectical index of desexualisation or even sublimation. But it seems that, in such a transmutation, a disunity of instincts occurs. After sublimation, the erotic component no longer has the strength to bind together the totality of the destruction that was adjoining it, and the latter becomes autonomous and uncontrollable, like a tendency to aggression and destruction. It is from this disunity that the ideal in general derives its trait of harshness and cruelty, that of imperative duty. Jacques Lacan in particular developed this Freudian concept. In his 1972–1973 seminar *Encore*,[27] he asserted that the superego is an agency that incites and invites the subject to exceed the pleasure principle. In fact, it would rather prescribe jouissance: 'Enjoy [Jouis]', at the risk of becoming the object of death instincts and perishing itself. Indeed, jouissance is to be understood here as 'beyond the pleasure principle'. Freudian and Lacanian psychoanalysis argues that the specific concept of jouissance can only be found in the entanglement of language with desire. This complex and specific notion of jouissance, which is linked to castration and lack, concerns unconscious desire, the desire of the 'Other' that imposes enjoyment [*jouir*], that makes it enjoy. For Lacan, the 'neurotic', who can respond with the signifier '*j'ouis*',[28] complies while trying to make this 'Other' within them enjoy. In this way, they desperately try to fill the chasm (castration), at the risk of encountering infinitude and death.

On the other hand, the ego is worried by three threats, which correspond to three kinds of anxiety: from the outside world, from the libido in the id, and from the severity of the superego. In *The Ego and the Id*, and, more specifically, in Chapter V about 'The Dependent Relations of the Ego', Freud (1923b) points out that the superego has the capacity to oppose the ego and control it. It is the memorial to the impotence and dependence that were formerly of the ego and perpetuates its authority even over the mature ego. It has a parental role to which the ego must submit. Similarly, he reminds us that:

> it may be said of the id that it is totally non-moral, of the ego that it strives to be moral, and of the super-ego that it can be super-moral and then become as cruel as only the id can be.

The superego torments the guilty ego with the same sensations of anguish, and watches for opportunities to have it punished by the outside world. According to one Freudian view, the severity of the superego, in other words the introjected parental couple, is simply an extension of the severity of external authority, which it has relieved of its functions and, in part, replaced.[29] However, as Melanie Klein and other English authors have pointed out, the severity of the superego that a child develops in no way reproduces the harshness of the treatment they have undergone.

The return of primary masochism

As I have already mentioned, Freud (1915c) claims in 'Instincts and their Vicissitudes' that the transformation of sadism into masochism would mean a return to the primary narcissistic object, while in both cases the person is exchanged through identification with another, foreign self. As a consequence, masochism, narcissism, and the feminine are closely intertwined. This idea is taken up again in 'A Child is Being Beaten' (1919e), which I discuss later, where Freud points out that masochism is not a primary instinctual manifestation, but arises from a reversal of sadism against the subject's own self, and thus coincides with a narcissistic regression (primary feminine) from the object to the ego.[30] Shortly afterwards, Freud put forward the hypothesis of a primary masochism, with the discovery of the death drive. It seems that, before 1920, sadism is more linked with a 'secondary' control instinct (different from the original cruelty of the child), i.e., with a sexual objective, masochism being merely a turning round upon the person. The notion of the death instinct completely revolutionises the 'sexual everything' and, thus, introduces a new metapsychology.

An earlier, first elaboration of the notion of the death drive therefore underpins the two articles of 1915 and 1919, 'Instincts and their Vicissitudes' and 'A Child is Being Beaten', respectively. Then came the fundamental turning point in 1920 (*Beyond the Pleasure Principle*) with the discovery of the death drive. With this last Freudian theory of drives, the intertwining and complementarity of sadism and masochism took on a new meaning. Subsequently, the notion of primary masochism emerges. Similarly, masochism is no longer simply the turning around of sadism towards the person, nor is it just a change of sexual objective. The notion of the death drive goes beyond the sexual. It seems, then, that the interweaving of sadism and masochism in this post-1920 reworking ultimately contains both the sexual (aggressive instinct, feeling of guilt) and the non-sexual (death instinct). The sexual includes a notion of pleasure and the effect of its prohibition involves guilt, punishment, and suffering. The death drive, which is both beyond and below the pleasure principle, nevertheless has a link with sexuality. According to Freud, even in those cases where the tendency to destruction is most evident, a libidinal satisfaction may still be present: object-orientated sexual satisfaction or narcissistic jouissance (cf. *Civilization and Its Discontents*, 1930a).

In his *New Introductory Lectures on Psychoanalysis* (1933a), and, more specifically, in the 32nd lecture entitled 'Anxiety and Instinctual Life', Freud points out

180 Feminine masochism

that masochism, apart from its erotic element, has the objective of self-destruction. Moreover, while it seems obvious for the destructive instinct that the ego originally harbours all instinctual impulses, it follows that *masochism is more ancient than sadism*. Sadism is a destructive instinct directed outwards, which, thus, assumes the mark of aggression. But a certain amount of the original destructive instinct can still remain inside. It can either be bound libidinally, hence masochism, or develop outwards as aggression, with a more or less significant erotic remainder.

However, if the destructive instinct does not find satisfaction in the external world, if it is prevented by solid adversity, then it can flow back and increase the destructive capacity that dominates inside the person. This self-destructive instinct is the figure of the original death drive, which remains silent and 'works' inside the self, unbeknown to the conscious mind. Indeed, the 'secret', mortifying force only reveals itself to the person when, as a destructive instinct, it moves outwards as an aggressive instinct.

In the same vein, Freud's 'Analysis Terminable and Interminable' (1937c) led him to hypothesise that the need for punishment could not be fully understood as the translation of the death instinct through the conflicting relationship between superego and ego alone. Because, while one part of the death instinct is indeed 'psychically bound by the super-ego', other parts 'whether bound or free, may be at work in other, unspecified places'.[31]

As a result, when the superego is formed, considerable assaults from the aggressive instinct get trapped inside the ego and act in a self-destructive way. Suppressed aggression is transferred to the superego and transformed into feelings of guilt and an unconscious need for punishment, where satisfaction is sought in pain and displeasure.

At the edge of displeasure: Jouissance

Following the analysis of dreams about the fulfilment of desires with painful content, Freud, from another perspective, essentially studied the intertwining of pleasure and suffering in the genesis of perversions. In this respect, let us not forget that satisfaction in masochism is intimately linked to pain and suffering.

Thus, for example, erogenous masochism appears to be characterised by an alliance or amalgam between satisfaction and the physical or psychic suffering endured by the sexual object.[32] In a kind of identificatory chiasmus, the satisfaction of the masochist is linked to the 'mirrored' jouissance of the sadist. This situation also involves a process of turning round upon the subject's own self through a change of object, since masochism is precisely sadism turned round on to the ego.[33] The masochist enjoys the pain, but also the fury directed at the subject's own self. In this regard, Freud points out:

> But when once the transformation into masochism has taken place, the pains are very well fitted to provide a passive masochistic aim; for we have every reason to believe that sensations of pain, like other unpleasurable sensations, trench upon sexual excitation and produce a pleasurable condition ... '[34]

Beyond his fundamental text 'The Economic Problem of Masochism' (1924c), the question of masochism was studied by Freud in his contribution to understanding the genesis of sexual perversions, more precisely in 'A Child is Being Beaten' (1919e). In this work, Freud highlights the masochistic phantasies of fustigation in the child (around their fifth or sixth year), to which feelings of pleasure are linked.

Three phases are described in the processual content of this clearly masochistic phantasy:

The first phase of this fustigation phantasy is represented by this statement: '*The father beats the child (hated by me)*'.

Between this first phase and the next one, important transformations have taken place. The beater is indeed the father, but the beaten has become the child author of the phantasy, with the following utterance: '*I am beaten by the father*'.

The third phase, which resembles the first, is marked by the imprecision of the 'fustigating' person, who may be replaced by a phallic and authoritarian paternal substitute. In this final phase, the subject's own self of the child author of the phantasy is now missing.

This phantasy, which is unquestionably masochistic in nature, is charged with strong excitation. This is undoubtedly sexual, in so far as this masochistic representation leads to onanistic satisfaction, notably through incestuous-type love. Thus. The child will say: '*He (the father) loves only me, and not the other child, because it's the other child that he beats*'. But with the manifestation of the consciousness of guilt and the accompanying punishment comes a reversal of the situation and a negation of this love phantasy of an incestuous and Oedipal nature: '*No, he doesn't love you, because he beats you*'. As a result, the phantasy – being beaten by the father oneself – becomes the direct emanation of the consciousness of guilt. Under the effect of regression and punishment for the forbidden genital relationship '*the father loves me*' becomes '*the father beats me*' (*I'm beaten by the father who doesn't love me*), the consciousness of guilt in alliance (*Legierung*) with eroticism no longer simply brings correction for the forbidden genital relationship, but triggers a libidinal arousal inherent in a regressive stage and discharges it in onanistic acts. In the same text, Freud points out that the consciousness of guilt is linked to the autoerotic activity of early childhood and not of adolescence, and that more often than not it is not with the onanistic act that it should be linked, but with what lies at the root of this act; that is to say, an unconscious phantasy stemming from the Oedipal complex. Jean Laplanche's theory of generalised seduction is of particular interest here.

Repetition compulsion, the displeasure principle, and the death drive

The notion of repetition compulsion, essentially studied in *Beyond the Pleasure Principle*, cannot be disassociated from other fundamental notions in Freud's work, such as the pleasure principle, the instinct and its destiny, the death drive, and the concept of binding.

From the outset, psychoanalysis has been confronted with the phenomenon of repetition. If we study symptoms in particular, some are themselves obviously

182 Feminine masochism

repetitive, such as obsessional rituals for example, and they reproduce, in a global and more or less masked way, certain elements of an earlier, inner conflictualisation.[35]

Generally speaking, the repressed tries to 'make a comeback' in the present: '... a thing which has not been understood inevitably reappears; like an unlaid ghost, it cannot rest until the mystery has been solved and the spell broken'.[36] In the course of psychoanalytic treatment, transferential manifestations force the repressed conflict to come to light in the relationship with the analyst. Alongside recollection, transferential repetition and working-through are major stages in the therapeutic process.

By placing at the heart of *Beyond the Pleasure Principle* (1920g) the notion of repetition compulsion, which, it should be remembered, had already been put forward as an argument in 'Remembering, Repeating and Working-Through' (1914g), Freud brought together a number of reproductions of events that had already been observed, and discarded others where repetition played a dominant role in the clinical picture, such as in destiny neurosis and traumatic neurosis. But in these clinical pictures, the analysis of negative repetitions seems to him to demand a new theoretical approach. These are undeniably unpleasant experiences that are repeated. Indeed, although these compulsions originate in the unconscious, it is difficult at first sight to see in these painful repetitions, even in the form of compromise, the realisation of a rejected desire.

And yet, in the first chapters of *Beyond the Pleasure Principle* (1920g), Freud goes in the direction of this fundamental hypothesis, which holds that underneath the manifest suffering – that of the symptom, for example – is the search for the fulfilment of a hitherto inhibited desire. Let us not forget that it was in this text that Freud put forward the famous thesis according to which *what is displeasure for one system of the psychic apparatus is pleasure for the other*. This shows the strange paradox of conscious and unconscious desires.

From this perspective, repetition compulsion is always underpinned by motives subject to the pleasure principle, the guardian of psychic life, and its close relationship with the principle of constancy, which results in the reduction of the organism's internal energy, bringing it back to an inorganic state (Barbara Low's principle of Nirvana or 'inertia'). The reduction of all excitation to zero, or the return to level zero, expresses the tendency of the death drive and its conservative character (self-preservation).

Through the repetition compulsion, the drive regresses and attempts to re-establish an earlier state (primary masochism) that the subject must have lost under the disruptive action of external constraints: 'a kind of organic elasticity, or, to put it another way, the expression of the inertia inherent in organic life'.[37] So, if 'the goal of all life is death', the death drive, in its close relationship with the pleasure principle, would be the drive *par excellence*.

While the destiny of everyone is death, some people have a veritable compulsion of destiny (*Schicksalszwang*), a fundamental need for repetition, an 'eternal return of the same', generally painful and unpleasant, event. At the end of Chapter III of *Beyond the Pleasure Principle* (1920g), Freud addresses the case of those people who 'give the impression of a destiny that pursues them, of a demonic orientation of their existence' (benefactors paid with ingratitude, friends betrayed, etc.).

These compulsions of destiny are characterised by the systematic recurrence of unpleasant experiences, unfolding according to an invariable scenario and appearing as an external fatality (*fatum*) of which the subject feels they are the victim. In fact, the subject has no access to an unconscious desire, which therefore comes to them from outside. Freud gives the example of a woman who, having been married three times, sees her three husbands fall ill soon after marriage, and nurses them until they die.

Freud also points out[38] that the pleasure principle does not regulate the flow of psychic processes on its own or in a dominant way. While there is a strong tendency towards the pleasure principle in the psyche, other forces or conditions also oppose it, so that the ultimate outcome may not always correspond to the tendency towards pleasure. So, for example, in repetition compulsion, the displeasure brought to the ego by repressed instinctual emotions is not in contradiction to the pleasure principle provided by the other system.

This idea can be taken up again, this time with regard to intra-systemic cleavage, as it generally occurs in melancholia, where the lost object is internalised and re-established in the ego. This creates a close association between the displeasure engendered by the difficult mourning of the deprivation, and the pleasure produced by the narcissistic regression and identification of the ego (by incorporation) with the disappeared object. The pleasure here is both sadistic and masochistic, where the jouissance of self-destruction can drive the ego to the point of annihilation.

Melancholy or death masochism

The psychoanalytical study of melancholy has allowed a more in-depth analysis of the feeling of guilt. We know that the accusations and self-deprecations that characterise melancholia can culminate in extreme self-punishment 'confused'[39] through suicide.

Through a process of internalisation of an intersubjective relationship, the ego is split into two opposing parts: one accuses (superego), the other is accused. This second, incriminated part represents the lost love object. Thus: '... self-reproaches are reproaches against a loved object which have been shifted away from it on to the patient's own ego ... *complaints* [of the melancholic] *are really 'plaints' in the old sense of the word*'[40] brought against the disappeared object now incorporated into the self. Attacks against the ego are in fact attacks directed towards another.

Melancholy, like mourning and obsessional neurosis, is a state in which the subject expresses their inescapable condition as victim in a different and apparent way. Melancholy has been a major focus of psychoanalytic reflection. While Freud attempted to study this mental state in his early work, for example in his F and G draft manuscripts (1895–1897), it is in his seminal text 'Mourning and Melancholia' (1917e) that we find an in-depth examination of this condition, linking it above all to compulsion neurosis, another psychic torment. 'The distinguishing mental features of melancholia,' he writes,

> are a profoundly painful dejection, cessation of interest in the outside world, loss of the capacity to love, inhibition in all activity, and a lowering of the self-regarding feelings to a degree that finds utterance in self-reproaches and self-revilings, and culminates in a delusional expectation of punishment.[41]

To sum up, the unlinking-disobjectalisation and incorporation of the object in melancholia lead to a major mobilisation of sadistic and hateful tendencies, directed against the own ego, confused with the loved-lost object. The disinvestment of the object-libido is replaced by a reinvestment of the narcissistic libido, in line with the identification process. Ego and object appear more fused than ever. To suffer is, therefore, to make the other suffer. To die is to make the other die. The masochism of the ego is, consequently, a sadism against the erection of the object internalised in the ego. It is in this perspective that Freud writes: 'The analysis of melancholia now shows that the ego can kill itself only if, owing to the return of the object-cathexis, it can treat itself as an object'.[42] In the end, a victim of others, the melancholic becomes a persecutor of themselves, now amalgamated and 'muddled' with others.

Death masochism and instinctual disintegration

One of the expressions of what we have called *death masochism* can be observed in the mechanisms of the *turning round upon the subject's own self*, and the *reversal into its opposite,* in other words, a transformation of the drives from activity to passivity and in content from love to hatred. In reversal and turning round, we are dealing here with narcissistic sadism, where the drive attacks the interior from within, *from the interior of the body, the interior of the person.* It is a form of internal traumatic invasion. In this way, the body is transformed into an instinctual object-source. Jouissance is auto-objectal, and sadism has become auto-erotic, where the death drive in its intense internal expression can go as far as stopping life.

As we have seen, death masochism, whose ultimate manifestation is suicide, is also very much present in the state of pathological mourning or melancholia.

In his final drive theory, Freud radically opposed the life and death drives. However, the pairing of the dual drives is most generally marked by a mixing (*Mischung*), an assembly of the two antagonistic forces.

In the 32nd lecture entitled 'Anxiety and Instinctual Life' (1933a), Freud makes these clarifications:

> It is our opinion, then, that in sadism and in masochism we have before us two excellent examples of a mixture of the two classes of instinct, of Eros and aggressiveness; and we proceed to the hypothesis that this relation is a model one – that every instinctual impulse that we can examine consists of similar

fusions or alloys of the two classes of instinct. These fusions, of course, would be in the most varied ratios. Thus the erotic instincts would introduce the multiplicity of their sexual aims into the fusion, while the others would only admit of mitigations or gradations in their monotonous trend.[43]

The aggressive component brings a feeling of existence and self-affirmation to sexuality. Aggression is, thus, largely at the service of sexuality. But the proportions in a logic of completeness between Eros and aggression are variable:

> Modifications in the proportions of the fusion between the instincts have the most tangible results. A surplus of sexual aggressiveness will turn a lover into a sex-murderer, while a sharp diminution in the aggressive factor will make him bashful or impotent.[44]

In contrast to the union of the instincts, disunion (*Entmischung*) is characterised by autonomy in terms of the instinct objective. This is a profound regression, an un-coupling between aggression and the sexual function. Let us not forget that the two types of instinct are each determined by an asymmetrical and contradictory logic. Indeed, while libido is a factor in bonding (*Bindung*), and uniting (*Vereinigung*), aggression, on the contrary, tends by itself to 'undo connections'.[45]

Consequently, the more aggression dominates, the more the instinctual union tends to break down; conversely, the more libido dominates, the more the union is achieved. The notion of sexuality has largely evolved within Freudian oppositional dualism: free energy – bound energy, primary process – secondary process, pleasure principle – reality principle, and, in the 'Project for a Scientific Psychology' (1895), inertia principle – constancy principle. Until then, sexuality had fitted in with the first terms, presenting itself as a predominantly explosive force. With the new conceptualisation of the drive (1920g), the death drive becomes this 'primary', 'demonic' force that is truly instinctual, while sexuality, on the other hand, moves to the side of bonding.

But, in the death drive and the tendency to destruction (self or another), libidinal satisfaction is always present, whether sexual satisfaction is orientated towards the object or narcissistic jouissance.[46] As a result, in death masochism, which has its source in primary, narcissistic and erogenous masochism, the instinct for aggression or destruction is present in a pure state, disunited from the life drive, as in the case of the melancholic whose sadism of the superego appears as 'a pure culture of the death instinct'.[47]

Life masochism or the primacy of moral conscience and Eros

Apart from extreme forms of pathological self-destruction or perversion, masochism is, to some extent, useful and necessary. Indeed, the 'enigmatic' and 'unintelligible' masochistic tendency does exist in the instinctual life of human beings.

186 Feminine masochism

As Freud writes in 'The Economic Problem of Masochism' (1924c): 'If pain and unpleasure can be not simply warnings but actually aims, the pleasure principle is paralysed – it is as though the watchman over our mental life were put out of action by a drug'.[48]

This idea that the pleasure principle does not dominate the course of psychic processes was already identified in *Beyond the Pleasure Principle* (1920g): '... there exists in the mind,' Freud explains, 'a strong *tendency* towards the pleasure principle, but that tendency is opposed by certain other forces or circumstances, so that the final outcome cannot always be in harmony with the tendency towards pleasure'.[49] While increased tensions and excitations essentially bring displeasure, according to Fechner's model of the 'tendency to stability', or that of the 'Nirvana principle', there is a disposition on the part of the psychic apparatus to restrict as far as possible the quantity of excitation reaching it, or to keep it as low as possible.

In this way, the pleasure principle, the guardian of life, seeks level zero in the lowering and calming of tension. In this state of extinction, it favours the death instinct,

> whose aim is to conduct the restlessness of life into the stability of the inorganic state, and it would have the function of giving warnings against the demands of the life instincts – the libido – which try to disturb the intended course of life.[50]

A certain form of (active) masochism is also used as a mode of defence against the (passive) masochism of unpleasant situations. This type of masochism, which is sometimes expressed through identification, is necessary for the maturity of the ego, for its strengthening and perhaps even its balance. Thus, for example, the child in the Fort/Da game no longer remains passive, suffering the painful absence of the love object. On the contrary, by reiterating this scene of loss, through symbolic playful expression, they assume an active role of control and power over the object. Repetition compulsions are, therefore, not exclusively unpleasant, nor do they oppose the pleasure principle. In the case of children's play: 'the compulsion to repeat and instinctual satisfaction which is immediately pleasurable seem to converge here into an intimate partnership'.[51]

Like the death drive and Eros, pleasure and displeasure are closely linked and strangely mixed, forming the paradoxical masochism that tends towards life.

The death drive at work in the organism (original sadism or masochism) must, nevertheless, be tamed by the libido. The libido displaces the internal destructive force towards external objects. Although a residual part does not join in this displacement and takes root in the organism, it is specifically proper masochism, original and erogenous, that conserves the individual's own being as a privileged object.

The outward-looking and externalised destructive instinct can, however, once again be internalised and turned inward, thus returning to its original situation. Secondary masochism is added to primary masochism. The increase of masochism in the ego, the result of introjected sadism directed against the subject's own self,

Feminine masochism 187

acts uniformly during the cultural repression of the instincts, which prohibits a large proportion of destructive instinctual components from being exercised in life. This imperative life masochism, initially imposed by external authority through frustrations, is indispensable because it creates morality and the 'moral conscience' that auto-refuses the ego from expressing certain instinctual forces. In the course of a person's gradual development, protecting allo-repression regularly gives way to masochistic auto-repression, which generates a feeling of guilt that gives rise to certain masochistic behaviours. But this auto-repression and the masochism it accompanies cannot take place without narcissistic libidinal satisfaction, since it is an amalgam of the inward-looking destructive tendency and sexuality. Essential auto-repression, or introjected sadism, generates moral pain and suffering which, eroticised in masochism, have an eminently beneficial role, since they act as a bastion against the mortifying disunity of the instincts.

All in all, we can see that masochism, in a rational quantity, is ordinary and necessary. It only becomes pathological or pathogenic when it 'works' hard against the subject's own self, as in certain mental conditions in which the subject's feeling and condition as victim are particularly and incessantly dominant.

Notes

1 Krafft-Ebing (1893). Available at: https://www.perlego.com/book/957137/psychopathia-sexualis-the-classic-study-of-deviant-sex-pdf (accessed on 11 October, 2023).
2 Named after the Austrian writer Leopold von Sacher-Masoch (1836–1895), author of *Venus in Furs* (1870), the word *masochismus was* probably coined by a Berliner in his important 1889 sexual autobiography addressed to Krafft-Ebing (1890). However, the notion of masochismus seems to have been preceded by the word *passivism* invented by Dimitry Stefanowsky (1888), inspired by the work of Alfred Binet (1857–1911).
3 Krafft-Ebing also speaks of '*seltsame* perversion'.
4 Krafft-Ebing (1893)[1969], p. 35.
5 *Id.* p. 159.
6 *Ibid.*
7 There are many examples in literature of women who write in this way, such as Pauline Réage or Vanessa Duriès. These are literary pseudonyms. See Duriès (1993) and Réage (1954; 1972)'.
8 Krafft-Ebing (1893)[1969]), p. 157.
9 Rousseau, J. J. (1770)[2019].
10 The 'Rousseau case' received early attention. See Mœbius P.-J. (1889); Châtelain D. (1890); Demole V. (1918); and the synthesis by Claude Wacjmann (1992).
11 Rousseau, J. J. (1770)[2019].
12 *Ibid.*
13 Binet (1887)[2001], p. 92.'
14 Femininity, p. 116, in Freud (1933a).
15 Freud (1896b), p. 169.
16 Freud (1915c).
17 Freud (1924c).
18 Freud (1923b).
19 Freud (1916d).
20 Freud (1923b).
21 Freud (1937), p. 242.

188   Feminine masochism

22 Freud (1923b).
23 Freud did not yet use the term 'reversal' and 'turning round upon the subject's own self'. He would do so more clearly in 1915 in 'Instincts and their vicissitudes'.
24 Intrasubjective sadomasochism cannot be separated from intersubjective sadomasochistic play. Deleuze stresses, however, that masochism is neither the opposite nor the complement of sadism. In *Venus in Furs*, it is Séverin who really coerces Wanda into a perverse practice. But could Wanda the cruel indulge in the abuse that excites her without identifying with the victim? (G. Deleuze, *Présentation de Sacher Masoch - le froid et le cruel* and the integral text of *La Vénus à la fourrure* [Venus in furs], Paris, Ed. de Minuit, 1967).
25 I explain the dynamics and scope of this masochistic phantasy in the paragraph entitled 'At the edge of displeasure: jouissance' (see *below*, same chapter).
26 Freud (1915c), p. 127.
27 Lacan (1972–1973).
28 'Jouis' comes from the verb 'jouir', to enjoy, but with the apostrophe, 'J'ouis', it also means 'I heard'.
29 Freud (1930a).
30 In the same 1919 text, we note that the transformation of sadism into masochism seems to take place under the influence of the consciousness of guilt, which takes part in the act of repression.
31 Freud (1937c), pp. 242–243.
32 Freud (1905d).
33 Freud (1915c).
34 *Id.*, p. 126.
35 Cf. the hysterical symptom of the mnesic symbol in Freud's early work, in his texts written around 1895: 'The neuro-psychoses of defence' (1894a); Further remarks on the neuro-psychoses of defence (1896b); *Studies on Hysteria* (1895d), etc.
36 Freud (1909b).
37 Freud (1920g), p. 36.
38 *Id.*
39 The term 'confused' is of interest here because of its double meaning. In effect, it holds the meaning of fusion, but also of unveiling the fault.
40 Freud (1917e).
41 *Id.*, p. 244.
42 Freud (1917e).
43 Freud (1933a), pp. 81, 112.
44 Freud, S. (1940a)[1938], p. 150.
45 *Id.*, p. 149.
46 Freud (1930a).
47 Freud (1923b).
48 Freud (1924c), p. 159.
49 Freud (1920g), pp. 9–10.
50 Freud (1924c), p. 160
51 Freud (1920g), p. 23.

Conclusion

In this work, I have focused primarily on the feminine as a theoretical and clinical concept that represents a mode of psychic functioning dominated by negative narcissism, impotence, and defeatism. This condition can invariably be found, beyond anatomical difference, in both men and women. There is no such thing as masculine or feminine purity. In psychic bisexuality, the feminine and the masculine are intertwined. The differences between qualities in men and women are accepted and not explained scientifically.

Similarly, the fundamental primary feminine (original seduction) is not a woman's secondary femininity. The primary body is of the female 'type' long before the distinction of the sexes. The originally seduced child, whether girl or boy, is a receptacle child, feminised and passivated.

This unavoidable primary feminine can, however, prove insurmountable and later become fixed and dominant in certain individuals, giving way to unhappiness, distress, passivation, and masochistic inclinations.

These severely 'feminised' people – both men and women – shout, sometimes cry out and denounce this state of stress, or deliberately and publicly display their narcissistic wounds and moral pain, which continue to eat away at them in the present day. As former victims, they therefore continue to endure in the real world the torments of their historical condition. This is generally organised around an individual myth that is based on early narcissistic deficiencies, narcissistic wounds or sexual trauma (Maïdi, 2008).

Not overcome, these difficulties manifest themselves particularly in the repetition compulsion, which finds here its full operational value. For these people who are both plaintive and complaining, placed in a position of passivation and resignation, the repetition compulsion denotes a mode of psychic functioning of the masochistic feminine type, a kind of multiform masochistic complacency, even a liminal or clearly pathological and psychotic state dominated by feelings of internal and external attack. In this instance, it is, more often than not, an organisation of the 'paranoid feminine' type, where the subject is, in effect, tyrannised by ideas of persecution and unremitting harassment, as well as by serious and extreme thoughts of self-destruction.

DOI: 10.4324/9781003414247-12

190   Conclusion

Close to Freudian thought, my aim in this work has been to analyse and understand the psychic phenomena that lead the subject to experience repeated unpleasant situations. This approach has led me to research and locate the genesis for the repetition of a traumatic 'feminine' in the subject's history, to look into their sometimes most archaic past, and even to consider the origin of the person's suffering from a phylogenetic and transgenerational point of view or in terms of individual mythology. In this situation, the person has the compelling feeling of having been the object of a trauma from birth, of having been prey to a cruel destiny in the sense of this equivocal, melancholic, paranoid and megalomaniac assertion: 'I was born to occupy the place of a living martyr.'

Furthermore, I have approached the inescapable notion of trauma, principally in the profound relationship between the feminine, sexuality and narcissism. This clinical, psychoanalytical and psychopathological text therefore focuses, globally, on traumatic mental organisations with the subject's clear and explicit affirmation of their restrictive and recurrent position as martyr, a status in which the notion of jouissance is not absent.

So, while I have excluded stress neurosis from this field of reflection, I have nevertheless gone beyond what, in the classical nosography, could be called traumatic neurosis or failure neurosis in my theoretical and clinical approach. Indeed, traumatic neurosis, which generally follows a violent emotional shock, like failure neurosis, do not sufficiently highlight the overdetermined expression of these disorders, the traumatic archaic feminine, the infantile conflicts, and above all – as psychoanalytical clinical practice has mainly identified through destiny neurosis – the impact of the unconscious and the value of the repetition compulsion.

In destiny neurosis, or, more accurately, in what Freud called destiny compulsion (*Schicksalszwang*), the subject is confronted, in spite of themselves, with their unconscious wish, which comes back to them from outside in the form of recurrent unhappy events, as the fruit of an external fatality. But this 'indirect' desire of the subject is often someone else's desire, real or imagined. A desire that is consequently borrowed and adopted by the person who makes it their own. Yet, this desire remains buried and repudiated, pushed from consciousness, although sometimes revealing itself to it and being expressed through symptomatic compromises.

Closely related to this issue of 'demonic', 'destinal' repetition, I've addressed the question of the feminine in relation to the deadly negative of the instinctual force, under the concept I call 'victimhood neurosis'. What seems to me to characterise this variety of 'neurosis' or, more clearly, psychopathological organisation, and could be described as 'victim syndrome' with an essentially descriptive value, are precisely the endless and genuine distressing situations, the vivid and intense sensations of an 'exceptional', *a priori* unpleasant, traumatic position. These experiences are as much displayed as described, thus manifesting complaint in its double sense of finding fault and registering a grievance, and seeking in this way a mythical reparation for their damage.

Consequently, whether the situation is real, linked to external reality, or 'lived' phantasmatically – that is, relating to an internal reality – the harm alleged by the 'feminised' subject is frequently accompanied by the vigorous expression of a need for reparation, a significant secondary guilt, and the translation of a masochistic psychic experience of a sacrificial type.

Supported by the observations presented in this text, clinical practice attempts to provide some answers to the problems of masochistic mental organisations of the 'feminine' type. It shows that this is, more often than not, a repetition of the harmful primary intersubjective relationship, or its failure, marked by real or perceived deprivation. If the subject has suffered from a pathogenic environment or a native deficiency in the primary homosexual relationship, they thus tend to retain these unpleasant moments, 'involuntarily' reproducing the same trauma. The position of 'secondary' genuine victim is, therefore, achieved *a posteriori* as a backlash to a fundamental and 'primary' position of early victim, a status initially imposed by an insecure, hostile or defective environment. It is in this sense that, paraphrasing Freud's (1905d) formulation, we can say: 'To lose the object is only ever to re-lose it'. Failure is re-found. The misfortune of the first 'bad encounter', the 'unhappy encounter', is perpetuated. As a result, studies are discovering that, in the majority of cases, while the individual has at first been an 'original' victim in the context of their early environment, it seems that, in the second instance, they unconsciously play an active role in repeating unpleasant conditions and producing a protean 'militant' feminine masochism.

This feminine masochism, which, it should be remembered, is inherent in the psychic processes of each individual, seems strange and contradictory to say the least. On several occasions, Freud was rightly led to describe the phenomenon of masochism as 'enigmatic' and 'unintelligible'. How, indeed, 'can pain and displeasure in themselves be goals, and no longer warnings?' How can suffering be sought by the subject themselves? How can an upsurge in excitation be accompanied by pleasure? How can a state of rest and tranquillity be strangely and paradoxically unpleasant?

Freud himself was at a loss to answer these questions. He noted, however, that the quantitative explanation of this phenomenon was clearly insufficient, and that a qualitative factor was required. In 1924, in his seminal text 'The Economic Problem of Masochism', which develops the ideas of *Beyond the Pleasure Principle*, including the function of the death drive and its significance in the clinical approach to masochism, he adds with regret: 'We'd be much further ahead if we could indicate what this qualitative character is... but unfortunately, we do not know'. Yet, this question of feminine masochism is of vital importance in psychoanalysis and psychopathology. It is, in fact, a constituent of, and basis for, many conditions or inconceivable behaviours through which certain subjects seem to be pursued by an unfortunate fate, a demonic destiny.

Psychoanalytic clinical evidence certainly indicates that some subjects actively desire, crave and indulge in painful or humiliating situations, even though they vigorously defend themselves against them at the conscious level, experiencing these same situations as exceptionally negative, unpleasant, and intolerable. Indeed, it is a masochistic attraction and tolerance that compels the subject, who has become

192 Conclusion

a martyr to their own unconscious, to iterate what is painful until, more often than not, in treatment, in the form of a negative therapeutic reaction. Of course, this type of feminine masochism, militant and active, sought-after and 'acted upon', rests on fragile narcissistic and identity foundations, shaken by this traumatic archaic history.

Ultimately, could the repetition of suffering and the negative masochism that goes with it be the expression of a tribute to infantile loyalty? Beyond this causal explanation of the original trauma, Freud's 'riddle' remains. The economic problem of masochism is far from resolved. Perhaps this riddle does not have to be solved, for it is quite simply rooted in the mystery of human nature, haunted by death (like Freud himself, heir to German Romanticism). Masochism, the 'guardian of life', clearly seems to be inherent to the psychic make-up of every individual. Yet, how does this notion of suffering also fit into Western culture, where the notion of destiny is important, as is individualism; a society in which the individual is confronted with Goethe's essential distinction: 'Be the anvil or the hammer'.[1] We can also wonder, on the other hand, about the universality of this problem. The unconscious, structured as language and indispensable to the emergence of language, has no border. It is certainly linked to, and impregnated by, culture, even though it claims the nature and truth of the subject. In this sense, the unconscious shows that it is animated by original culture and religion. This is why some of the studies presented raise the question of the significance of belief and the sacred. Let us not forget that different religions favour dolorism and asceticism. We could mention here the myth of original sin and the Christian theme of redemptive suffering.

As a result, is it ultimately possible to treat, heal or simply hear and relieve suffering? I think so. In fact, these psychically victimised people are becoming commonplace for psychoanalysts. They hate themselves through introjective identification with the negative other, and suffer cruelly from a narcissistic wound and deficiency. Notwithstanding, these patients are considered 'difficult', as they tend to resist treatment. For them, repetition of the repressed is stronger than recollection. What is bad becomes good, an asset, the renunciation of which proves painful. The patient is afraid of being changed in spite of themselves. This can make therapeutic work arduous and complicated. Indeed, the patient may take advantage of their capacity for resistance and defy the therapist's help, like those people who provoke their pathology through jouissance. I am thinking, for example, of Münchhausen syndrome and other pathomimias.

Yet, treatment, which risks repeated failure given that this is part of the subject's morbid and deadly logic, is certainly not impossible. These people are not 'un-analysable'. So, once the patient has expressed the need for recognition of the harm they have suffered – a prerequisite that must be heard and taken into consideration – the treatment will primarily enable the subject to move from repetition to recollection; help them become aware of the part they play in the occurrence of unhappy events, and of their jouissance through the autosadistic internal Other, understand the need for punishment and identification with the aggressor, but, where the object of aggression is the patient's own ego, dis-identify with the lost object, emerge from their status as negative exception, and ultimately offer the patient the freedom to be and to decide: in other words, quite simply, to disengage from their specific condition of the pathological feminine.

Note

1 This word by Goethe is used by Sacher-Masoch in *Venus in Furs* (2006), applying it in a distinctive way to the relationship between man and woman. He writes, in a very personal style:

All a woman's power lies in the passion a man may feel for her, and which she knows how to take advantage of if he is not careful. Indeed, he can only choose between the role of slave and that of tyrant. Let him surrender, and the yoke will begin to weigh on his head, and he will feel the approach of the whip.

References

ABRAHAM K. (1907–1914), 'Giovanni Segantini, essai psychanalytique', in *Œuvres complètes, Vol. I*. Paris: Payot, 1965.

ABRAHAM K. (1907–1914), 'Les différences pyschosexuelles entre l'hysterie et la démence précoce'. In *Œuvres complètes*, Vol. 1. Paris: Payot, 1965.

ABRAHAM K. (1915–1925), 'Développement de la libido'. In *Œuvres complètes, Vol. 2* (I. Barande, Trans.), Paris: Payot, 1966.

AESCHYLUS (1902), *Prometheus Bound* (E. R. Bevan, Trans.). London: David Nutt.

AISENSTEIN M., FINE A., PRAGIER G. (1995) *L'hypochondrie*, in *Monographies de la Revue française de psychanalyse*. Paris: PUF.

ANDRÉ J. (1995), *Aux origines féminines de la sexualité*. Paris: PUF.

ANDREAS-SALOMÉ L. (1916), 'Anal und sexual'. *Imago*, *IV*(5), 249–273.

ANDREAS-SALOMÉ L. (1921), *L'amour du narcissisme*. Paris: Gallimard, 1980.

AULAGNIER, P. (1975), *The Violence of Interpretation: From Pictogram to Statement* (A. Sheridan, Trans). Hove: Brunner-Routledge, 2001.

AULAGNIER P. (1985), *L'apprenti historien et le maître sorcier*. Paris: PUF.

AULAGNIER P. (1986), *Un interprète en quête de sens*. Paris: Ramsay.

ANZIEU D. (1974), 'Le moi-peau'. *Nouvelle Revue de Psychanalyse*, *9*, 195–208.

BAK R. (1946), 'Masochism in paranoia'. Published online 30 April 2018. Available at: https://doi.org/10.1176/appi.psychotherapy.1947.1.4.548.

BAUDELAIRE C. (1857), *The Flowers of Evil* (W. Aggeler, Trans.). Fresno, CA: Academy Library Guild, 1954.

BAUDELAIRE C. (2012), *Paris Spleen: little poems in prose* (K. Waldrop, Trans.). Middletown, CT: Wesleyan University Press. Available at: https://muse.jhu.edu/book/425/.

CHAMBERS R. (1987), *Mélancolie et opposition, les débuts du modernisme en France*. Paris: Corti.

CHÂTELAIN D. (1890), *La folie de J.-J. Rousseau*. Paris: Neuchâtel.

CIORAN E. M. (1973), *The Trouble with Being Born* (R. Howard, Trans.). London: Penguin Books, 2020.

COTARD J. (1882), 'Le délire des négations'. In *Textes essentiels de la psychiatrie* (Jacques Postel, Ed.). Paris: Larousse, 1994.

COURNUT J. (1991), *L'ordinaire de la passion : Nevroses du trop, nevroses du vide*. Paris: PUF, 'Le Fil Rouge' Collection.

COURNUT J. (2002), *L'ordinaire de la passion – Névroses du trop, névroses du vide*. Paris: PUF.

196   References

COURNUT J. (2006), 'Why are men afraid of women?' (A. Weller, Trans.). *International Journal of Psychoanalysis*, *83*, 970–974.

COURNUT M., COURNUT J. (1993), 'La castration et le féminin dans les deux sexes'. *Revue française de psychanalyse*, *LVII*, spécial congrès, 1335–1557.

DAVID C. (1973), Les belles différences. *Nouvelle revue de psychanalyse*, *7*, 99–122.

DE BEAUVOIR S. (1949). *Le deuxième sexe* [*The Second Sex*], Vol. I, *Les faits et les mythes* [*Facts and Myths*]. Paris: Gallimard.

DEBRAY R. (1983), *L'équilibre psychosomatique: organisation mentale des diabétiques* [Psychosomatic balance: the mental organisation of diabetics]. Paris: Dunod.

DEGOS L. (1994), *Les greffes d'organes* [Organ transplants]. Paris: Flammarion.

DE HEUSCH L. (1986), *Le sacrifice dans les religions africaines* [Sacrifice in African religions]. Paris: Gallimard.

DE MAISTRE J. (1796–1797), *Les sacrifices*. Paris: Pocket, 1994.

DEMOLE V. (1918), 'Analyse psychiatrique des *Confessions de J.-J. R.*'. *Schweizer Archiv für Neurologie und Psychiatrie*, *II*(2), 270–304.

DE MUSSET A. (1834), *Lorenzaccio*. A play of the Romantic Period.

DEUTSCH H. (1944), *The Psychology of Women, Vol. 1*. London: Research Books, 1946–1947.

DUBOIS D'AMIENS F. (1833), *Histoire philosophique de l'hypocondrie et de l'hystérie*. Paris: Deville-Cavellin.

EHRENBERG A. (1998), *La fatigue d'être soi*. Paris: Odile Jacob.

ENRIQUEZ M. (1984). *Aux carrefours de la haine – Paranoïa, masochisme, apathie*. Paris: EPI.

ERNST L. (Ed.) (1961), *Letters of Sigmund Freud 1873–1939* (T. & L. Stern, Trans.). London: Hogarth Press.

EVANS-PRITCHARD E. E (1956), *Nuer Religions*. Oxford: Oxford University Press.

EY H. (1960), *Manuel de psychiatrie* (6th edn). Paris: Masson, 2010.

FAIN M. (1990), 'À propos de l'hypocondrie'. *Cahiers du Centre de Psychanalyse et de psychothérapie*, *21*, 177–184, 2010.

FAIN M. (1993), 'Spéculations métapsychologiques hasardeuses à partir de l'étude des procédés autocalmants'. *Revue française de psychosomatique*, *4*, 59–69.

FAIRBAIRN W. R. D. (1945), 'Considerations arising from the Schreber Case'. *British Journal of Medical Psychology*, *29*(2), 113–127, June 1956.

FÉDIDA P. (1995), 'L'hypocondriaque médecin'. In *Monographies de la Revue française de psychanalyse*. Paris: PUF.

FELLINI F. (1969), *Fellini Satyricon*, film.

FRAZER J. G. (1910), *Totemism and Exogamy: A Treatise on Certain Early Forms of Superstition and Society*. London: Macmillan.

FRAZER J. G. (1911), *The Magic Art and the Evolution of Kings* (Vol. 1 of *The Golden Bough*). London: Macmillan, 1911–1915, 12 vols.

FREUD S. (1894a), Draft K, The Neuro-Psychoses of Defence. *S. E.*, *1*, 220–228. London: Hogarth Press.

FREUD S. (1895), 'A Project for a Scientific Psychology'. *S. E.*, *1*. London: Hogarth Press.

FREUD S. (1895a), 'Psychopathology', in *The Origins of Psychoanalysis*. London: Imago, 1954.

FREUD S. (with BREUER J.) (1895d), *Studies on Hysteria. S. E.*, *2*. London: Hogarth Press.

FREUD S. (1896b), Further Remarks on the Neuro-Psychoses of Defence *S. E.*, *3*, 159–187. London: Hogarth Press.

References 197

FREUD S. (1897), *The Complete Letters of Sigmund Freud to Wilhelm Fliess 1887–1904* (J. Masson, Trans.). Cambridge, MA: Belknap Press, 1986.

FREUD S. (1899), An Accomplished Premonition. *S. E.*, *1*. London: Hogarth Press.

FREUD S. (1900a), *The Interpretation of Dreams. S. E.*, *4–5*. London: Hogarth Press.

FREUD S. (1905d), *Three Essays on the Theory of Sexuality. S. E.*, *7*, 125–243. London: Hogarth Press.

FREUD S. (1905e), *Fragment of an Analysis of a Case of Hysteria. S. E.*, *7*, 1–122. London: Hogarth Press.

FREUD S. (1907a), A Few Theoretical Remarks on Paranoia, in *The Freud/Jung Letters: The Correspondence between Sigmund Freud and C. G. Jung* (R. Manheim, Trans.). Princeton, NJ: Princeton University Press, 1979.

FREUD S. (1907b), Minutes of 6 February 1907, in H. Nunberg & E. Federn (Eds), (M. Nunberg, Trans.), *Minutes of the Vienna Psychonalytic Society, Vol. 1, 1906–1908*. New York: International Universities Press, 1962.

FREUD S. (1908a), 'Hysterical Phantasies and Their Relation to Bisexuality'. *S. E.*, *9*, 155–166. London: Hogarth Press, London.

FREUD S. (1909b), *Analysis of a Phobia in a Five-Year-Old Boy. S. E.*, *10*, 3–149. London: Hogarth Press.

FREUD S. (1909d), *Notes Upon a Case of Obsessional Neurosis. S. E.*, *10*, 153–249. London: Hogarth Press.

FREUD S. (1910c), *Leonardo da Vinci and a Memory of his Childhood. S. E.*, *11*, 59–137. London: Hogarth Press.

FREUD S. (1911c), *Psycho-Analytic Notes on an Autobiographical Account of a Case of Paranoia: Dementia Paranoides* (The Schreber Case). *S. E.*, *12*, 3–84. London: Hogarth Press.

FREUD S. (1912b), 'The Dynamics of Transference'. *S. E.*, *12*, 97–108. London: Hogarth Press.

FREUD S. (1912c), 'Types of Onset of Neurosis'. *S. E.*, *12*, 229–238. London: Hogarth Press.

FREUD S. (1912–1913), *Totem and Taboo. S. E.*, *13*, ix–163. London: Hogarth Press.

FREUD S. (1913i), 'The Disposition to Obsessional Neurosis'. *S. E.*, *12*, 317–326. London: Hogarth Press.

FREUD S. (1913j), 'The Claims of Psycho-Analysis to Scientific Interest'. *S. E.*, *13*, 165–199. London: Hogarth Press.

FREUD S. (1914c), 'On Narcissism: An Introduction'. *S. E.*, *14*, 67–102. London: Hogarth Press.

FREUD S. (1915a), 'Observations on Transference-Love'. *S. E.*, *12*, 157–174. London: Hogarth Press.

FREUD S. (1915c), 'Instincts and their Vicissitudes'. *S. E.*, *14*, 111–140. London: Hogarth Press.

FREUD S. (1915e), 'The Unconscious'. *S. E.*, *14*, 161–215. London: Hogarth Press.

FREUD S. (1915f), 'A Case of Paranoia Running Counter to the Psycho-Analytic Theory of the Disease'. *S. E.*, *14*, 261–272. London: Hogarth Press.

FREUD S. (1916d), 'Some Character-Types Met with in Psycho-Analytic Work'. *S. E.*, *14*, 309–334. London: Hogarth Press.

FREUD S. (1916–1917), *Introductory Lectures on Psycho-analysis. S. E.*, *16*. London: Hogarth Press.

FREUD S. (1917b), 'A Childhood Recollection from *Dichtung une Warheit*'. *S. E.*, *17*, 145–156. London: Hogarth Press.

198 References

FREUD S. (1917e), 'Mourning and Melancholia'. *S. E.*, *14*, 239–260. Hogarth Press, London.

FREUD S. (1918b), *From the History of an Infantile Neurosis. S. E.*, *17*, 3–124. London: Hogarth Press.

FREUD S. (1919e), 'A Child is Being Beaten'. *S. E.*, *17*, 177–204. London: Hogarth Press.

FREUD S. (1919h), 'The "Uncanny"'. *S. E.*, *17*, 219–256. London: Hogarth Press.

FREUD S. (1920a), 'The Psychogenesis of a Case of Homosexuality in a Woman'. *S. E.*, *18*, 145–175. London: Hogarth Press.

FREUD S. (1920g), *Beyond the Pleasure Principle. S. E.*, *18*, 3–64. London: Hogarth Press.

FREUD S. (1921c), *Group Psychology and the Analysis of the Ego. S. E.*, *18*, 67–143. London: Hogarth Press.

FREUD S. (1923b), *The Ego and the Id. S. E.*, *19*, 3–67. London: Hogarth Press.

FREUD S. (1923d), 'A Seventeenth-Century Demonological Neurosis'. *S. E.*, *19*, 69–108. London: Hogarth Press.

FREUD S. (1923e), 'The Infantile Genital Organisation'. *S. E.*, *19*, 141–148. London: Hogarth Press.

FREUD S. (1924c), 'The Economic Problem of Masochism'. *S. E.*, *19*: 287–297. London: Hogarth Press.

FREUD S. (1924d), 'The Dissolution of the Oedipus Complex'. *S. E.*, *19*, 173–182. London: Hogarth Press.

FREUD S. (1925j), 'Some Psychical Consequences of the Anatomical Distinction between the Sexes'. *S. E.*, *19*, 243–260. London: Hogarth Press.

FREUD S. (1926d), *Inhibitions, Symptoms and Anxiety. S. E.*, *20*, 77–174. London: Hogarth Press.

FREUD S. (1928b), 'Dostoevsky and Parricide'. *S. E.*, *21*, 175–197. London: Hogarth Press.

FREUD S. (1930a), *Civilization and its Discontents. S. E.*, *21*, 59–147. London: Hogarth Press.

FREUD S. (1931b), *Introductory Lectures on Psycho-Analysis* (Female Sexuality). *S. E.*, *9*, 225–245. London: Hogarth Press.

FREUD S. (1933a), *New Introductory Lectures on Psychoanalysis. S.E.*, *22*, 112–135. London: Hogarth Press.

FREUD S. (1937c), 'Analysis Terminable and Interminable'. *S. E.*, *23*, 211–254. London: Hogarth Press.

FREUD S. (1937d), 'Constructions in Analysis'. *S. E.*, *23*, 255–270. London: Hogarth Press.

FREUD S. (1939a), *Moses and Monotheism. S. E.*, *21*, 3–137. London: Hogarth Press.

FREUD S. (1940a[1938]), *An Outline of Psychoanalysis. S. E.*, *23*, 141–207. London: Hogarth Press.

FREUD S., ABRAHAM K. (1907–1925) *The Complete Correspondence of Sigmund Freud and Karl Abraham* (C. Schwarzacker, Trans.). London: Karnac, 2002

FREUD S., BULLIT, C. W. (1966), *Thomas Woodrow Wilson: Twenty-Eighth President of the United States, A Psychological Study*. Houghton Mifflin.

FREUD S., FERENCZI S. (1908–1914), *Correspondence of Sigmund Freud and Sàndor Ferenczi*, Vol. 1. (E. Brabant, E. Falzeder, P. Giampieri-Deutsch, Eds, P. Hoffer, Trans.). Cambridge, MA: Belknap Press, 1993.

GIRARD R. (1972), *La Violence et le Sacré* [Violence and the sacred], Paris: Grasset.

GIRARD R. (1982), *Le bouc émissaire* [The scapegoat]. Paris: Grasset,

GREEN A. (1983a), 'La mère morte'. In *Narcissisme de vie, Narcissisme de mort*. Paris: Éd. de Minuit, pp. 222–253.

References 199

GREEN A. (1983b), *Narcissisme de vie, Narcissisme de mort*. Paris: Éd. de Minuit.

GREEN A. (1990), *La folie privée (Psychanalyse des cas limites)*. Paris: Gallimard.

GREEN A. (1993), *Le travail du négatif*. Paris: Éd. de Minuit.

GRODDECK G. (1923), *The Book of the It*. Northport, AL: Vision Press, 1961.

HENTIG H. VON (1948), *The Criminal and his Victim*. New Haven, CT: Yale University Press.

HERITIER F. (1996), *Masculin/féminin, La Pensée de la différence*. Paris: Odile Jacob, 2002.

HUBERT H., MAUSS M. (1899), *Essai sur la nature et la fonction du sacrifice* [Essay on the nature and function of sacrifice]. *Sociétés*, *1*(107), pp. 63–71, 2010.

JANET P. (1926–1928), *De l'angoisse à l'extase* (2 vols). Paris: Société P. Janet, 1975.

JANIN C. (1996), *Figures et destins du traumatisme*, Paris: PUF, 2nd edn. 1999.

JEANNEAU A. (2002), 'L'hypocondrie ou le corps ailleurs qu'en lui-même'. *Revue Française de Psychosomatique*, *22*, 119–138.

JONES E. (1933), 'The Phallic Phase'. *International Journal of Psychoanalysis*, *14*. 1–33.

JONES E. (1961), *The Life and Work of Sigmund Freud*, New York: Basic Books.

JUNG, C. G. (1909), 'The Significance of the Father in the Destiny of the Individual'. In *Freud and Psychoanalysis*, *Vol. 4*. London and New York: Routledge.

JUNG C. G. (1991), *Psychology of the Unconscious* (B. Hinkle, Trans.). Routledge.

KHAN M. (1973), 'L'alliance perverse'. *Nouvelle Revue de Psychanalyse*, *8*: 195–206.

KHAN M. (1974), *Le Soi caché*. Paris: Gallimard, 1976.

KESTEMBERG E. (1984), 'Astrid ou homosexualité, identité, adolescence'. *Les Cahiers de Centre de psychanalyse et de psychothérapie*, *8*. Reprinted in *L'Adolescence à vif*. Paris: PUF, 1999.

KIERKEGAARD S. (2011), *In vino veritas* (C. Bellinger, Trans.). In *Selected Essays*. Benediction Classics.

KLEIN M. (1932a), 'The effects of early anxiety situations on the sexual development of the girl', *The Psychoanalysis of Children*. London: Vintage, 1997.

KLEIN M. (1932b) *The Psychoanalysis of Children* (A. Strachey, Ed. & Trans.). London: Vintage, 1997.

KLEIN M. (1940), 'Mourning and its relation to manic-depressive states'. In *Love, Guilt and Reparation and Other Works, 1921–1945*. New York: Vintage, 1998.

KLEIN M. (1952), 'Some theoretical conclusions regarding the emotional life of the infant'. *The Writings of Melanie Klein, Vol. 8* (pp. 61–94). Vintage

KRAFFT-EBING R. VON (1893), 'Les formes du masochisme'. In *Étude Médico-Légale: Psychopathia sexualis avec recherches spéciale sur l'inversion sexuelle* (S. Csapo & E. Laurent, Trans.). Paris: Payot & Rivages, 1969.

KRAMER H., SPRENGER J. (1486), *The Malleus Maleficarum* (S. Mackay, Trans.). Cambridge: Cambridge University Press, 2009.

KREISLER L., FAIN M., SOULÉ M. (1974), *L'enfant et son corps*. Paris: PUF.

KRETSCHMER E. (1918), *Der sensitive Beziehungswahn* (S. Horinson, Trans.). *Paranoïa et sensibilité*. Paris: PUF, 1963.

LACAN J. (1932), *De la psychose paranoïaque dans ses rapports avec la personnalité*. Paris: Éditions du Seuil, 1980.

LACAN J. (1938), 'Les complexes familiaux', in *Encyclopédie française, La vie mentale, Volume VIII*. Paris: Larousse.

200 References

LACAN J. (1948), 'Aggressiveness in Psychoanalysis' (B. Fink, Trans.). In *Ecrits*. New York: Norton, 2002.

LACAN J. (1954–1955), 'The ego in Freud's theory and in the technique of psychoanalysis'. *The Seminar of Jacques Lacan, Book II* (S. Tomaselli, Trans.). Cambridge: Cambridge University Press, 1988.

LACAN J. (1955–1956), *The Seminar of Jacques Lacan, Book III, The Psychoses* (J.-A. Miller, Ed., B. Fink, Trans.). New York: Norton, 1993.

LACAN J. (1956–57), *The Seminar of Jacques Lacan, Book IV, The Object Relation,* (J.-A. Miller, Ed., B. Fink, Trans.). Norton, New York, 1998.

LACAN J. (1957–1958a), *The Seminar of Jacques Lacan, Book V, Formations of the Unconscious* (R. Grigg, Trans.). Polity Press, 2017.

LACAN J. (1957–1958b), 'On a question prior to any possible treatment of psychosis'. In *Ecrits*. New York: Norton, 2004.

LACAN J. (1959–1960), *The Seminar of Jacques Lacan, Book VII, The Ethics of Psychoanalysis* (D. Porter, Trans.). New York: Norton, 1992.

LACAN J. (1960–1961), *The Seminar of Jacques Lacan, Book VIII, Transference* (B. Fink, Trans.). Cambridge: Polity Press, 2015.

LACAN J. (1962–1963), *The Seminar of Jacques Lacan, Book X, Anxiety* (J.-A. Miller, Ed., B. Fink, Trans.). New York: Norton, 1998.

LACAN J. (1960), Propos directifs pour un Congrès sur la sexualité féminine. *Écrits*. Paris: Éditions du Seuil, 1966.

LACAN J. (1972), 'L'étourdit', 14 July, 1972, *Scilicet, 4*, 1973, 5–52.

LACAN J. (1972–1973), *The Seminar of Jacques Lacan, Book XX, Encore* (J.-A. Miller Ed., B. Fink, Trans.). New York: Norton, 1988.

LACAN J. (1975), Talks and Conferences in North American Universities, Yale, 29 November, *Scilicet, 6/7*, 38–41.

LAGACHE D. (1937), Deuil, mélancolie, manie [Mourning, melancholia, mania], presented to the Paris Psycholanalytic Society on 25 March (dactylo 44p).

LAGACHE D. (1956), Deuil pathologique, in *Œuvres IV, Agressivité, structure de la personnalité et autres travaux*, 1956–1962. Paris: PUF, 1982.

LAGACHE D. (1960), 'Agressivity', in *The Work of Daniel Lagache: Selected Papers 1938–1964*. Routledge, 1993.

LAGACHE D. (1961), 'La psychanalyse et la structure de la personnalité' [Psychoanalysis and the structure of the personality], in *Œuvres IV*, 1956–1962. Paris: PUF, 1982.

LANOUZIERE J. (1990), 'Schreber et le sein', *Psychanalyse à l'université, 15*(57), 23–56.

LANOUZIERE J. (1991), *Histoire secrète de la séduction sous le règne de Freud*. Paris: PUF.

LAPLANCHE J. (1968), *La révolution copernicienne inachevée – Travaux 1967–1992*. Paris: Aubier, 1992.

LAPLANCHE J. (1970a), Réparation et rétribution pénales. In *Vie et mort en psychanalyse*. Paris: Flammarion. Also in *Psychanalyse à la Université*, 1983, *30*, 211–224.

LAPLANCHE J. (1976), *Life and Death in Psychoanalysis*. Baltimore, MD: Johns Hopkins University Press.

LAPLANCHE J. (1981), *Problématiques 1, L'angoisse*. Paris: PUF.

LAPLANCHE J. (1987a), *The Temptation of Biology: Freud's Theories of Sexuality*. New York: Unconscious in Translation, 2015.

LAPLANCHE J. (1987), *Nouveaux fondements pour la psychanalyse*. Paris: PUF, 1990.

LAPLANCHE J. (1992), 'Masochisme et théorie de la séduction généralisée'. *Psychanalyse à la Université, 17*(67): 3–18.

References 201

LAPLANCHE J. (1993), 'Séduction, persécution, révélation'. *Psychanalyse à la Université*, *18*(72), 3–34.

LAPLANCHE J. (2003), 'Gender, Sex and the Sexual'. *Studies in Gender and Sexuality*, *8*(2), 201–219.

LAPLANCHE J., PONTALIS J.-B. (1967), *Vocabulaire de psychanalyse*. Paris: PUF.

LORAUX N. (1990), *Les mères en deuil* [Mothers in mourning]. Paris: Seuil.

MACALPINE I., HUNTER R. (1953), The Schreber case; A contribution to schizophrenia, hypochondria, and psychosomatic symptom-formation. *Psychoanalytic Quarterly*, *22*, 328–371.

MACDOUGALL J. (1996), *Eros aux mille visages*. Paris: Gallimard.

MACDOUGALL J. (1998), 'La solitude somatique'. *Topique*, *64*, 25–43.

MAÏDI H. (1996), 'Trauma, séduction et répétition à l'adolescence', *Perspectives psy*, *XXXV*(3), 221–227.

MAÏDI H. (2000), 'Masochisme et destin dans une névrose de victimité' [Masochism and destiny in victim neurosis], in *Destin, infortune, névrose de destinée, Champ psychosomatique*, *17*, 101–116.

MAÏDI H. (2003), *La plaie et le couteau*. Paris: Lausanne, Delachaux et Niestlé, 'Champs psychanalytiques' collection.

MAÏDI H. (2008), *Les souffrances de l'adolescence – Trauma et figurations du traumatique* [The sufferings of adolescence – Trauma and figurations of trauma]. Besançon: Presses universitaires de Franche-Comté.

MAÏDI H. (2012), *Clinique du narcissisme – L'adolescent et son image* [A clinical approach to narcissism]. Paris: Armand Colin, 'U' collection.

MAKARI G. J. (1991), 'German philosophy, Freud, and the riddle of the woman'. *Journal of the American Psychoanalytic Association*, *39*, 183–213.

MASSON J. M. (Ed. & Trans.) (1985), *The Complete Letters of Sigmund Freud to Wilhelm Fliess 1887–1904*. Cambridge, MA: Belknap Press.

MAUSS M. (1924), *The Gift: The Forms and Reason for Exchange in Archaic Societies* (M. Douglas, Trans.). London: Routledge, 2002.

MAUSS M. (1968), *Les Fonctions sociale du sacré, Oeuvre I*. Paris: Les Éditions de Minuit.

MELTZER D. (1988), *The Apprehension of Beauty*. London: Karnac Books.

MICHELET J. (1862), *La Sorcière*. Paris: Garnier Flammarion, 1993.

MIJOLLA-MELLOR de S. (1998), *Penser la psychose. Une lecture de l'œuvre de Pierra Aulagnier*. Paris: Dunod.

MŒBIUS P. J. (1889), *J.-J. Rousseau Krankheitsgeschichte*. Leipzig.

MONTRELAY M. (1977), *L'Ombre et le nom. Sur la féminité*. Paris: Les Éditions de Minuit.

NIETZSCHE F. (1887), *The Joyous Science*. Penguin Classics, 2018.

NUNBERG H., FEDERN, E. (1962), *Minutes of the Vienna Psychoanalytic Society Vol. 1 1906–1908* (S. Freud, session of 6 November 1907, p. 232). New York: International Universities Press.

PARAT C. (1988), *Dynamique du sacré*. Lyon: Césura.

PERRIER F. (1980), Le *désir et la perversion*. Paris: Aubier.

POMMIER G. (1985), *L'exception féminine* [The feminine exception]. Paris: Aubier.

RABAIN J. F., WELLER, A. (2002), Pourquoi les hommes ont peur des femmes? [Why Are Men Afraid of Women?]: Jean Cournut (A. Weller, Trans.). Paris: Presses Universitaires de France, 2001. *International Journal of Psychoanalysis* [Book Review], *83*(4), 970–974.

RACAMIER P.-C. (1990), 'La paranoïa revisitée'. *Perspectives psychiatriques*, *21*(I), 8–21.

202   References

RACAMIER P.-C. (1991), 'Souffrir et survivre dans les paradoxes'. *Revue française de psychanalyse*, 4/

REIK T. (1957), *Mythe et culpabilité (Crime et châtiment de l'humanité)*. Paris: PUF, 1979.

RIEDER I., VOIGT D. (2021), *The Story of Sidonie C.* (1st edn). Helen History Press. Available at: https://www.perlego.com/book/2876086/the-story-of-sidonie-c-freuds-case -of-female-homosexuality-pdf (accessed 8 November, 2023).

RIVIERE J. (1929), 'Womanliness as a Masquerade'. *International Journal of Psychoanalysis, X*, pp. 303–313.

ROSENBERG B. (1991), *Masochisme mortifère, masochisme gardien de la vie*. (Coll. des "Monographies de la RFP"). Paris: PUF.

ROSENFELD H. (1958), 'Some Observations on the Psychopathology of Hypochondriacal States'. *International Journal of Psycho-Analysis, 39*. 121–214.

ROSOLATO G. (1969), 'Paranoïa et scène primitive'. In *Essais sur le symbolique*. Paris: Gallimard.

ROSOLATO G. (1976a), 'L'expulsion', in *La relation d'inconnu*. Paris: Gallimard.

ROSOLATO G. (1976b), 'Le narcissisme'. *Nouvelle revue de psychanalyse, 13*, 7–36.

ROSOLATO G. (1987), *Le sacrifice*. Paris: PUF.

ROUSSEAU J. J. (1734), *Narcissus, Or the Lover of Himself*. New York: Contra Mundum Press, 2015.

SACHER-MASOCH L. VON (2006). *Venus in Furs*. London: Penguin.

SADGER I. I. (1910), 'Ein Fall von multipler Perversion mit hysterischen Absenzen' [A case of multiple perversion with hysterical absences]. *Jahrbuch für psychoanalyt. Und psychopat*, Forschungen, vol. II.

SARTRE J.-P. (1963), *St Genet, Actor and Martyr*. New York: George Brazillier.

SCHILDER P. (1935), *The Image and Appearance of the Human Body*. London: Kegan Paul.

SCHNEIDER M. (1992), *La part de l'ombre – Approche d'un trauma féminin*. Paris: Aubier.

SCHOPENHAUER A. (1851), *Parerga and Paralipomena, Vol. 2*. E. F. J. Payne (Ed.). Clarendon Press.

SCHREBER D. P (2000), *Memoirs of My Nervous Illness*, I. Macalpine (Ed.), R. Hunger, (Trans.). New York: New York Review of Books.

SEARLES H. F. (1959), 'The effort to drive another person crazy'. *British Journal of Medical Psychology, 32*(1), 1–18.

SMADJA C. (1993), 'A propos des procédés autocalmants du moi.' *Revue française de psychosomatique, 4*, 9–26.

SMADJA C. (1994), Préliminaires techniques à l'analysibilité de patients atteints d'affections somatiques. *Revue française de psychanalyse, 4*, 1059–1076.

STAROBINSKI J. (1989), *La mélancolie au miroir. Trois lectures de Baudelaire*. Paris: Julliard.

STEIN C. (1987), *Les Erinyes d'une mère. Essai sur la haine*. Paris: Calligrammes, PUF.

STOLLER R. J. (1975). 'Symbiosis Anxiety and the Development of Masculinity'. *Archives of General Psychiatry*, 1974, *30*.

STOLLER R. J. (1985). Presentations of Gender. New Haven, CT, Yale University Press.

SZWEC G. (1993), Les procédés autocalmants par la recherche répétitive de l'excitation. Les galériens volontaires. *Revue Française de Psychosomatique, 4*: 27–51. See also *Les galériens volontaires*. Paris: PUF, 1998, 2014.

TAUSK V. (1919), *Œuvres psychanalytiques*. Paris: Payot, 1975.

VALABREGA J. P. (1980), *Phantasme, mythe, corps et sens* [Phantasm, myth, body and meaning]. Paris: Payot.

TELLENBACH H. (1961), *Melancholie – zur Problemgeschichte, Typologie, Pathogenese und Klinik*. Berlin: Springer-Verlag.

VERNANT J.-P. (1980)[1965], *Myth and Society in Ancient Greece*. J. Lloyd (Trans.). Chichester: Harvester Press.

VOLTAIRE M. de (1759). *An Essay on Universal History, The Manners and Spirits of Nations* (Mr Nugent, Trans.). London: J. Nourse. Available at: https://www.google.co.uk/books/edition/An_Essay_on_Universal_History_the_Manner/cLUvAAAAYAAJ?hl=en&gbpv=1&printsec=frontcover.

WACJMANN C. (1992), *Fous de Rousseau. Le cas Rousseau dans l'histoire de la psychopathologie*. Paris: Éditions L'Harmattan.

WEIBERGER-THOMAS C. (1996), *Cendres d'immortalité – La crémation des veuves en Inde*. Paris: Seuil.

WINNICOTT D. W. (1947), 'Hate in the Counter-Transference', in *Through Paediatrics to Psychoanalysis.* London: Karnac Books, 1975.

WINNICOTT D. W. (1971a), 'Creativity and its Origins', in *Playing and Reality.* London: Routledge, 2005.

WINNICOTT D. W. (1971b), 'The Split-Off Male and Female Elements to be Found in Men and Women', in *Playing and Reality. Potential Space*. London: Tavistock Academic Press.

WINNICOTT D. W. (1988), *Human Nature*. London: Free Association Books.

Index of names

Abraham K. 23, 57, 63, 83, 85, 90, 92–3, 139, 159, 167, 195, 198
Adam 5, 6
Aeschylus 121, 195
Aisenstein M. 131, 195
Alcibiades 108
André J. 41, 195
Andreas-Salomé L. 23, 74, 195
Anzieu D. 108, 164, 195
Aphrodite 39
Aristophane 94
Artaud A. 110
Aulagnier P. 89, 93, 121, 142–3, 155, 166–7, 195

Bak R. C. 140, 165, 195
Bateson G. 136, 165
Baudelaire C. 6, 69–70, 78, 195
Bazin H. 41
Binet A. 170, 187
Bonaparte M. 10, 22
Brunswick R. 22

Chambers R. 78, 195
Cioran E. M. 57, 195
Cournut J. 4, 22, 57, 195–6
Cournut M. 4, 22, 196

David C. 4, 196
D'Avila T. 24
Da Vinci L. 164, 197
De Beauvoir S. 3, 10, 22, 196
De Bergerac C. 108
Degos D. 116, 122, 196
De Heusch L. 66, 77, 196
De Maistre J. 66, 76–8, 196
De Mijolla-Mellor S. 69, 78, 201
De Musset A. 196

Deutsch H. 22, 106, 109–10, 196
Dolto F. 22
Dubois d'Amiens F. 123, 131, 196
Duflos H. 164

Ehrenberg A. 196
Enriquez M. 137, 165, 196
Evans-Pritchard E. E. 77, 196
Ey H. 131, 150, 196

Fairbairn W. R. D. 133, 164, 196
Ferenczi S. 125–7, 131, 139, 198
Fine A. 131, 195
Frazer J. G. 73, 77–8, 97, 196
Freud S. 1–5, 7–17, 19, 22–34, 39–44, 57–65, 67, 72, 73–4, 76–8, 80, 85, 87–8, 90–102, 104–6, 108–10, 112, 115–16, 119–22, 124–8, 131–5, 137–41, 151–3, 159–60, 163–5, 167, 170–84, 186–8, 190–2, 196–200

Girard R. 66, 77, 198
Green A. 23, 198–9
Groddeck G. W. 28, 39, 199
Guthkelch A. N. 57

Héritier F. 199
Hermès 39
Hugo V. 78
Hunter R. 165, 201

Janet P. 88, 93, 132, 199
Janin C. 58, 199
Jeanneau A. 132, 199
Jesus 5, 63, 72, 93, 162–3, 167
Jones E. 9, 19, 22, 24, 199
Jung C. G. 93, 104, 197, 199

206 Index of names

Kestemberg E. 39, 199
Khan M. 69, 78, 199
Kierkegaard S. 7, 22, 199
Klein M. 13, 19, 23–4, 65, 92–3, 118, 122,
   138, 140–1, 165, 167, 179, 199
Kohut H. 92
Krafft-Ebing R. v. 135, 168, 187, 199
Kramer H. 6, 22, 199
Kreisler L. 44, 57, 199
Kretschmer E. 58, 136, 165, 199

Lacan J. 7, 10, 19–22, 24, 32, 34, 40–1, 57,
   78, 80, 87, 90–3, 95, 106, 108–10, 120,
   122, 131, 141–2, 144, 148, 164, 166,
   178, 188, 199, 200
Lagache D. 77–8, 85, 92, 106, 200
Lanouzière J. 108, 142, 144, 166, 200
Laplanche J. 2, 4, 18–19, 24, 34, 39,
   65, 74, 76–8, 140, 142–4, 165–6,
   200–1

Macalpine I. 138, 165, 201–2
Mac Dougall J. 20
Maïdi H. 3, 23, 25, 39–40, 63, 78, 108, 132,
   164, 189, 201
Makari G. J. 22, 201
Mauss M. 76–7, 119, 199, 201
Meltzer D. 40, 201
Michelet J. 22, 201
Montrelay M. 102, 109, 201

Napoleon B. 1, 3
Nietzsche F. 7, 9–10, 22, 201

Parat C. 63, 77, 201
Perrier F. 102, 109, 201
Pommier G. 104, 109, 201
Pontalis J.-B. 39, 201
Pope Innocent VIII 6
Pragier G. 131, 195
Prometheus 165, 195
Puttkammer V. L. 30

Racamier P.-C. 136, 165, 202
Réage P. 187
Reik T. 87, 93, 202
Rieder I. 40, 202
Rosenberg B. 88, 109, 202
Rosenfeld H. 131, 202
Rosolato G. 65, 67, 77–8, 100, 110, 165,
   202
Rousseau J.-J. 4, 29, 39, 169–70, 187, 195,
   201, 202–3

Sadger I. I. 164, 202
Sartre J.-P. 3, 202
Schopenhauer A. 7, 9, 22, 202
Schreber D. P. 51, 57, 109, 126, 133–5,
   138–40, 142–7, 149–50, 152–9, 161–7,
   196–7, 200–2
Searles H. F. 165, 202
Segantini G. 83–4, 92, 195
Smadja C. 43, 57, 202
Socrates 108
Soulé M. 57, 199
Sprenger J. 6, 22, 199
Starobinski J. 78, 202
Stefanowsky D. 187
Stein C. 109, 202
Stoller R. J. 17–18, 23, 202
Szwec G. 57, 202

Tausk V. 110, 203
Thebes 3, 68
Tiresias 3, 21, 68

Valabrega J. P. 112–13, 121, 203
Venus of Lespugue 5
Vernant J.-P. 68, 92, 203
Voigt D. 40, 202
Von Hentig H. 77, 199

Wacjmann C. 187, 203
Winnicott D. W. 10, 14–18, 23, 28, 34, 39,
   95, 108, 203

Milton Keynes UK
Ingram Content Group UK Ltd.
UKHW021706041224
451949UK00018B/339

9 781032 537375